Waddington

Village Life in

the Nineteenth Century

Carnegie Publishing Ltd, 1994

WADDINGTON

Village Life in the Nineteenth Century

MARY BRIDGE

Carnegie Publishing Ltd, 1994

Waddington: Village Life in the Nineteenth Century
by Mary Bridge

Copyright © Mary Bridge, 1994

Published by Carnegie Publishing Ltd., 18 Maynard Street, Preston
Typeset in Monotype Ehrhardt and origination by Carnegie Publishing
Printed by Cambridge University Press

British Library Cataloguing-in-Publication Data
Bridge, Mary
  Waddington: Village Life in the
  Nineteenth Century
  I. Title
  942.76081

  ISBN 1-85936-000-9

Contents

Acknowledgements

I DISCOVERED Waddington some twelve years ago. That I have been able to write a book about the village is due largely to the information and assistance so readily given by a great number of people.

The staff of the institutions referred to in the bibliography section 'Main Sources' have been unfailing in their help. My thanks are also due to individuals who placed a variety of documents and records at my disposal. I am especially grateful to the Parker family of Browsholme Hall, and to the Revd J. Needham, Superintendent Minister of the Methodist Church, for allowing me to use their archives before they were deposited at the Record Office in Preston; and to the Revd A. Bailey, the Churchwardens of St Helen's, and the Hospital Trustees for making their archives available to me. Mr C. Ainsworth, Mr H. Banks, Miss E. Bishop, Mr I. Dearing, Mr J. Dugdale, Mr J. Herd, Mr A. Holden, Mr F. Leeming, Mrs A. Maudsley, Mr A. Pye, Mr M. Rothwell, Mr B. Stott and the Girl Guides' Association, Waddow Hall kindly allowed me to make use of their private records.

I am indebted to Miss M. Hulme and Miss W. Slater for the illustrations; to Mr D. Booth and Mr R. J. Hayhurst for photographic work, and to Miss E. Bishop and Mr P. Cunliffe, Mr J. Dugdale, Mr J. Herd, Mrs V. Kenyon, Miss H Whittern, Clitheroe Library and the Masonic Lodge, for the loan of photographs. Mr R. R. Parker kindly gave permission for the portraits of Robert Smith and William Parker to be photographer; Mrs Patrick Gordon-Duff-Pennington, owner of the Ramsden papers deposited in the WRAS, Leeds, kindly allowed me to reproduce the plan on page 47, and the British Library gave permission for the reproduction of the illustration on page 99.

Local historians readily passed on information and gave advice; friends have cast an eye over the manuscript and added their comments. My sincere thanks are due to them and to typists and critics, among whom members of my family have been the most severe and most helpful.

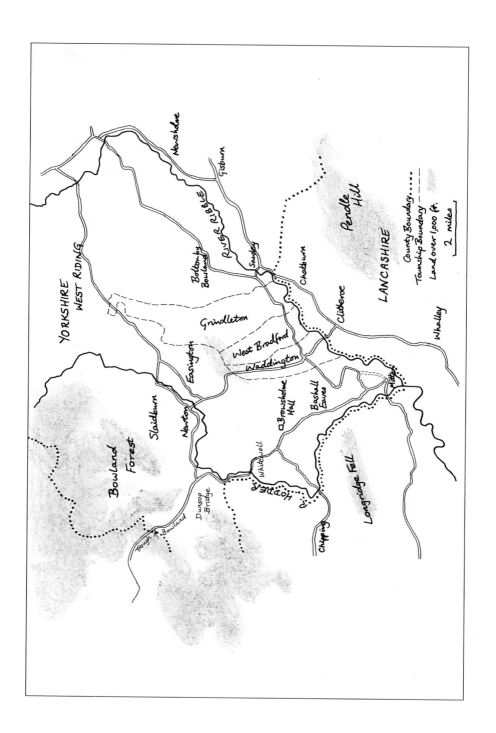

Waddington—a West Riding township.

I

Waddington, 1801

'AN OUT OF THE WAY little Yorkshire village'[1] was how Waddington was described in 1890. The description was even more appropriate at the beginning of the century when the population was smaller and poor communications ensured its isolation. Situated in the south-west corner of the West Riding it was remote from the main towns of the county. Though only two miles from the rapidly growing town of Clitheroe, until there was a bridge over the Ribble at Brungerley contact with Lancashire was also limited. The rather longer journey to the neighbouring village of Newton was thought by Robert Smith, the vicar, to be like a crossing of the Alps.

Leaving the vicarage, a Georgian building, and turning his horse northwards towards Newton he passed the Reader's House and the Leawood cottages across the way and began the ascent. Soon, he passed Hollins Farm and Baileys Farm, one on either side of the road, and saw the track to Feazer and the old walk mill where cloth had been fulled and then stretched on tenters. (There was talk of its becoming a mill for spinning cotton with machines driven by water from the stream.) There were more farms with their farmhouses near the roadway—Bowkers, Thornbers and Leemings and beyond them several others which, until recently, belonged to Thomas Weddell, Lord of the Manor. After his death in 1788 his widow, now Mrs Clarke, had been forced to sell them to clear his debts.

Another track led to the corn mill. Like the old Feazer mill this was worked by water power. There were a few more farms before Newy Nook, the most northerly one, came into sight. This was a low building sheltered by the hills from the rough weather of winter, which, they said, lasted for nine months in these parts.

As Newy Nook disappeared from view, the vicar passed through the Fell Gate and entered a wild, desolate country, 300 acres of moorland claimed by the freeholders of Waddington and bounded by similar common land belonging to Bashall Eaves, Newton and West Bradford. There were no walls to interrupt the sweep of land but occasional merestones marked the boundaries. These were known to the vicar who, during a freeholders' dispute with Mrs Clarke about the common, was arranging to 'walk the bounds'.[2] In summer, sheep found rough grazing there; grouse had their haunts in the heather until disturbed by sportsmen. Sheep stealers were not unknown: in 1801 a Grindleton man was caught stealing a ewe and lamb; trial at York assizes

---

[1] *Manchester Weekly Times*, 17 October 1890.
[2] Lancashire Record Office (LRO), DDX/118/149.

Thornbers—one of the oldest farmhouses. The cruck structure remains.

and the death sentence awaited him.[1] In the late spring turves were cut. When dry these were carted to the village for winter fuel. Heather and bracken were carted for bedding for cattle; ling was used for thatching when straw was not available; stone was quarried for building and repairing the roads. No wonder the vicar, himself a freeholder, supported his fellow freeholders against Mrs Clarke: 'Gaffer' Smith's interests were not confined to church matters.

The track which he now followed was an old drovers' road used by farmers and cattle dealers like old George Battersby who, in 1783, walked from Slaidburn through Newton and Waddington, forded the river at Brungerley and sold his cattle at Clitheroe Fair. He never made the return journey: he was murdered just as he left the town. People still talked of how his body had been hidden for a time in the stream which flowed into the Ribble opposite Waddow Hall. Each year on 29 March, the anniversary of his death, blood stains were said to appear on stones in the stream: there were those who had stones as proof. The trial at Lancaster and surprise acquittal of the four accused of Battersby's murder still gave rise to comment and speculation.

At the boundary between Waddington and Newton Fell the road reached a height of over 1,100 feet. Peaks of the Pennines were to be seen to the north-east; Bowland Forest lay to the north-west, spectacular country even when partly hidden by mist. Turning to look back over the two miles he had travelled the vicar could see that Waddington lay on the edge or 'eaves' of the forest and not far from the Pennines. Pendle Hill and Longridge Fell closed in the view to east and west. On fine days it was difficult to believe that witchcraft still lingered in these parts but each year people took candles up on Longridge at Hallowe'en to 'leet' the witches. Tales of the Pendle witches who had passed through the Trough of Bowland to be tried at Lancaster were, after nearly two hundred years, still familiar to most. The vicar knew of the superstitions of his parishioners for it was a common practice to hang holed or 'hag' stones above the shippon doors to ward off evil.

---

[1] Public Record Office (PRO), Assi 144/117 Part 2.

In the valley between Pendle and Longridge flowed the Ribble and Hodder to join at Mitton, four miles to the south of Waddington. The parish of Mitton had included the three townships of Waddington, West Bradford and Grindleton until 1483, when the three formed a separate parish in the deanery of Craven in the see of York; the parish church was built at Waddington. Certain payments were still made to Mitton, the mother church, and people were expected to worship there at Easter.

Below the fell the remainder of Waddington's 2,000 acres were divided into twenty-six farms some of 40 to 60 acres, some even smaller. With several springs, and streams flowing into the Ribble, they were certainly well watered and were fairly well wooded. Most of the land was pasture and meadow with enough arable to make the village largely self-supporting. Oats were fed to the horses which by 1801 had replaced oxen on the farms. There was little wheat, but barley was grown for beer.

Over half the land was held by Mrs Clarke of Waddow Hall; the enforced sales she had made brought new landowners, most of them connected with manufacturing, into the township. Of Waddington's population of 481 approximately one third were farmers or agricultural labourers. Some combined farming with another occupation such as that of innkeeper or weaver. Almost a third of the men were weavers; their number was still growing. The rest were craftsmen, clogmakers, tailors, joiners, masons and blacksmiths who between them were able to satisfy most people's requirements.

For the last eight years the war with France had caused prices to rise and the poor harvest of 1800 had made food dear. However, wages too were increasing, albeit not at the same rate. A mason could earn 3s. 6d. a day and his apprentice 1s. 6d., while weavers were receiving even more.

The vicar knew the village scene well, having lived in Waddington for nearly forty years. About half the township's 142 houses clustered around the Square and along the roads, if roads they could be called, leading from it to West Bradford, Newton, Clitheroe and Bashall Eaves. The houses, thatched and whitewashed, were not unlike the old vicarage, with two rooms downstairs and two bedrooms; Back Fold houses were even smaller. Although picturesque in appearance the cottages were dark, damp and verminous with flags or earth floors and small windows. Springs, wells and the brook were the main water supply although some houses had pumps. Coal, peat and wood were used for fuel; candles for lighting. There was little furniture but the houses were often overcrowded especially where a loom had been set up. Outdoor priv- ies—'the little houses' or petties—were shared by several households. A number of barns in the village had been converted into weaving sheds. Newcomers may well have lived in them until they could move in with another family or find a place of their own.

When work finished for the day there was little for the men to do apart from go to one of the three ale-houses. For the women as they gathered around the fire there was knitting to be done, wiskets and besoms to be made and tales to be told and re-told. Favourites among these were the stories of Peg O'Nell who every seven years claimed a victim at the river crossing, and of the Diel and Dun Inn from where the devil, outwitted by a tailor, rode off on a dun horse.

There were occasional celebrations at rush-bearing time and plenty of noise and excitement when bulls were baited in the Square. Sunday was different. Men who

The Square

worked away from home returned to wash and put on their Sunday clothes. Some attended church where the vicar was assisted by a curate, his son. There was small chance, however, of the latter's becoming vicar when his father died. The advowson was held by the Parkers of Browsholme and Thomas Lister Parker would be sure to appoint one of his five brothers when the opportunity arose.

During the last decades of the eighteenth century the vicar had recorded in the parish register an increasing number of christenings and weddings. In 1800 there had been fifteen baptisms, six marriages and ten burials of Waddington people; a total of fifty-six ceremonies for the three townships.

The church itself, built in the sixteenth century, was showing signs of decay though the tower had weathered well. Repair work would soon be needed but the vicar, in his seventies, was reluctant to think about this. Meanwhile a churchwarden appointed by him and three others from the townships faithfully performed their duties; ringers and singers took part in the services and the dog-whipper controlled the dogs brought by farmers to church.

So far there was only talk in the village about a meeting house for dissenters similar to that in West Bradford where followers of John Wesley worshipped. The vicar sincerely hoped that certain fellows in the village 'no better than Levellers' would not do mischief among the lower classes by pursuing this matter. 'We used to be sociable and quiet here,' he reflected.[1]

---

[1] St Helen's Church Archives, letter to T. Parker of Newton.

View towards Pendle

In the small churchyard one or two seventeenth-century tombstones were to be seen. Prominent amongst the eighteenth-century ones was that of Robert Parker, founder of the Hospital. There were only ten almshouses when the Hospital had been endowed a hundred years earlier: now there were sixteen for local widows unable to support themselves. The Reader held services for them twice a day.

Others who were poor received help from the poor law overseers who, with the constable and highway surveyors, were responsible for dealing with the affairs of the township. There was little interest in parliament, for although freeholders were entitled to vote for the two county members there had been no contested election since 1746. War-time taxes affected only those who were wealthy enough to keep servants and carriage horses; land, income and windows were also taxed. Near the church were the pinfold and stocks, the former for strayed animals and the latter for errant villagers. If their crimes were serious, local magistrates and assize judges dealt with the offenders.

There were not many buildings of note in the village, no chapel, no Sunday school, no day school. The Old Hall, former home of the lords of the manor and one-time refuge for Henry VI, had lost its former glory and was now just one of several farmhouses along the village street. Whitaker, well on with his *History of Craven*, wrote of the hall: 'Though constructed of strong old masonry it has nearly lost all appearance of antiquity. One room retains the name of King Henry's chamber.'[1] Across the way from the hall geese were kept on Gander Green, hens wandered about, cows came to drink at the stream which flowed through the village.

New Hall and Waddow Hall were the only other houses of importance. The former, recently sold along with the tannery by the Parker family, was occupied by

---

[1] T. D. Whitaker, *History and Antiquities of the Deanery of Craven*, vol. 2, 3rd edn (London, 1878), p. 31.

Robert Walker, a newcomer to the village. He, like other newcomers, was already beginning to prosper. Waddow Hall, the home of Jane Clarke and her second husband, with its view across the river towards Pendle, had been enlarged and furnished by Thomas Weddell who had taken great pride in 'his mansion'. In his day the river had been crossed by hipping stones but the inhabitants of Clitheroe and Waddington were about to build a wooden footbridge. This would certainly help those who attended Clitheroe's markets and fairs and might in time encourage people to go there for work: mill owners were already advertising for labourers.

There were not many, however, who had occasion to leave the village. The people could provide their food and clothing. Oatcakes made on the bacstone, porridge and broth were their basic diet. Cheese, boiled meat and bacon were eaten occasionally. Cottage gardens provided fruit and some vegetables. Amongst those who did leave the village from time to time were the constable who had to report to Slaidburn and take annual payments to Settle for the county's administration, church officials visiting Skipton and the agent of the Hospital Trustees attending to their business at Hellifield and Keighley. Even fewer people had occasion to visit Waddington, seemingly an insignificant place of no great interest or importance.

But,

> Let not Ambition mock their useful toil,
> Their homely joys and destiny obscure;
> Nor Grandeur hear with a disdainful smile
> The short and simple annals of the Poor.

> Thomas Gray.

2

Population and Housing, 1801–1901

The most important production of a country is its population.[1]

THE POPULATION in England and Wales as a whole increased from six million in 1760 to nine million in 1801. This was due in part to the falling death rate brought about by the gradual improvement of social conditions and greater medical knowledge. Using the method adopted by Dr Cox and advocated by Tate,[2] the eighteenth century population of Waddington can be calculated. It doubled in the second half of the century with the last decade showing the biggest increase. In the next twenty years, while the population of some of the neighbouring villages was declining, there was a further increase in Waddington as the population rose from 481 in 1801 to 687 in 1821.

After 1821, apart from the small rise shown in the 1841 statistics, there was a steady fall in Waddington's population with the result that in 1881 it was smaller than at the beginning of the century. Thereafter, another period of growth led to a population of 583 by 1901.

Population changes

Date	Total population	Males	Females
1801	481	240	241
1811	580 (estimated)	–	–
1821	687	336	351
1831	624	294	330
1841	644	319	325
1851	580	287	293
1861	513	248	265
1871	466	228	238
1881	447	202	245
1891	510	240	270
1901	583	252	331

Waddington and West Bradford figures were combined in 1811.

[1] Census of Great Britain Abstract, 1851, p. 64.
[2] W. E. Tate, *The Parish Chest* (Cambridge, 1946), p. 81.

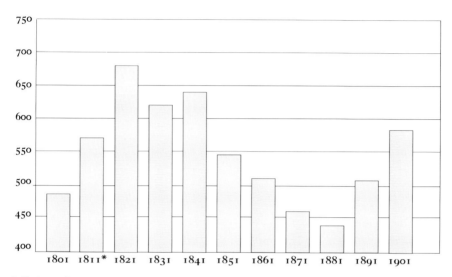

* Estimated

Graph illustrating population change during the nineteenth century.

The 1821 total is all the more remarkable as there were then only sixteen widows at the Hospital as compared with twenty-six by 1831 and thirty after 1853. In 1841 there were ten boarders (eight boys, two girls) at James Grimshaw's school and thirty-two boarders (nineteen boys, thirteen girls) in 1851.

A study of the parish registers from 1801 to 1841 throws some light on the reasons for the fluctuating population figures. The registers—although a few Wesleyan parents had their children baptised in Clitheroe during these years—may be taken as a fairly complete record prior to the compulsory registration of births, marriages and deaths after 1836. They show an excess of baptisms over burials in the first four decades of 61, 99, 129 and 84. These figures alone do not explain the population figures and account has to be take of the movement of people to or from the village.

Population Mobility

In these four decades changes in the cotton industry were the main factors in determining population mobility. A cotton spinning mill, sometimes referred to as 'the Waddington factory', was established at Feazer and there was another mill two miles south of the village at Low Moor. Both were producing a steady supply of yarn at the beginning of the century and this attracted hand-loom weavers from nearby villages. They crowded into the cottages, weavers' sheds and barns. When power-looms were installed at Low Moor Mill in 1824 a dramatic change took place and a great exodus of hand-loom weavers from Waddington occurred. Their wages were falling and Low Moor offered the double attraction of higher wages in the factory and the chance of a cottage in the newly built factory village.[1] Over sixty Waddington-born people were living there by 1841.

Population mobility (1)

	Population at beginning of decade	Excess of births over deaths per decade	Population plus excess	Census population at end of decade	Number of migrants per decade
1801	481	69	550	580 (est.)	+30
1811	580 (est.)	99	679	687	+8
1821	687	129	816	624	−192
1831	624	84	708	644	−64

A local paper commenting in 1846 on the early censuses referred to this development: 'The villages around Clitheroe were inhabited by an industrious and well-employed people chiefly in hand-loom weaving. This has now been superseded by the power-loom. The people have had to follow and find employment in other districts.'[2]

The names in the marriage and baptismal registers supply further evidence of this population mobility. At least seventy new surnames appear in these registers between 1801 and 1831. Fifty of these are missing from the 1851 census, some as the result of marriage. Twenty-five surnames existing in 1801 had also disappeared by 1851.

The drift to the towns to which the agricultural depression of the 'seventies contributed continued until 1881. By that date Waddington had declined into a 'state of quietude and rural simplicity'. Gradually the trend was reversed as workers like Caleb Bishop from Oxfordshire and others from parts of the country where the depression was even more severe moved into the village. There were some, like the Garnetts, who found Waddington a desirable place of residence as it afforded them a country home not far from their mill.

Population mobility (2)

Date	Population	% born in Waddington	% born elsewhere in Yorkshire	% born elsewhere
1841	644	94% born in Yorkshire including those born in Waddington		6
1851	580	53	30	17
1861	513	48	27	25
1871	466	49	28	23
1881	447	44	28	28
1891	510	47	23	30

The boarders at the school in 1841 and in 1851 have been excluded from the calculations.

[1] Census returns.
[2] LRO, DDX/28/316, *Clitheroe Monthly Advertiser*, 5 December 1846.

Several such records are to be seen in the churchyard.

The later census returns give evidence of increasing population mobility—due partly to improvements in communication. In 1851 83 per cent of Waddington's population had been born in Yorkshire and the majority of newcomers to the village were from West Bradford, Grindleton, Sawley, Slaidburn and other villages within ten miles of Waddington. By that year the railway had reached Clitheroe and of those who came from a distance two came from Durham, one from Staffordshire and one from Doncaster. Forty years later when 70 per cent of Waddington's population had been born in Yorkshire there were people from Lincolnshire, Oxfordshire, Shropshire, Staffordshire, Derbyshire, Cheshire, Westmorland, Wales, Ireland and Scotland. Lancashire continued to be the main supplier of settlers from outside the county.

There were more females than males in Waddington throughout the century. In 1801 there was a difference of only one, whereas the greatest difference—of forty-three—was recorded in 1881. Contributing to this discrepancy were the thirty almshouses the majority of whose inhabitants usually came to reside in Waddington at the age of sixty or over. Their presence also helps to explain why there was a greater percentage of women over sixty than men. There were more boys than girls up to the age of fourteen in the village.

The inhabitants of Waddington had a reputation for longevity and the total percentage of people over sixty steadily increased. In 1851 twenty men and forty-nine women, 8 per cent of the population, were over sixty. In 1891 twenty-two men and forty-seven women, 14 per cent of the population, were over sixty.

The working population (male)

Precise figures relating to occupations are not available before 1841. The 1801 census states that sixty people were engaged in farming and sixty-five in trade, manufacture and craftsmanship. The Muster Roll of 1803 shows over a third of the men to have been farmers and agricultural workers with two slightly smaller groups of weavers and craftsmen. The remainder were classed as labourers. The 1821 census comments on the local increase of those engaged in manufacturing and trade. The 1831 census divides the males over twenty years of age into three groups: fifty-eight engaged in

The working population (male)

Date	Male population	Workers	Non-workers	Agric. workers %	Indust. workers %	Craftsmen %	Services %	Profes- sionals %	General labourers %
1841	311 (319 – 8)	159	162	43	22	21	10	4	–
1851	268 (287 – 19)	170	98	44	22	17	12	3	2
1861	248	153	95	35	29	15	16	3	2
1871	228	142	86	31	26	21	13	4	5
1881	202	125	77	28	30	15	17	4	6
1891	240	154	86	26	33	14	17	4	6

The non-workers include most children under the age of thirteen; the scholars, retired, unemployed, paupers, those of independent means.
1841: No occupation is given for a number of possible workers, even for some farmers' sons though it is likely that they worked on the farm. Eight boarders are excluded from the calculations.
1851: Nineteen boarders are excluded from the calculations.

agriculture, thirty-one in manufacturing and industry, thirty-eight in retail trade or handicrafts. There were also five professionals and three male servants. This division was roughly the pattern for the rest of the century.

The percentage engaged in farming declined in the later decades, a reflection of what was happening throughout the country. In England in 1801 a quarter of the men had been farming, only one twelfth were farming at the end of the century.

Before 1841 most of the industrial workers were involved in the cotton industry as hand-loom weavers. After 1841 the number of mill workers steadily increased, except when changes at Low Moor Mill led to workers being laid off.

Quarrying was an expanding industry—there was a greater demand for stone for new houses and road improvement. The manufacture of bricks and tiles (drain pipes) was established in 1873. Some half-dozen men were employed at the tannery which was in business throughout the century. The industrial workers included two lime-burners, and a lead miner living at Feazer and presumably working the Newton Fell lead mines. There was a smelt mill nearby. General labourers could find work on the roads and wherever seasonal demand created opportunities.

Early in the century local craftsmen could meet most people's needs in terms of clothing, furniture, tools and houses. Industrialisation led to their decline. The presence of a shoe-dealer in the village in 1881 was indicative of mass production which threatened the livelihood of shoemakers and tailors. Even so, in 1891 there were still shoemakers, a tailor, blacksmiths, a wheelwright, a joiner and a rope-maker in the village.

Other services were offered. In addition to the shopkeepers, one of whom was a chandler, and publicans the numbers of gardeners, grooms, coachmen, servants and carters increased. In later years there were errand boys, huntsmen, gamekeepers and estate agents and before the century ended a tea-dealer, wine merchant, coal-dealer, insurance agents, a file-maker, a rural postman and a policeman.

The vicar, the Reader and then the schoolmaster were for some time the only members of the professional class. A solicitor, doctor, book-keeper and a pupil teacher were later recorded.

There were also the retired and unemployed. As many as seven retired farmers were living in the village in 1881 but most men had to continue working until prevented by failing health. Those who were classed as paupers received outdoor relief despite the 1834 Act. Some, after 1895, like John Pinder, unable to support himself as a shoemaker because of failing sight, were given a pension by the Hospital Trustees.

Further details about the workers are given in the following sections.

The working population (female)

The trend was for an increasing number of women to find employment. The majority of working women were hand-loom weavers or factory workers. When re-organisation took place at Low Moor Mill, women were the first to be laid off—hence the fall in numbers in 1871.

The Vicarage, Waddow Hall and New Hall were the main employers of domestic servants—cooks, housekeepers, maids, washerwomen, manglers. One or two women of independent means employed a servant or companion, and servants were employed on the larger farms.

The professional class included a few teachers and governesses. Others in employment were the shopkeepers, sometimes working with their husbands, dressmakers—eight in 1891—publicans, the occasional farmer and dairymaid, nurses and those in domestic service.

The majority of those in employment were unmarried women and young girls; some widows became housekeepers. The handicapped, chiefly the few who were deaf and dumb, worked at home as dressmakers. The maximum number of those under fourteen recorded as employed was nine, in 1851; thirty years later the number was down to three. Apart from one servant girl all in this age group worked in factories.

The working population (female)

Date	Female population	Workers	Cotton industry	Domestic service	Professionals	Others
1841	325	60	40	15	–	5
1851	293	62	41	10	2	9
1861	265	72	42	19	–	11
1871	238	54	29	14	2	9
1881	245	40	24	12	3	1
1891	270	89	40	27	3	19

33 per cent of the female population was working in 1891 as compared with 18 per cent in 1841.

Housing

The number of houses recorded as occupied varied between 143 in 1841 and 123 in 1881 and the average number of occupants between 3.5 and 5 (approximately). These figures are affected by the existence of the Hospital cottages each with a single inhabitant. The exclusion of these and of the children boarding at the school in 1841 and 1851 gives an average number of occupants ranging from nearly four to six.

Date	Inhabited houses	Population	Av. per house	Uninhabited houses	Total number of houses	Av. per house excl. almshouses
1801	142	481	3.4	0	142	3.7
1811	137 (est.)	580 (est.)	4.2	6	142 (est.)	4.7
1821	131	687	5.2	1	132	5.8
1831	135	624	4.6	12	147	5.5
1841	143	644	4.5	16	159	5.0
1851	131	580	4.4	11	142	5.0
1861	135	513	3.8	5	140	4.5
1871	130	466	3.6	18	148	4.2
1881	123	447	3.6	13	146	4.4
1891	139	510	3.7	17	156	4.4
1901	136	583	4.3	–	136	5.2

Some houses had more than ten inhabitants; there were sixteen at the vicarage in 1871. Though families of eight to ten children were not uncommon the children do not always appear together on census returns, some of the older ones having left home by the time the youngest were born. Illegitimate children appear to have been accepted into families. Their number rose from 5 per cent in the first decade to 11, 10, 10 and 14 per cent in the following decades.

As well as the family, including in-laws, some households had servants, others agricultural labourers and apprentices, 'living in'. Some took in lodgers, mainly elderly paupers or single men or women new to the village. The term 'visitor' may have been used instead of lodger. In some cases, especially in 1811, two families were sharing a house. If the family was very large some of the children were sent to live with grandparents.

The uninhabited houses may have resulted from a decreasing demand or, like the old vicarage, have been abandoned because of their age.

The houses

Of the 142 houses existing in 1801 some seventy remained at the end of the century. Others, which were thatched, mostly remained until at least mid-century. Proctors and Chancery Cottage survived until the 'nineties. Those houses which disappeared were small cottages, three in Pilling Close, the cottages in Church Croft, some near Belle Vue, others near the Old Hall and three in the Hospital Close. Stones from these buildings were re-used in the building of walls or new houses.

Picturesque but primitive.
Waddington, 1842: 'a neat, white-looking village, with a clear rivulet running through it, over which is a small picturesque bridge, with an old house or two near it, combining to make a scene we thought worth sketching.'
(*C. Redding,* An Illustrated Itinerary of the County of Lancaster.)

Chancery—the last of the thatched cottages.

Mascar Row—eighteenth-century cottages built with stone staircases.

Although the population was increasing rapidly in the early part of the century little appears to have been done to provide new houses. The Old Hall was said by Whitaker to have been divided into cottages,[1] barns were converted into houses and two families, or more, shared a house. The widows at the Hospital were the ones who gained most from such new building as occurred: ten additional cottages were built in the 'twenties and four more in 1853. Thomas Taylor had a new house built for himself in 1824 and three more were built shortly afterwards in Spring Gardens.

With the decline in population in 1841 there was no great demand for additional houses but the old ones were increasingly in need of repair or total rebuilding. The Public Health Acts after 1848 showed a growing awareness of the danger to health arising from poor houses. According to a local doctor, Dr Musson, 'There is no more fruitful source of diseases common to children than living in a damp and ill-ventilated house.' The Rural Sanitary Authority wasted no time in condemning a number of houses, amongst them the Reader's House and houses at the Hospital.

The Hon. Isabella Ramsden, Lady of the Manor, was the first to show concern for her tenants by building them new houses. The first of these were the Ramsden Terrace houses. The plans show a kitchen, pantry and 'house' downstairs; two bedrooms above; a chairmaker's shop with room above attached to one house; coal houses, petties and a place for ashes. A pig yard and two gardens were also provided.

---

[1] T. D. Whitaker, *History and Antiquities of the Deanery of Craven*, p. 31.

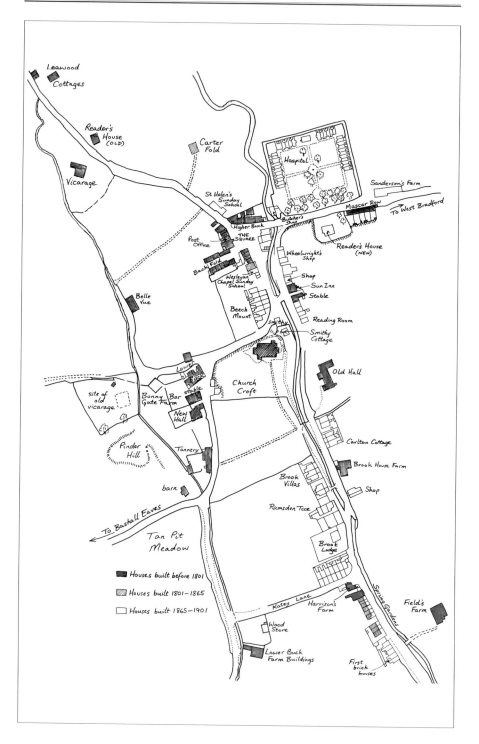

Housing development during the nineteenth century.

Ramsden Terrace, 1869—the beginning of a building era.

The rents were £6 and £10. These houses were built in 1869 with stone obtained from an old thatched cottage to the north of the terrace. The estimate of £407 included payments for pulling down the cottage, the work of the glazier, plumber, mason, joiner, carpenter, painter, and fitments such as ovens, boilers and grates.[1]

After 1876 further work was undertaken for the Ramsdens. Four houses were built along Katey Lane to replace 'Rat Row'. The state of the five old houses in Rat Row had been such that even drastic reductions of the rent had failed to induce the tenants to stay. By 1891 three more houses had been built along the lane. A new house and 'shop' were provided for William Boothman, the blacksmith. Money was borrowed from William Dewhurst, farmer and jeweller, for this purpose. Two houses were built adjoining the Sun Inn and the wheelwright also had a new house and workshop to the north of the inn.

These houses were unpretentious but solidly built; they still lacked inside lavatories and bathrooms. Some rather more substantial ones, however, were being built. The first of these, the Reader's House, was built in 1872. Brook Lodge was built in 1881 for a retired farmer and beyond this were two houses built in 1890 and three built in 1893.

These developments encouraged further building. Edward Chester, stone merchant, added two houses and the Reading Room to the Sun Inn row in 1882. In 1896

---

[1] West Yorkshire Archive Service (WYAS), Leeds, Ramsden Papers, bundle 25.

Brook Villas, 1890.

Mrs Carding built Carlton Cottage and two other houses in West View. Caleb Bishop built the first brick houses, a row of five, in the village. They were advertised as:

> Lobbied houses, parlour, kitchen, scullery with boiler and pantry, two bedrooms: good view back and front. Rent 2s. 10d.

Bishop also had a pair of stone houses built along the West Bradford road in 1898. They were opposite the schoolhouse which Edward Burton had paid for. The building of thirty cottages for the Hospital was the most ambitious undertaking.

If not replaced, some of the cottages were improved by alterations and additions. Thatch roofs disappeared. Though Back Fold inhabitants still had to make do with a communal privy, where two houses were joined together they benefited. The old Reader's House was eventually improved and as the century closed the Old Hall was about to be restored to its former glory. Not surprisingly, a visitor was not a little struck with the amount of building going on in the village.

3

Occupations

Farmers and Farming

FOR FARMERS the nineteenth century brought 'the best of times and the worst of times'. The increase in population and the cutting off of supplies of corn from the Continent during the Napoleonic Wars caused prices to treble and encouraged farmers to enclose and improve their land. When the wars ended in 1815 a parliament of landowners gave farmers protection from foreign competition by passing the Corn Laws to restrict the import of corn.

The post-war boom was short-lived and farmers suffered from the high poor rates and other charges which fell heavily on them. A slow improvement came after the Poor Law Amendment Act of 1834 and, two years later, the Tithe Commutation Act which removed the long-standing grievance of payment in kind. Though the Corn Laws were repealed in 1846, those farmers who adopted the practices advocated by the agriculturalist writer Caird found 'high farming' a sufficient defence against competition. They enjoyed something of a golden age until the prairies were opened up and cheap corn was shipped to England. When refrigerated meat came from New Zealand, chilled beef from the Argentine, cheap wool from Australia and dairy products from Denmark, even high farming was unable to survive one of the severest depressions in British agriculture. Farmers went bankrupt and some 300,000 out of an estimated total of one million agricultural labourers left the land. These developments had their repercussions in Waddington.

In the early nineteenth century farming in Waddington was still largely subsistence farming. Though rising prices encouraged farmers to increase production and improvements associated with the Agricultural Revolution made this possible, the population increase meant there was little surplus food. The mild, wet climate of the area was best suited to the rearing of sheep and cattle but restrictions on the import of corn and transport difficulties meant that corn had to be grown to supply local needs. Little wheat was grown because of the high rainfall but oats, for man and horse, and barley were grown in greater quantities. Potatoes and beans were field crops.

The land, flat and low-lying near the Ribble, rose to over 1,100 feet on the fell. It was mainly meadow, pasture and rough grazing for sheep and cattle. There was in 1801, however, more arable than the 11 per cent cultivated in 1850. In the summer, farmers were allowed to keep as many animals on the common fell as they could winter on their enclosed fields. Cattle, mainly of the longhorn or Craven breed, were reared;[1] surplus animals were sold in Clitheroe's street market.

Though some farms had the shippon near to the farmhouse, cows were sometimes milked in the fields or in a cowshed away from the farm and the milk was carried to the dairy in a back-can. This arrangement had the advantage of reducing the amount of carting to be done. Hay, stored in the cowshed loft, was fed to the cows during the winter and in the spring the manure was there for the spreading. Most of the milk was used in the making of butter or cheese: the skimmed milk and whey were fed to the pigs. As the century progressed it is evident that land was being taken out of cultivation and put down to grass. The Hospital records of 1814 show that grass seed was sown in one field after stone for drainage had been gathered and carted. Two years later, £2 11s. 4d. was spent on clover seed and in 1840 almost as much was paid for white clover seed for the field opposite the Hospital, 'thereafter to remain as grassland'. When Mrs Clarke leased Waddow the agreements included penalties for any reversion to arable.[2]

The year's work

Change, however, came slowly and the pattern of work during the first half of the century varied little. There was ploughing to be done in January, followed by harrowing, manuring and sowing. Fences and walls were repaired, hedges laid and ditches cleared. Lambing was the most important work in the early spring. In May, the sheep were collected by the farmers and brought to the fold on the fell for washing in the nearby stream. Shearing, another collective effort, took place in the following month. June was hay-making time. An expert with the scythe could cut an acre in a day, and every available person was called upon to help cut or turn the hay, rake it with wooden rakes into rows and then make it into cocks. Given a fine spell of weather, the hay was carted before July was out. If the hay was wet and had to be spread and turned the work could drag on till August. A second crop, or fog, was normally cut in August. A good supply of food and drink, the company of many workers and a spell of fine weather made the work more enjoyable.

The corn harvest in July or August meant another busy time. The field was first 'opened out', then from dawn till dark men, working as a team, cut the corn in readiness for the women to bind it into sheaves to be stooked. Threshing and winnowing were a winter occupation. Flails were used, and wind, blowing through the barn, separated the chaff from the grain which was then thrown into the air with a casting shovel. The heavy grain, which was carried beyond the 'tailings' was put into four-bushel sacks. The little wheat that was grown had sometimes to be dried in a kiln before being ground.

---

[1] Rennie Broun and Shirreff, *A General View of the Agriculture of the West Riding* (1794 pub., Board of Agriculture).
[2] Indenture, 19 November 1831.

In autumn there was some ploughing to be done and wheat to be sown. Pigs were killed and the bacon salted. Ale was brewed. Peat, cut in the early summer and allowed to dry, was carted from the fell. There was other carting to be done. Bracken and rushes were used for bedding the cattle when they were brought in at Martinmas (11 November). Lime had to be carted from the kiln at Brungerley, stones from the quarry for road work. In November, coppices were cut for faggots, woodland cleared of brushwood, trees pruned and young trees planted.

Though the seed drill and horse hoe had been invented in the previous century, it is unlikely that much machinery was used as most farms were too small to warrant it and labour was cheap. The plough, sickle and scythe were much in evidence. Even so, chaff-cutting machines and winnowing machines were beginning to appear. Other improvements were being made: lime produced locally for 1s. 6d. a load was widely used to reduce the acidity of the soil and was in high repute as a manure.[1]

Almost every farm had a garden, an orchard and a close near the house. Adjoining the house or grouped round the yard were a barn, sometimes a shippon, and a stable: one thirty-acre farm had stabling for three horses. Feazer had a wain-house, hay barn, stable, cow barn, corn barn and swine-cote. Hollins had a barn, stables, fold, yard, garden and calf croft. Gannies, the neighbouring farm, had a barn, stable, fold yard, orchard and garden. In the kitchen garden, more important than the small front garden, apples, plums, damsons and gooseberries were grown.

Women's work

The dairy was the province of the women. As the cows calved in the spring there was milk for cheese-making from May to October. The sieve, breaker, cheese vats and, most important, the cheese kettle, were all needed, along with the press which squeezed out the whey.

When butter-making took place the cream was skimmed off the milk and then, using the plunger in the stand-up type of churn, the butter was 'made to come' and the remaining buttermilk was removed. The flagged floors of the dairy were scrubbed, and the walls were whitewashed twice a year. The butter muslin and cloths were dried on elder bushes grown near the door to keep flies away.

Poultry keeping was another job for the farmer's wife and daughters. Hens, ducks and geese were kept and the eggs were sold in the village or at the market. Such was the work done on the twenty-six farms in the village.

Landowners

Details of the farms, their owners, tenants and acreage are obtainable from land tax returns and from the land sales registered at Wakefield. In 1801, the land, approximately 2,000 acres, was owned by thirteen people, eleven listed on the land tax return

---

[1] Baines, *History, Directory and Gazetteer of the County Palatine of Lancaster*, p. 612.

The landowners

Farms	Acreage	Owner in 1801	Later owners
Manor farms:			
Waddow	136	Clarke	1838 Ramsden: 1879 Garnett
Brungerley	144	Clarke	1838 Ramsden: 1879 Garnett
Fields House	110	Clarke	1838 Ramsden: 1879 Garnett
Fields	42	Clarke	1838 Ramsden: 1879 Garnett
Brook House	25	Clarke	1838 Ramsden: 1879 Garnett
Old Hall	37	Clarke	1838 Ramsden: 1879 Garnett: 1899 Waddington
Sun Inn	16	Clarke	1838 Ramsden: 1879 Garnett
Proctors (Sandersons)	50	Clarke	1838 Ramsden: 1879 Garnett
Baileys	46	Clarke	1803 Calverley: 1836 Oddie: 1843 Stewart: 1851 Shaw: 1893 Walmsley
Bowkers	40	Clarke	1803 Calverley: 1815 Taylor: 1824 Fenton: 1867 Burton
Manor farms sold in or before 1801:			
Gannies	52	Brocklehurst	1847 Holker
Hollins	99	Brocklehurst	1847 Holker
Cuttock Clough	268	Leach	1892 Hartley Baldwin
Leemings	24	Leach	1848 Garstang: 1873 Holker
Newy Nook	26	Isherwood, G.	1823 Isherwood, J.:1856 Grimshaw
Freeholders (Daisy Hill)	40	Walmsley	1825 Taylor: 1828 Brennand (Taylor's niece): 1836 Fenton: 1867 Burton
Thornbers	98	Walmsley	1825 Taylor: 1828 Brennand: 1836 Fenton: 1867 Burton
Dam (Mill)	47	Walmsley	1825 Taylor: 1828 Brennand: 1836 Fenton: 1867 Burton
Feazer	59	Taylor	1824 Fenton: 1867 Burton
Other farms:			
Lane Side	27	Taylor	1824 Fenton: 1867 Burton
Bonny Bar Gate	41	Bradshaw	1866 Walker: 1879 Walmsley
Elms	20	Bradshaw	1866 Walker: 1879 Walmsley
Carter Fold	30	Hospital	
Twitter (Alass)	20	Hospital	
Buck Inn	33	Parker	1820 Hospital
Helm (Mitchells)	153	Parker	1807 Brocklehurst: 1847 Holker
The Glebe	49	The vicar	

These farms were in existence at the end of the century. The size of some, especially Baileys and Leemings, changed following sales and subsequent reorganisation.
Acreages are those given in late nineteenth-century sales or in the 1850 tithe award.

and two others who bought land later in the year. The most important landowner was Mrs Clarke, Lady of the Manor. Her first husband, Thomas Weddell, had left her a life interest in an estate of some 1,100 acres but his considerable debts obliged her to sell off some of the property. She and her second husband, Major Clarke, lived at

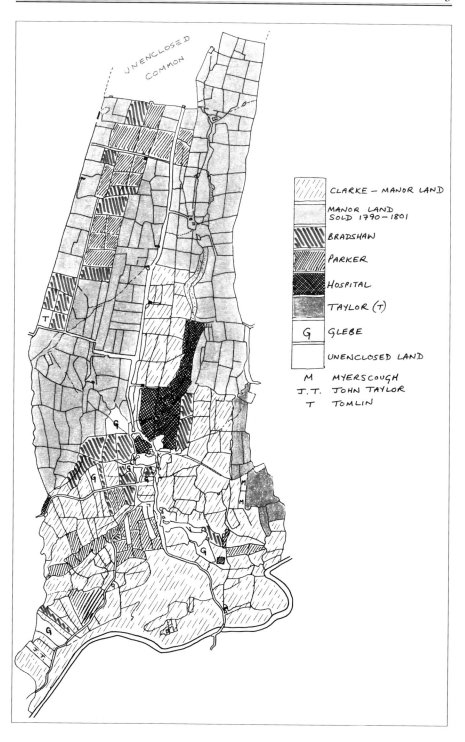

Landownership, 1801.

Merestone: boundary stone to mark
Thomas Parker's section of Lillands.

Waddow Hall which, along with gardens, orchard and woods, had 143 acres of arable, pasture and meadow land in what was still called 'the demesne'. Seven farms had been part of the manor for a considerable time. The two largest of these were Fields House Farm to the west of the hall, and Brungerley, extending to the Ribble, to the east. North of Brungerley were Fields, Brook, Old Hall, the Sun, whose innkeeper was part-time farmer, and Proctors, next to the Hospital. These were small farms of some 20 to 30 acres.

To the north again and extending to the fell were nine farms at one time part of the manor but sold at the turn of the century to existing or to new landowners. George Isherwood was one of the first to buy: in 1790 he bought Newy Nook. George Walmsley of Rochdale bought the three farms Freeholders, Thornbers and Dam Head with the corn mill for £2,150 in 1792. In the same year, Thomas Taylor of Eaves House, owner of Lane Side farm, bought Feazer Farm. In 1801 Cuttock Clough was sold to Mrs Clarke's sister, Elizabeth Leach; Leemings also became hers—a gift from her sister. John Brocklehurst of Burnley bought Gannies and Hollins, adjacent farms. Bookers and Baileys were sold a few years later.

John Bradshaw, magistrate, of Lancaster and later of Manchester, had for some time owned land in Waddington. His farms—the Elms, along Cross Lane, and Bonny Bar Gate—were usually held by one tenant. The Parkers of Browsholme according to a survey made in 1765 owned almost 200 acres in Waddington including New Hall, the tannery, Carter Fold, the Roebuck Inn and farm and Helm Farm near the fell; most of this they still held in 1801. As soon as they were prepared to sell, they found the Hospital Trustees, some of whom were members of the Parker family, ready purchasers.

Forty-nine acres farmed by the vicar or his tenants lay in eight different parts of the village, a legacy from open field days. Some of the fields and the old vicarage in Dobson Croft were let to weavers and craftsmen.

The remaining landowners included John Tomlin of Little Harwood, who was soon to sell Colthurst and land on the Bashall Eaves–Waddington boundary to the Brocklehursts. John Smith, shopkeeper, owned cottages and a croft near the Square. John Myerscough, yeoman, owned the Mascar Row cottages and a few acres near Lane Side (Healings).

All except two of the thirteen landowners lived in or within five miles of the village. An increasing number of industrialists like Tomlin and Brocklehurst from the cotton towns of Lancashire, were now investing in land.

The enclosure award[1]

By the time the Enclosure Act was passed in 1812 further sales, notably to the Calverleys and to Robert Walker, had increased the number of landowners to twenty. The Act and resultant enclosure award of 1819 led to further changes.

By custom the landowners, who were freeholders, or their tenants, had grazing rights for sheep and cattle on some 300 acres of fell known as The Common. The right of turbary provided them with fuel once they had cut and dried the peat. They were also allowed to cut rushes, bracken and ling for bedding for the cattle and for thatch. Shortly before the end of the eighteenth century Mrs Clarke began to enclose the Lord's Moss, claiming it to be the private property of the owner of the manor. There was an immediate outcry from a number of freeholders who held Lord's Moss to be common land on which they had rights of pasture and turbary, rights which they were determined to maintain. John Walmsley, nephew of the Walmsley who had bought three farms from Mrs Clarke, led the opposition to her when sheep belonging to one of his tenants were 'dogged' on Lord's Moss. Thomas Taylor, John Brocklehurst, the vicar and even Thomas Lister Parker of Browsholme, himself busy at the time enclosing a few acres on the neighbouring moor, readily pledged Walmsley their support. Attempts to settle the matter at a meeting in 1805 failed. A few years later the leading landowners, 'aware of the advantages which would result from enclosure', joined the landowners of the neighbouring townships and secured an Act of Parliament for the enclosure of their fells.

William Harper of Salmesbury was appointed commissioner responsible for the implementation of the Act. Notice of a meeting at which freeholders could put forward their claims was given at Mitton Church; other notices appeared in the *Blackburn Mail* and in West Riding newspapers. Then Harper sold parts of Waddington Fell to raise money towards his expenses of 2 guineas a day. At the auction, Walmsley bought 20½ acres for £290 and Taylor bought 42½ acres for £251. Later, Joseph Whittle of Whalley, by arrangement with the commissioner, bought 9 acres for £125. Nearly a quarter of the common was disposed of by these sales.

Next, Harper proceeded to 'view and value the land, set out the public highways and carriage ways over the heath, set out watering places for the cattle, arrange for the getting of stone, slate, flags and other materials for repairing buildings, bridges and walls and for the making and repairing of roads'.[2] As a result, a road 30 feet wide from the north end of Waddington Moor Lane across Waddington Fell to Newton Fell was made. From this road another one of the same width led to a public stone quarry at Cob Castle. The grazing of the quarry allotment was to be let by the highways surveyor to help pay for road repairs.

Following the surveying of the common came the main part of the work, the 'setting out, dividing and allotting the said tracts of common'. Those responsible for fencing the allotments were named.

---

[1] LRO, PR 3031 13/1.
[2] LRO, Enclosure Award, PR 3031/1.

The principle which Harper applied to Grindleton of dividing the common amongst the landowners according to the extent and value of their estates in the township appears to have been applied also to Waddington and a map showing their holdings was prepared for Harper.[1] Owners of estates who could give proof of rights of pasture and turbary were considered entitled to part of the common.

Of the twenty freeholders to whom allotments were made three were allocated waste land in the village near to their 'ancient enclosures'. Nine others were also granted part of the village waste land in addition to an allotment on the fell. All those who had allotments on the common were allowed to get marl, clay, stones, sand and gravel for their own use but not for sale.

Jane Clarke, who appears to have acquired Lord's Moss by this time, was acknowledged as 'owner of the soil and royalties upon the waste ground and common called Waddington Fell'. She received an allotment of a 'twentieth part in the value of the whole'. This amounted to 18 acres with mineral rights in and under the common reserved to her and to future lords of the manor. Two quarries were included in her allotment, although the public had the right to obtain stone from them.

Her sister, Mrs Leach, was allocated 106 acres 3 roods not only 'in respect of her freehold messuages, lands and hereditaments in Waddington'—this was said of the other landowners—but also 'in compensation and satisfaction of her right and interest in and over the said common and waste grounds'.

John Bradshaw and John Brocklehurst had both died before the enclosure was completed. Their trustees received 15 acres and 10 acres. John Walmsley received 11 acres adjoining the common land which he had purchased and Thomas Taylor was allotted 12 acres near to his purchase. The vicar, the Hospital and Thomas Lister Parker had approximately 5 acres each. Of the remaining freeholders, John Altham had 2½ acres: others had 1 acre or less, Richard Isherwood's 19 perches being the smallest allotment. These arrangements were completed by 1819. Eight of those with small allotments decided to sell them: the expense of enclosing a few roods some distance from the village was hardly worthwhile. Five of them sold to Taylor and the others to the Brocklehurst trustees; John Altham also sold his share of the common and his other property. However, the number of freeholders in Waddington was not greatly reduced by enclosure and although some might regret the loss of summer pasture for their sheep and were no longer able to get peat, they were not reduced as elsewhere to the position of landless labourers.

Enclosure entailed expenses for the encloser. The Hospital accounts show that they paid £5 1s. 0d. towards the commissioner's expenses and £1 12s. 2d. towards the survey of the fell. They employed a pair of men at 6s. a day to build walls. Quicks were planted as hedge boundaries, the land was drained and later a plantation was established. Some owners were content to pay the commissioner, fence the land as directed and leave their tenants to use the land for grazing. A few owners whose allotments adjoined their farms improved the land for pasture: Isherwood of Newy Nook, with the advantage of a lime-kiln, was one owner to do this. Most of the land, however, remained rough moorland with the quarries the most valuable asset.

---

[1] WYAS, Leeds, Waddington Hospital, box 14.

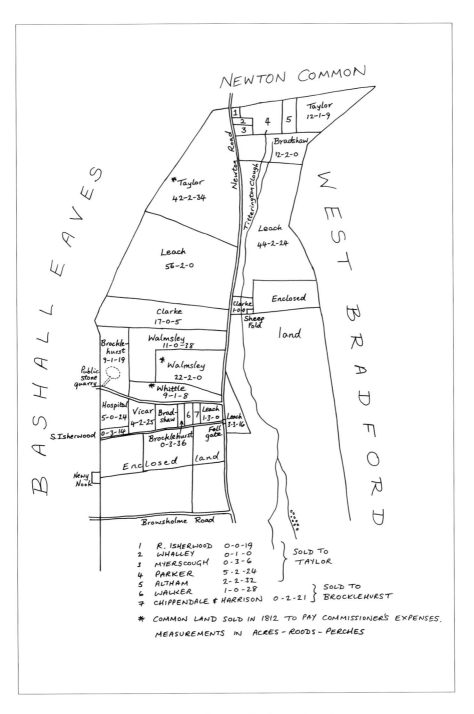

Waddington Common Enclosure Award.

The farms

Of the twenty-six farms seven were approximately 100 to 150 acres. (A 100-acre farm was considered to be large.) Ten farms were from 40 to 60 acres; the other nine were 20 to 40 acres. There were in addition a few smallholdings.

A typical farm had arable, meadow and pasture land. Horses were used, and cows, pigs and poultry were kept. Cheese and butter were made. Among the items included in the Sun Inn sale in 1808, were a cart which went for £5, collar, saddle, barkham, the haimes, a harrow, gig, two wheelbarrows, a cheese press and churn. There were two calves, a cow and calf, mare and foal, four pigs and wool. There were two silos and hay which 'sold at 7s. 2d. and 10s. 1½d. per yard upon scaffolds'.[1]

Field names

Fields varied in size from 2 to over 10 acres. Names which were used in the eighteenth century and even earlier remained in use, giving an indication of the nature and usage of the land or referring to the size, shape and position of the field.

Crofts, Great and Little, were pieces of land attached to a house. There was a Four Acre Field, Near and Far Four Acre Fields, Straight Field and Long Field. Irregular pieces of land were known as Butts. Probably the names West Field and South Field relate to the large open fields later divided into Higher and Lower West Fields.

Names such as Moor Field, Fleet (stream), Chapel Meadow, Laith Close were associated with man-made or natural features. Others—Parker, Dewhurst—were named after people, as were some of the farms. The character of the land is suggested in such names as Rough Field, Riddings, Heys, Limed. Barley Croft, Clover Land Meadow, Calf Croft, Horse Heys refer to farming; Mill Field, Tenter Field, Bleaching Spot to local industries.

Leases

The terms on which the farms were let varied. In the early part of the century seven-year leases were not unusual. In 1831 Mrs Clarke let Waddow Hall and some land on a seven-year lease beginning at 'Candlemas [2 February] Old Style'. Her husband's will declared eleven years to be the maximum lease, though she herself leased her own property for forty years at a low rent on condition that improvements were made and some land enclosed. On the other hand some leases were renewed annually.

Whatever the original lease, in practice many tenants stayed for life and were succeeded by either their widow or son. When Robert Turner had occupied one of the Hospital farms for forty years the Trustees made him an allowance in recognition of this and he remained as their tenant for another eight years. In 1801 five of Mrs Clarke's tenants had been in possession for twenty years or more: one remained as her tenant for another twelve years and two families remained for a further twenty years. Occasionally tenants were given notice, as was Robert Pye by John Brocklehurst in 1801.

---

[1] LRO, DDX/54/72.

The leases referred not only to the length of tenure but to rent and other conditions. Customarily, rents were due half-yearly on Lady Day (25 March) and at Michaelmas (29 September). The Hospital and other landowners kept up the practice of giving their tenants a small payment or dinner on rent day. In 1808 John Pilling was paying a yearly rent of £95 for the Buck and accompanying farmland (33 acres): he also paid all taxes. Incoming tenants might have to face an increase. Both Mrs Clarke and, after her death in 1838, the Hon. Isabella Ramsden when letting Waddow Hall and its land, stipulated in the lease that the meadows were to be manured: tenants were to 'spread and bestow all the hay straw fodder manure compost dung and ashes which shall grow arise be gotten upon or from the said premises and to leave some at a convenient place at the termination of the lease'.[1] Other clauses referred to the care and preservation of woodland and to the owner's hunting rights and the right to cut trees.

The landlords varied in their attentiveness to their tenants' needs. The Hospital Trustees appear to have been good landlords. They accepted responsibility for the repair of farmhouses and outbuildings. In 1829 they built a barn on their Twitter Bridge Farm—the first building on the site. In 1839, following storm damage, they built a new house at Carter Fold at a cost of £200. (The stone had to be carted by the tenant from two old cottages on the farm.) A new shippon and barn were built at the same time and later a liquid manure tank was put in. The Buck had a new barn, calf house, a small shippon and pig-cote. The Trustees attended to minor repairs, to gates and bridges, provided a new hay-hole door, repaired a stable and put in two milkhouse stones. They provided clover seed, fruit trees, lime and drain pipes and paid for the work of drainage. Trees, alder, poplars, beech and larch were planted. They even paid a mole-catcher who was frequently employed at Carter Fold.

The farmers

It was customary, but not obligatory until 1875, to pay the tenant for improvements. By the time some of the farmers had paid the rent and met their other commitments of tithe, poor and highway rate, they had not much money in hand. If they worked hard, however, they generally had enough to eat and a house which, although possessing few comforts, was at least warm. Some of the older farmhouses, such as eighteenth-century Brook House Farm, with their thick walls, remain. Downstairs there were two main rooms, the 'house' or kitchen, and parlour. Each had a fireplace but the parlour, though it sometimes served as a bedroom, was seldom used. Fields House, a late eighteenth-century three-storey building, and the new farmhouse at Carter Fold (1839) had extra rooms. In the kitchen, wood, peat or coal was burned. Large pans over the fire were used for boiling bacon and, less frequently, beef. Bread was baked in the oven and oat and haver cake were made on the bacstone. Hams, sides of bacon and pickled beef were in evidence.

Beyond the essential table and chairs, and chest or sideboard, some of which items were made in the village, there was little furniture. Beds (the bedstocks were often

---

[1] Indenture, 3 September 1846.

*Views of the front
and rear of the
Old Hall in 1842.*

mentioned in wills) had feather mattresses though chaff was also used as a filling. Candles supplied the lighting. Water was pumped from wells or was taken from a spring.

One description of a farmhouse and its occupants made in 1841 leaves no doubt as to what some conditions were like.

> Meanness and dirt, cows and cowhouses, dogs and stables, with shattered implements of husbandry, alone saluted our sight … Turning a little to the right, however, we found that it was 'feeding time' for others besides the quadrupal live-stock. There around a clothless table, and up and down a filthy room, sat or stood grand-father and his wife, master and his wife, a serving woman and several brawny lads, with one intelligent-looking girl, literally devouring fried fat bacon and boiled potatoes. The condition of their persons we pass, lest we should be charged with caricature … At length, having finished his meal and wiped his mouth with the back of his hand, grandfather became communicative.[1]

This was Thomas Leeming, who was then farming 42 acres at the Old Hall. However uncouth his person and his home he took sufficient interest in politics to vote in the 1841 election and, unlike other villagers, he voted Whig.

---

[1] C. Redding, 'An Illustrated Itinerary of the County of Lancaster', *England in the Nineteenth Century*, VI, *Lancashire* (How and Parsons).

Agricultural labourers

At the beginning of the century at least one third of the villagers were making a living from farming. In addition to the farmers and their families there were twenty-one servants or labourers, many likely to be agricultural labourers, included in the muster roll (1803). The 1831 census states that thirty-eight labourers were employed in agriculture by ten out of twenty farmers. Labourers who 'lived in' slept in a loft or attic and usually had their meals with the family though later in the century they ate apart. Once they could afford to marry and had found a cottage they were more independent. Farmers' sons, if not needed to work at home, worked on another farm. In the late eighteenth century labourers had been supplied with food and clothing and up to £5 a year. In the early nineteenth century wages were rising; in 1812 for stone wall building and other labouring jobs men were paid 3s. a day. For agricultural workers the wages would have been much the same. By 1850 things were beginning to improve.

The Tithe Award

1850 was a landmark in the farming history of the village. Though the Tithe Commutation Act had been passed in 1836 it was fourteen years before it was implemented in Waddington. Tithe, one tenth of crops and produce, had originally been paid to support the clergy. Waddington had paid the great tithe on corn and grain to Cockersand Abbey until the dissolution of the monasteries. Then it was paid to a lay person, usually the owner of the manor. The small tithe, paid originally to the Rector of Mitton, in 1850 was being paid to the trustees of Cardinal Weld.

Payment of produce, inconvenient for both payer and recipient, led to many disputes and irregularities. Individual landowners such as Thomas Taylor made arrangements to buy the tithe from the holders. In 1832 Mrs Clarke and her sister made tithe agreements with Thomas Weld for Leemings, Lord's Moss and Cuttock Clough. Walmsley paid £340 for the small tithe on his 150 acres. In most cases these tithes were then 'merged' with the rent.

By 1850 tithes, great and small, had been merged and accepted on 773 acres, more than a third of all the land in Waddington. Great tithe had been commuted on a further 615 acres so that when the Tithe Award was made in 1850, Mrs Ramsden was receiving tithe on only 162 acres. As not much corn was being grown, she was allowed £4 10s. od. payment of which was apportioned to the various properties. The trustees of Cardinal Weld were allowed £50 14s. 8d. instead of small tithe on 724 acres. A sum of £19 7s. od. was apportioned to owners who had bought tithe but had not converted it to a rent charge.

Felix Leach made the survey upon which the award was based and he determined the sums of money to be paid to the tithe owners by averaging the prices of wheat, barley and oats over the last seven years.

The award contains much information relating to the farms, owners, tenants and crops, though there are discrepancies between Leach's figures for the size of farms and those given in the census a year later.[1] In 1851 five families—Ramsden, Bradshaw, Fenton, Leach, Brocklehurst—held 82 per cent of Waddington's 2,000 acres. Some, like James Grimshaw, schoolmaster, John Harrison and Robert Whittle of the Moor-cock, owned only a few acres, enough to qualify for the vote. Those who rented such smallholdings usually had another occupation. William Hanson, who farmed a part of the glebe, was a mason, and the Cunliffes farmed two fields while still working as hand-loom weavers. Even some of those with medium and small farms had to rely on another source of income: two of them were innkeepers and one farmer was a shoemaker. Mrs Foulds was a dressmaker with two apprentices; three members of the family at Carter Fold were employed in industry.

Changes in land ownership

Changes in land ownership occurred in the second half of the nineteenth century. When the Bradshaws sold their land in 1866 and retired to the south, Robert Walker, the sitting tenant, became owner. The Fenton Estate was sold to Edward Burton, a wealthy manufacturer. Leemings and Brocklehurst–Holker land became Lady Holker's Colthurst Estate after her husband's death.

The most important sale was that of the manor. In 1879 the Ramsdens sold the 587-acre estate which included Waddow Hall and 159 acres of parkland to William Garnett, cotton manufacturer. Garnett sold part of the estate—the Old Hall and a few acres—in 1899 to John Waddington. The Leaches sold Cuttock Clough in 1892 to Hartley Baldwin of Winkley Hall (see table on p. 22).

Their tenants

Of the twenty-six farmers living in Waddington in 1851 only three had been born there. The others came from the nearby villages of Sawley, Slaidburn, Easington, Grindleton and Harrop Fold. Several of the families—the Rushtons, Tattersalls and Chesters—became related by marriage. Other farmers found their partners in neigh-bouring villages, usually from farming families. Tenants, unless moving to a bigger farm, were not inclined to move. Of the 1851 tenant families, twelve were still tenants in 1861; nine were tenants in 1871 and one in 1881. Felix Leach occupied Brungerley for over fifty years; the Foulds were at Brook House Farm for sixty years and the Tattersalls at Hollins for forty years. 'A good tenant is never disturbed and even a poor one is long borne with' appears to have been the prevailing custom.

Landowners continued to be responsible for buildings, and the Agricultural Hold-ings Act of 1875 was designed to improve the position of tenants. The act, like others, was not always observed: 'The provisions of the Act shall not apply to the Contract of Tenancy' stated one Waddington agreement in 1882. In 1887, William Altham's agreement when he took over the Buck Farm stated that 'the conditions of the Act of 1883 except such as cannot lawfully be excluded by agreement shall not apply'. Other agreements stated that the landlords reserved all game for themselves. Dogs hunting on an estate could be shot.

---

3 LRO, Tithe Award, PR 3031/4/6.

Brook House Farm: built in the village c.1762.

Brungerley—the eastern extension is early nineteenth-century.

Agricultural labourers after 1850

On the larger farms the family and one labourer appear to have done the work, with extra labour at busy times. Leach was the exception. When he was farming three farms (400 acres) he had eight labourers, four of whom lived in; one was the son of a neighbouring farmer. In 1851 there was one shepherd and forty-seven labourers in Waddington, nineteen of whom had been born there. Apart from one from Long Preston, the rest came from an area within ten miles of the village, and half of them were already married when they came to Waddington. Seventeen labourers lived in—a practice more common in the north than in other parts of England. Some, coming from the same village as their employer, were probably known to him or had been recommended. Others may have been hired at the March or October fairs in Clitheroe, though the practice of standing with a straw in their billycock, waiting to be given a shilling on being hired, was dying out. Only three of the forty-seven labourers were in their teens and twenty-three were over thirty-five. Already towns and factories were attracting workers from the land.

Most farmers regarded March as the beginning of the year, at least as far as their male employees were concerned. Their wages, with keep, were from £10 to £12 a year, a shepherd expected to earn 2s. a week more than other agricultural labourers. Those in their own homes, for which they would pay £2 to £4 a year rent, could earn from 12s. to 14s. a week. Caird reckoned their earnings to be 37 per cent higher than the earnings of southern labourers. In 1858 men working in the hay fields were paid from 2s. to 3s. a day, with drink; women received half that amount. Some labourers' wives supplemented the family's income by working at the mill.

Conditions for labourers remained much the same in the second half of the century as in the first. A few kept a pig and there was a greater interest in gardening. As the working day was not shortened by legislation labourers started work at six, taking breakfast with them into the fields and having dinner brought out to them. Despite this they had a longer life expectancy than most other labourers.

Farming practices

At the time when Waddington's tithe award was being made *The Times* commissioned James Caird to write a series of letters describing the state of agriculture in thirty-two counties in England. Of the West Riding he wrote 'Farming cannot claim a very prominent place.' Although there were eminent exceptions he claimed that there was a great extent of imperfectly drained land, foul stubbles, light, and in many cases, carelessly managed turnip crops. 'Much yet remains to be done by landlord and tenant.'[1] As he went by train up the Lune Valley and on to the dales he noted that there was scarcely a ploughed field. Although he did not visit Waddington, several of his observations would have applied.

---

[1] J. Caird, *English Farming 1850–51*.

By the late 1850s and '60s there were indications that the high farming practices advocated by Caird were being followed and something of a golden age had dawned. Nearly fifty years after Sanderson's sale at the Sun Inn there was a farm sale in 1856 a few miles out of Waddington. At this, in addition to the churn and butter bowls, the scythe and harrow, were a threshing machine, winnowing machine, a Ransome plough, horse rake, turnip drills, turnip chopper, scarifier, haycutter and a corn crusher.[1] When Dewhurst took over Brungerley (1871) he intended to do some river banking and drainage. He also planned to fix a small engine to drive a chaff cutter, root pulper, cake crusher, and a mill for grinding seeds etc. As, however, his tenancy was then only yearly he did not feel justified in undertaking the improvements for the time being.

Land was being improved by the application of manure, lime and fertilisers: bone manure was bought for Carter Fold. There were two lime-burners in the village in 1851 and the kilns at Brungerley were still in use. Jeremiah Garnett of Low Moor, a relation of the Waddow Garnetts and a man greatly interested in science, was one of the first in the country to have guano imported. Drainage, 'the great improvement of the age' was encouraged by government grants. When drain pipes were made locally by Caleb and William Bishop the Hospital Trustees and others used pipes to replace the old drainage system of filling trenches with stone topped with straw. The Hospital Trustees paid £5 8s. 6d. for drainage 'tiles' for the Buck Farm in one year and a further £3 9s. 10d. in 1874. A number of combined barns/cowsheds were built and old hay-lofts were repaired. A farmhouse was built in 1883 at Twitter Bridge at a cost of £400.

The golden age

During this so-called golden age farms were difficult to get. Tenants competed for the farms and were prepared to pay for lime and drainage. 'Do not delay offering your Browsholme Farm for competition' wrote Edward Parker to his son. 'Farms are very much wanted.' An increase in rent was usual when a new tenant took over.

The Clitheroe Agricultural Show, first held in 1862, gave publicity to the latest methods of farming and machinery and the local newspaper encouraged further improvements with articles on silage, poultry rearing and dairying. The tithe award showed that of the 1,135 acres under consideration 121 acres or 11 per cent were arable, 227 or 20 per cent were meadow and 736 acres or 65 per cent were pasture. Most of the farmers in 1851 had some arable land even if only an acre or two; Leach had 47 acres and grew potatoes, mangolds and turnips as well as corn. In 1860 his lease stated it was lawful for him to 'lay down and sow with approved grass seeds any of the closes'. The old clause about cultivating arable with wheat was removed for though 1855 was the peak year for cereal growing in England corn growing had already passed its peak in this area. The miller, a part-time farmer by 1851, had ceased to operate the mill before 1871. When the manor was sold in 1879, only 4 of its 197 acres were arable. In August 1889, the local paper stated that 'Grain growers about this time are anxious for the ripening sun. Happily, in this part there is not much grain growing.'

---

[1] LRO, DDX/28/286.

Decline of arable farming

In 1892 it was said that 'the district is essentially a grazing district and consequently the chief consideration is the hay harvest'. The remark could have been made in 1867 when the Post Office Directory stated that 'the chief crop is grass'. In 1874 Sir John Ramsden's agent commented thus on a request made for a new barn and shippon at Brungerley: 'There is need for some building to supply the place of the one in ruins especially as the whole of the farm is now in grass thereby carrying a greater number of cattle and requiring more accommodation in winter.'[1] Before the end of the century it was reported that 'ploughing has become unknown in our midst' (1898).

Corn had never been grown extensively in the district and when better transport made it easy for farmers to obtain cheap corn from America they began to specialise in dairy farming for which, for climatic reasons, they were better suited. Land was put down to permanent pasture. Agreements made it clear that it was in order for tenants to 'lay down and sow with approved grass seeds'. In 1864 the Hospital paid a tenant 19s. 11d. for grass seed for this purpose. The meadows were producing more grass, and hay-making methods changed. In 1861 John O'Neil noted in his diary, 'I saw the mowing machine at work this morning [near Clitheroe] for the first time in my life; with two horses it can do the work of ten men.' In 1890 at a farm sale in Bashall Eaves there was a mowing machine and a shadray amongst the implements advertised for sale. Though it was increasingly common to see the mowing machine lay the well-grown grass in swathes, extra men were still being hired for hay-making at Bolton-by-Bowland fair in June 1890. In that year those waiting to be hired stuck out in the early part of the day for higher wages. Demand proved to be slow and in the end the following terms were agreed upon: 'Best English £4 to £6: others and Irish £3 10s. to £5: youths £2 to £4 for the month.' The following year between two and three hundred Irish labourers were waiting to be hired. Women still worked in the hay fields, some from the Hospital joining in the hay-making in their holiday week.

In 1889 hay-making had begun early as it was an exceptionally dry summer. There was soon a cry for water as the pastures scorched and there was not likely to be much grass. Even so an observer noted that 'passing through Waddington we noticed several places where the loaded and stacked hay looked somewhat too green for our liking. It would be better to ensilo it.' At the time, talks on ensilage were being given at meetings of the Clitheroe Agricultural Association.

As the mowing and other machines replaced men on the farms there was an increased demand for horses and the Horse Fair was started in Clitheroe in 1883. This meant that horses, mainly Shire and Clydesdales, could be bought in May ready for the hay-making and sold off in October for £28 to £40.

With 3 acres considered sufficient to support one cow, dairy farmers were able to keep several cows, mostly shorthorns. Turnips, kale and lucerne were grown as part of their feed. By the 'eighties the Low Moor Mills and Dugdales were delivering to farmers 'dairy cake for better milk and butter'.

---

[1] WYAS, Leeds, RA 65/12, Ramsden papers.

Dairy farming had become sufficiently important by 1861 for dairymaids, one of whom came from Northampton, to be employed on three farms. Classes for butter-making were held in Clitheroe, demonstrations and competitions took place at the Agricultural Show and in 1892 a ten-day school with theory and practical work was held. Much of the dairy work was done in the summer when butter could be made from 'grass milk'. The new up-and-over type of churn made the work easier but with the inspection of dairies and cowsheds greater attention had to be paid to cleanliness.

In 1885 one farmer was selling 26 lbs. of butter a week at 1s. 4½d. a pound; cheese sold for 33s. to 43s.

Extract from the Account Book kept by George Holden, who farmed at Bashall Eaves and Waddington.

a hundredweight. Dewhursts at the Old Hall were getting 2½d. a quart for milk and 1d. for skimmed or 'blue' milk. Milk was sold in the village or taken in kits to Clitheroe station—a perilous journey in winter when roads were icy—for Manchester and other towns.

In April and May, winter-fed cattle were sold off and young beasts for summer feeding were bought at Clitheroe cattle market, opened in 1878, or at the new Gisburn market. Cows sold for £12 to £17, calving cows for £16 to £27. Local farmers attended the shows at Clitheroe and Whalley and won prizes for their bulls and cows.

Pigs, especially Yorkshire Whites, were to be found on most farms. Pig meal and bean meal were fed to them in addition to whey. Farmers, especially those with some rough fell country, kept sheep. The black-faced ones were popular though there were some pure Leicester and Lonks at Brungerley. Ducks, hens, and, towards the end of the century, turkeys were reared. The Michaelmas goose was still popular. Marsden and Wallbank of Waddington advertised eggs for hatching from their prize poultry. Their hens and pullets had 'unlimited grass runs' and the eggs sold at thirteen for 7s. 6d.; some no doubt were hatched in incubators. When there was a sale at Brungerley in 1900 it included two Shire horses, sixty head of cattle, ten sheep, ten pigs, geese, ducks, poultry, implements and 300 yards of rich mow hay. Farming appears not to have changed greatly during the last decades of the century.

Depression

Though the golden age of farming lasted longer here than in the corn-growing areas of England there was no escaping the agricultural depression.

The arrival of refrigerated meat meant that a Clitheroe shop could sell legs of New Zealand lamb for 5d. a pound. Chilled beef from the Argentine also meant competition. There was competition too from foreign dairy products. A series of poor harvests aggravated the situation. There were wet summers in 1878 and 1879 with worse to come. In 1890 hay was out in the fields in September and half the crop proved worthless; prayers were said at St Helen's when the wet weather continued in the following year. The harshness of the previous winter had beaten all previous records and many sheep had been lost in snow drifts. A late spring and poor growing season followed and disease broke out. An outbreak of foot and mouth disease closed the Clitheroe markets in 1892. Earlier there had been outbreaks of scab, rinderpest and liver rot.

When a meeting was held in Clitheroe in 1892 to consider the state of agriculture, Mr Kay Shuttleworth declared the depression to be unparalleled in extent and severity, with tenant farmers finding it impossible to pay the rent and make ends meet.

In Waddington farms were proving difficult to let—farm bailiffs had taken over four as early as 1871. The Deans gave up Gannies to become cattle dealers. In 1881 eight farmers 'out of business' were living in Waddington. In 1892 a tenant applied to the Hospital Trustees for a reduction of his rent owing to the bad times. Landowners had a choice of evils:

> Forgive the arrears and reduce their rent or make a distress and have the farm thrown on your hands. It is quite true that tenants now dictate their own terms and it is better to yield as far as possible in order to keep the farms occupied. (1883)

Lady Holker offered her tenants the inducement of lower rents and William Garnett reduced rents by 10 per cent for his tenants. When Leemings and Gannies were to let the advertisement appeared in the *Clitheroe Times* for over three months. Feazer proved equally difficult to let in 1895.

Food prices were falling; butter sold for 1s. a pound and meetings were held to try to obtain a better price for milk. Farmers' income, the wages of the labourers and their chances of employment diminished. Only eleven agricultural labourers remained in Waddington in 1881 as compared with forty-seven in 1851: machines and pastoral farming as well as the depression had driven them off the land. Joseph Arch addressing a meeting at Clitheroe urged the labourers who were left to join the agricultural union.

Though farmers made little profit in the closing years of the century, other people had cheaper food. They at least could join in the harvest thanksgiving services newly introduced to the village.

Textile Workers

The hand-loom weavers

Long before the Industrial Revolution affected Waddington, wool and flax, both produced locally, had been spun by the women and then woven by men on looms set up in their homes. Preston was a flourishing market for linen produced in north-west Lancashire and in Waddington, on the fringe of this area, flax had been grown on land known as 'Lillands'.

Woollen cloth was taken to a walk mill near Feazer for fulling and dyeing. Afterwards it was stretched on wooden frames or tenters in Higher and Lower Tenter fields. In 1792 when Thomas Taylor purchased 'all the buildings, lands, tenements being at Feizor Houses ... with the walk mill or fulling mill, the dyehouse and tenters', the tenters were said to be 'in ruin'.[1] Some weavers, influenced by developments in Lancashire, were turning to the production of fustian, a coarse cloth with a linen warp and a cotton weft, and, by the beginning of the nineteenth century, to the weaving of cotton.

By this time spinning as a domestic industry had been replaced by the factory system. One of the first and largest of the spinning mills to be built in the area had been built in the late eighteenth century at Low Moor two miles from Waddington. By 1824 twenty spinning frames with 1,200 spindles and seven with 720 spindles powered by a water wheel were producing an ample supply of fine strong yarn suitable for the local weavers to use as warp and yarn for the weft. That Waddington weavers were using cotton is apparent from the Muster Roll of 1803.

Twenty-nine men between the ages of seventeen and fifty-five—30 per cent of those listed—were given as weavers on the roll. Older men with children acting as their winders were also weavers, as were some women. There are few statistics relating to them but between 1813 and 1822 seventeen of the twenty mothers who had illegitimate babies were weavers.[2]

Some farmers, especially those with 20 acres or less, probably did the same as Cornelius Ashworth, another Yorkshire farmer, who, on 'a fine frosty clear droughty day sized a warp and churned in the forenoon. In the afternoon wove 5 yards'.

Twenty-four of the twenty-nine Muster Roll [3] weavers were Waddington-born; four were from Grindleton and West Bradford, the other townships in the parish. Ten under thirty were unmarried. Marriages led to many inter-relationships between the weavers. The Hansons were related to the Wilsons and the Nowells and through them to the Thornbers and Earnshaws. The Earnshaws were related to the Garners, Chippendales and Fishwicks. The Nutters and Seedals were also related by marriage.

Some of their children, Benjamin Mitchell, Hannah Nowell, Richard Parker, Ellen and Mary Whitehead, became weavers, as did at least two of the Read family, two of George Wilson's family and three of James Wilson's family.

---

[1] WYAS, Wakefield Land Registration DK. p.273.363.
[2] Church Archives, Parish Register.
[3] *The Craven Muster Roll, 1803* (North Yorkshire County Council, 1976).

There was a further increase in the weaving population as more people moved to Waddington and settled there in the early decades of the century. James Windle of West Bradford, James Slinger and twenty-five others whose names appear in the parish registers were amongst the newcomers.

This was the time when 'Every lumber room, even old barns, carthouses and outbuildings of every description were repaired, windows broke through the old blank walls and all fitted up for loom shops'.[1] There were at least two weaving sheds in the village. An indenture of lease and release dated 1816 related to a 'messuage with the weaver's shop and garden tenanted by George Read'.[2] There was another 'messuage, with a weaving shop and yard with stairs, nearby'.[3] When William Lawson came to Waddington in 1838 he saw weavers being given weft in a room beside the Higher Buck. They were paid when they delivered their pieces. An old barn in Back Fold appears to have been converted into a weavers' shop and in the Square the back-to-back houses with cellars were not unlike the Lancashire type of weaver's house.

There were hand-loom weavers' shops alongside the garden wall adjoining the westerly side of Back Fold Chapel. When they fell into disuse they were taken down at the expense of the vicar so (it is said) that he might have an uninterrupted view of the parish church from the vicarage.

The weavers set up their looms in the manner described by the Lancashire weaver Samuel Bamford. He sized the warp by brushing it over with a mixture of boiled flour and water, dried it with hot irons and beamed it in the loom. Winders meanwhile wound the yarn on to cops ready for the shuttle which, with the help of picking sticks, was sent from side to side of the loom.

Though weavers sometimes imposed long working hours upon themselves there was no 'tackler, no gaffer, no bell, no manager' to harass them. Monday was a slack day and weavers were to be seen in the afternoon 'playing marbles and enjoying themselves like schoolboys'.[4] Some found they need only work four days a week.

For them, the early years of the nineteenth century were, on the whole, times of prosperity. Families in Mellor, twelve miles away, were earning from 40s. to 100s. a week. In Blackburn weavers earned from 40s. to 50s. a week and boys and girls of twelve could earn a guinea. Earnings in Waddington, if perhaps not on this scale, must have been high until ever-increasing production had an adverse effect.

Towards the end of the Napoleonic Wars trade fluctuations produced some 'long faces and short purses' amongst the merchants. In one of his letters the Revd Thomas Wilson referred to the stagnation of trade in 1811:

The families of weavers, from want of economy in better times, and from want of employment or being employed at reduced wages, impose upon the parishes an overwhelming load of taxes for their relief, and what increases the evil is, that the persons who have been employed as weavers are incapable of other

[1] W. Radcliffe, *Origin of the New System of Manufacture, Commonly Called 'Power Loom Weaving'*, p. 60.
[2] WYAS, Wakefield, Land Registration GN, p. 479.
[3] WYAS, Wakefield, Land Registration, HN, p. 171.
[4] *Clitheroe Advertiser and Times*, 3 December 1926.

business; they cannot handle a spade or a pick-axe, and become a dead weight upon the townships to which they belong.[1]

A further fall in wages resulted from the perfecting of Cartwright's loom. By 1815 the finest cloth could be produced mechanically and a young weaver in a mill looking after two looms could weave fifteen pieces (60 to 100 yards) in the time that an experienced hand-loom weaver produced two. Wages fell to 3½d. a yard in 1826 as compared with 3s. a yard before Cartwright's invention.

Although elsewhere at this time men were trying to wreck the looms which were depriving them of work, power looms were no immediate threat to the weavers of Waddington. It was not until 1824 that a weaving shed was built at Low Moor and power looms installed. The mill expanded rapidly and in 1826 was marketing its finished goods in Manchester for export to the Far East. That year was one of severe trade depression which inevitably affected Waddington and district. There were many violent uprisings and during the Lancashire riots starving weavers determined to destroy the power looms in what proved to be 'one of the most dramatic events in the history of the English cotton industry'.[2] Hardly a loom was spared at Accrington and Blackburn. Six rioters were shot at Ramsbottom. As the men advanced against Low Moor, horse soldiers with swords glittering in the air tried to persuade them to return home. The mob were not impressed by promises of better times to come and continued to advance. At the factory they found the owners had barricaded the gates, there was a cannon in the middle of the road and the yeomanry had taken over from the soldiers.[3] Remembering the savagery of the yeomanry at Peterloo, the rioters turned back when they saw them and the cannon.

In 1829, another bleak year, there were further demonstrations at Low Moor. Garnett and Horsfall were reported to be cutting a 'gulph' of considerable width and depth around the outer wall of their premises. When filled with water this was expected to render the place almost impregnable. The demonstrators were again defeated. To survive, the hand-loom weavers worked longer hours only to force prices and wages down still more.

In the 'thirties conditions were desperate. In the five years 1830–4 an average of £200 a year was 'expended for the maintenance and relief of the Poor' in Waddington.[4] Petitions were addressed to the government—so many that eventually a select committee was set up to consider the position of the hand-loom weavers. Taking Bolton, Oldham and Preston as representative towns the committee examined conditions there from 1834–5.

In Bolton it was found that the weavers ate chiefly oatmeal, porridge and potatoes, with occasionally a small piece of butcher's meat. They were literally clothed in rags whereas forty years earlier they had had a Sunday suit. As to their bedding, 'they appear to be very bare of clothing'. 'I have seen many houses,' stated one witness,

---

[1] F. R. Raines, *Miscellanies: Memoirs of the Life of Revd Thomas Wilson* (Chetham Society, 1857–8).
[2] D. Bythell, foreword to *Riot!*.
[3] W. Turner, *Riot!: the story of the East Lancashire loom breakers in 1826* (Lancashire County Books, 1992), p. 18.
[4] Poor Rate Returns 1830–4 (1835), p. 241.

'with only two or three three-legged stools, and some I have seen without a stool or chair, with only a tea-chest to put their clothes in and to sit upon.'[1] Fielden, MP for Oldham, stated that many slept on straw. 'Their labour is excessive, not infrequently 16 hours a day.' Figures relating to weekly wages tell their own story.[2]

1797–1804	26s. 8d.
1804–1811	20s. 0d.
1811–1818	14s. 7d.
1818–1825	8s. 9d
1825–1832	6s. 4d.
1832–1835	5s. 6d.

Meanwhile, prices had risen and what would have been bought in wheat, malt, butter and cheese for 5s. in 1801 cost 22s. in 1839.[3]

Conditions in Waddington may not have been as grim as those in the towns but inevitably there were hardships. The government, in spite of the expressed opinion that the sufferings of the hand-loom weavers have 'for years continued to an extent and intensity scarcely to be credited or conceived', took no action other than amend the poor law.

Their aim was to end the system of outdoor relief and compel those seeking help to enter a workhouse. The Act was viewed with dismay by the workers and petitions were presented to the government against the measure. Waddington, Bolton-by-Bowland, Chatburn, Clitheroe, Gisburn, Sawley, Slaidburn and West Bradford were among the petitioners.[4] They achieved nothing. In 1842 Dr McDonall, the Ramsbottom Chartist, reported to a select committee on wages that he had seen as many as five hundred hand-loom weavers and factory workers begging through the villages around Blackburn and Clitheroe.

Local weavers were fortunate in one respect. Once the Board of Guardians had established the workhouses they continued to pay outdoor relief regardless of the Poor Law Amendment Act. They subsidised wages and supplied food to hand-loom weavers. Their minute book shows that in 1859 one family where the husband earned 5s. a week, his wife 3s. 6d., his ten-year-old daughter, who was a winder, 1s. 3d., were allowed 1s. in money and 1s. in kind. The other member of the family, a son, acted as winder for his parents.

> Knackety, Knickety, Knickety Knack
> Thin water porridge and hardly that

were the words set to their looms by those weavers who still worked.[5]

Rather than rely on charity the weavers made efforts to help themselves and in 1838 a branch of the Ancient Order of Foresters was formed in Waddington. The

1 An Analysis of the Evidence taken before the Select Committee on Hand-Loom Weavers' Petitions, p. 3.
2 *Ibid.*, p. 10.
3 Report from the Select Committee on Hand-Loom Weavers' Petitions, XII, PP 1835, p. 29.
4 PP 1837/8 (681) XVIII part 1, pp. 48–9.
5 S. Clarke, *Clitheroe in the Old Coaching Days*, 2nd edn (1929), p. 34.

first secretary was Henry Fishwick, schoolmaster, and son of a weaver. Members paid a small subscription and were entitled to sick and unemployment pay.

Gradually the number of weavers dwindled. In 1841 there were ten men and thirty-one women who were weavers in Waddington. The census of that year does not differentiate between hand- and power-loom weavers but as most of them were young and were power-loom weavers in 1851, they might well have been factory workers in 1841. By then the initial reluctance to work in factories had been overcome; families were moving from the village to live as well as work at Low Moor. Ten years later there were only seven hand-loom weavers left in the village and only three in 1861.

The fate of some of the 1803 weavers is known. John Chippendale continued to work as a weaver until in his seventies. He died in 1850 aged eighty-one. John Halstead became an agricultural labourer and died at the age of eighty in 1853. James Wilson died in 1836 when he was seventy-four. All three died in the workhouse and were brought to Waddington for burial. Richard Garner worked for a few years in a factory. In his seventies he entered Holden workhouse and presumably died there. Some, like William Mitchell and William Nutter, too old to find other employment, continued to work at their looms, Mitchell until he was seventy-six. Roger Fishwick, Richard Hanson, John Howarth, John Seedal and Roger Nowell died in Waddington before the worst of the depression.

Some of the younger ones left Waddington. William Burgess moved to Low Moor to work as a twister. Edward Whitehead and Thomas Parker were employed there as power-loom weavers. Thomas Blackburn was employed at the Primrose Mill, Clitheroe. Some stayed in Waddington but found other work: the second Thomas Parker became a farmer and Thomas Hanson a bobbin maker. John Ormerod, Luke Howard and George Wilson had become agricultural labourers by 1841. The rest were still weaving in the early 1830s: it is not known what happened to them in the end.

Children of weavers were amongst the first to leave the village and settle in Low Moor which had the double attraction of houses and work. By 1827, 146 cottages had been built there and fifty-two more were built in the next five years. With the building of the first weaving shed at the mill there was work for weavers as well as for spinners. Members of the Chippendale, Ormerod, Boothman, Mitchell, Siddal, Nowell, Smalley, Tomlinson and Whitehead families were among those who moved to Low Moor.

Weavers who had come to Waddington in the early part of the century left as hand-loom weaving declined. James Windle settled in Clitheroe. John Vicars and Thomas Edmundson went to Low Moor in the 'twenties: the Martins left in the 'forties. Some time after 1861 James Slinger joined his daughter-in-law and family who had been at Low Moor for thirty years. By 1841 sixty-five people who had been born in Waddington were living at Low Moor. John Foulds, grocer, and others who were dependent on the weavers, finding it impossible to make a living in the village also left. Seven more families moved to Low Moor in the next ten years. The decline of hand-loom weaving largely accounts for the fall in population in Waddington from 687 in 1821 to 580 in 1851.

Low Moor Mill had a great influence upon Waddington. Although it contributed to the decline of the hand-loom weavers, it later gave employment to others. Waddington also had its own cotton mill, much smaller and less well documented than Low Moor but not without interest. This was Feazer Mill.

Feazer Mill

In 1792 when Thomas Taylor bought 'two messuages out of the east end of the old Feizor House' he also bought the walk or fulling mill.[1] By the time he sold the property in 1824 to Joseph and John Fenton the mill had been adapted or rebuilt and was used as a cotton spinning mill. Some cottages were included in the sale.[2]

Information about the mill, especially in the early days, is slight. John Shepherd, recently settled in Waddington, was the only person to appear on the muster roll of 1803 as a spinner; later he was referred to as a cotton spinner and manufacturer.[3] For some years, in partnership with Christopher Hartley, he used the mill at Feazer as a spinning mill. In 1805 the parish register refers to Isaac Bramley, Waddington factory engineer. He may have had responsibility for the waterwheel which was used to drive the machinery and for a small engine-house built beside the mill.

To be Sold by Auction
for Ready Money

Six Spinning Frames, Roving Engines,
Blowing Frames, Warping Mills,
& other machinery belonging to
the Cotton Spinning business.
The property of
Messrs John Shephard & Christopher Hartley
At Faizor House & Cotton Spinning Factory.

Also Mahogany household furniture & Kitchen Utensils.
Six head of horned cattle, Horse, Coach ...

This notice appeared in the *Blackburn Mail* on 4 June 1817. The partnership may have been ending then; in 1822 Shepherd was living at Withnell. By 1824 James Ashworth had leased the mill and occupied one of the five cottages which had been built by this time at Feazer.

Among the early mill workers whose names appear in the parish registers were John Spencer, cotton rover, 1829: James Ellison and Thomas Edmondson of Feazer House. In 1830 Isaac Corbridge and William Brown, partners, were running the mill. William Brown of Waddington had married Rebecca Thornber of West Bradford in 1829. They were living at Feazer when their first child was born in 1831. During this partnership the mill was extended and produced cotton waste for the Bolton trade. Children, brought to work there, were said to have slept in the attics.

According to tradition raw cotton was brought from Lancaster, then a port, through the Trough of Bowland to the mill. Corbridge, a qualified voter after 1832,

---

[1] WYAS, Wakefield, Land Registration, DK p. 273 No. 363.
[2] WYAS, Wakefield, Land Registration, D p. 501 No. 511.
[3] *Baines's Yorkshire*, Vol. 1, *The West Riding* (1822).

continued in business until 1839 when he left for Blackburn. Shortly afterwards this notice appeared in local papers:

Feizor Cotton Mill
To be Let by Private Treaty
For a Term of Years

All that valuable water mill called Feizor Cotton Mill (lately occupied by Messrs Corbridge and Brown) situate at Waddington 2 miles from the market town of Clitheroe together with power from water-wheel 14 yards in diameter latterly erected by Messrs Whittaker of Moon's Mill; also the machinery in the same mill used for spinning cotton waste for the Bolton trade, consisting of four roving billys containing 872 spindles, 2 pairs of mules containing 472 spindles, three double carding engines and two single ones, blowing machine; willow; and a quantity of other machinery, etc.

Feizor Mill comprises 7 lofty rooms and the atticks. The west side of the mill [on lower ground] substantially built within a few years is 4 storeys high exclusive of the atticks, each storey being 14 yards by 7, and the other part is 3 storeys high exclusive of the atticks each storey being 9 yards by 8. Immediate possession may be had. The premises may be viewed, and further particulars obtained on application to Joseph Fenton Esq. of Bamford Hall near Rochdale (the owner) or at the office of Mr Trappes, Solicitor, Clitheroe.

From the machines mentioned it is evident what work was done. The raw cotton, brought mainly from America, was taken to the blowing room where it was blown and cleaned by a special machine. A carding machine removed the short fibres and drew out the cotton into slivers. These, when put on the draw frame had the fibres straightened and laid parallel. Slivers were combined and spun into a roving wound on to a bobbin, a slight twist being put in during the operation. The mule was generally used for this work. As the machine carriage, mounted on wheels, ran forward, the thread was drawn out and attenuated and when the carriage reversed the twist was put in and the yarn was wound on to spindles to form cops. A pair of mules had a spinner or minder to operate them: a considerable amount of strength and skill was required. Working with him as a team was a big piecer, also experienced, and a young piecer or apprentice. Their duties were to replenish the roving, mend the broken threads, doff the full cops and keep the mules clean and in good working order. Operatives (tenters) when attending to the running of the machines had to remove 'fly', the short fibre liberated during spinning.

Feazer Mill, a mile upstream from the village, used water from the brook which flowed in the clough. As a stream 3 feet wide and 6 inches deep flowing at 3 m.p.h. and turning a water wheel 11 feet in diameter can generate 5 h.p., this was quite sufficient to operate the small mill.[1]

---

[1] J. Porter, *The Making of the Central Pennines* (Moorland Publishing Co., 1980), p. 122.

As a result of the 1839 advertisement the mill was let to Messrs Constantine and Waring, carpet manufacturers and printers. Soon after they had taken the lease this report appeared in the *Blackburn Standard* on Wednesday 26 February 1840:

Destructive Fire at Clitheroe

A fire attended with very considerable loss of property occurred in the neighbourhood of Clitheroe in the morning of Friday last. The premises which have suffered from the ravages of the flames are those of Messrs Constantine and Waring, Carpet Manufacturers and Printers, Feazer Factory. The fire originated in the blow-room of the building on the above-named morning, whilst the people were at work. There was, as is too often the case, a great want of water, and though every effort was made to arrest the raging element the entire building was burnt to the ground. About £200 worth of finished goods were preserved, as well as the large water-wheel, but the actual loss cannot be estimated at less than £500.

Fires were not unusual: there had been two at Feazer before 1840.

A four-storey mill was built in replacement and was working by 1841. The census of that year shows that five cottages were all occupied by mill workers. Hannah and Henry Bulcock, weavers, and their son, a rover, occupied one. Next to William Waring, the carpet manufacturer, were the Cooks: the parents and one son were weavers, and their other sons a rover and a doubler. Of the Metcalf family two daughters were carpet weavers, one son a printer and one a piecer. William Brown, former partner, was now employed as a carder, as was his eldest son; Helen and James Slinger, who lived in the village and previously worked as hand-loom weavers, were carpet weavers at the mill in 1843.

Taylor Constantine lived in Clitheroe, attended the Wesleyan Church and sent his son to the grammar school. His name appeared on the 1849 electoral roll as joint occupier of the mill and buildings. By 1851 he had moved from Clitheroe to Blackburn and was dealing in cotton waste. Possibly he left in 1849 as the highway surveyors' accounts indicate that the mill was then empty. Waring remained at Feazer.

After the fire of 1840, in addition to the machinery for spinning, some looms for carpet weaving were installed. The carpets, cheap and of coarse weave, were printed. Using engraved rollers it was possible to apply a dye which had been mixed with a starch-containing paste. Later, calico printing machines were in use.

Cotton waste was a by-product of ordinary spinning or was broken down by the deviller from waste produced in winding and weaving. The yarns produced from it were weak, soft and fluffy and were used to make curtain materials and cheap flannelettes.

Further changes took place before 1851 when William Waring was employing five men, six boys and four girls. Ten of his employees lived in the cottages near to the mill. Three of them were spinners, two were piecers and one a rover. Two children were putting in bobbins and one was cleaning up. The Cooks were the only family along with the Warings who had been at the mill in 1841. The father was now a cotton deviller and the son a rover, as in 1841. The carpet weaving appears to have had

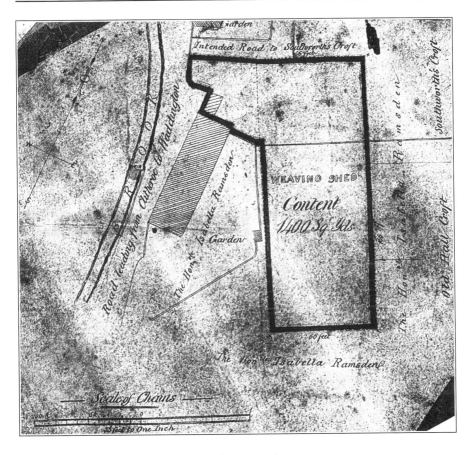

Plan of weaving shed.

limited success: the Slingers had returned to their hand-loom weaving in the village by 1851 and the mill had reverted to spinning.

In 1855 James Holgate of Grindleton moved to Feazer and was running the mill with Waring. Towards the end of the year, an accident in the devil room was reported in the *Preston Guardian*.[1]

Two thirteen-year-old piecers, one from Glasgow and one from Liverpool, were living with him in 1861. Robert Smith, a spinner from Burnley and three women, two from Rimington and the other from Todmorden, also lived at Feazer. A cotton tenter from Haslingden lived nearby at Mill Farm. According to a newspaper report 'about fifty hands were employed'. It is not clear how many people from the village worked at the Feazer mill. There was no footpath from the village to the mill: when, in 1852, some of the Feazer cottagers made a stile and prepared to walk across the fields, the Hospital Trustees accused them of trespassing and forced them to remove it. The

---

[1] *Preston Guardian*, 20 October 1855.

Holgates had plans to develop their enterprise and the Hospital accounts for 1860 refer to John Holgate of Feazer applying for land on which to build a mill. A letter to Edward Parker in July of that year mentions a draft agreement proposed to be entered into with Holgate concerning water from Waddington Clough. Holgate had applied for permission to take water from the clough to work a water-wheel at the proposed new mill. A plan, dated February 1860, shows a pipeline from Feazer to a reservoir in Simon Parrock and thence to a point behind the Higher Buck. Some negotiations took place and the Trustees' accounts of 1861 refer to the additional trouble given to their clerk 'in relation to the intended arrangement with Mr John Holgate for the water privileges'. Nothing came of the scheme, however: the Trustees needing the permission of the Charity Commissioners decided not to pursue the matter.

Holgate also applied to Mrs Ramsden for the lease of land behind the Sun Inn with the intention of building a weaving shed there. Work was started, for the diary of John O'Neil contains this entry for 29 April 1860:

After I got my tea I had a walk round Waddington to see a new shed that is building there for weaving, which as soon as it gets started will take a number of weavers from our place, as neither Waddington nor West Bradford weavers will come to Low Moor when they can get work nearer hand.

The Cotton Famine of 1861–5, resulting from the civil war in the United States, may have interrupted the work. Feazer, like other mills must have suffered from the shortage of raw materials and at least one employee, Robert Smith, received payments from the relief fund. A further setback was reported in the *Preston Guardian* on Saturday 14 February 1863.

Fire: A Cotton Mill Burnt Down

About five o'clock on Wednesday morning, it was discovered that the Feerser [sic] Cotton Mill which is situated one mile from Waddington and three from Clitheroe, was on fire. A messenger was dispatched to Clitheroe for the fire-engine, when the small one was immediately placed in a cart and taken to the scene of the conflagration; but on its arrival the place was completely gutted, nothing remaining but the bare walls. The building was four storeys high, and employed about fifty hands who will be thrown out of work. The mill was the property of Mr John Holgate, and the loss is estimated at near £3,000; it was insured to about half that amount. This is the fourth time this mill has been burnt down. The last time was in February 1840.

William Robinson as an old man recalled that 'there had been a fire amongst some cotton at Feazer factory. They devilled cotton there, and a good deal that had been damaged by water was brought to the kiln at the corn mill [Grindleton] to be dried.'[1]

As a result of the fire 'John Holgate, Feazer Mill, Cotton Manufacturer, quarry-master and farmer' was made bankrupt on 9 March 1863.[2]

---

[1] *Clitheroe Advertiser and Times*, 3 December 1926.
[2] *Preston Guardian*, 11 April 1863.

An attempt may have been made to restart the mill; rates were paid on it in 1865 though a refund was made for the previous year, when, according to the rate book, the mill was empty.

By June 1866 Holgate, as shown by his letter to Mrs Ramsden, had other plans based on the use of steam power.

> I wish to take about 1,200 yards of land in addition to that I have already taken (1,400 yards) at 1½d. per yard, that is, the whole of Southworth's Croft but leaving a 4 yard wide road to the Sun Inn Garden. I want it for a storage yard for coal. I purpose building a shed at once at a cost for building from £2,000 to £3,000.
>
> You are aware that some 4 or five years since I had a promise from the Trustees of Waddington Hospital that I should have a water lease for water power but finding they could not give me a lease without applying to the Charity Commissioners for powers they refused me. I have now to use steam if I make any use of the land.[1]

Feazer Mill.

Mrs Ramsden was prepared to grant a ninety-nine-year lease but a letter to her from John Holgate, waste dealer, dated 6 December 1866 shows that his plans were abortive.

> Enclosed I sent you a cheque for £5.16.8 rent (for the half year). I am intending giving up the place in the spring if you require it for any purpose previous to that time if you can make use of it.[2]

That was the end of factory work at Waddington. By 1871 some of the cottages at Feazer were standing empty. The farmhouse and two cottages were occupied ten years later; stones were taken from the old mill and were used for building a barn. Evidence of the four-storey mill remained until 1989; now there is only indication of the ground plan: 'an evocative ruin',[3] indeed.

---

[1] WYAS, Leeds, Ramsden papers, 64/15.

[2] *Ibid.*

[3] M. Rothwell, *Guide to the Industrial Archaeology of the Ribble Valley* (Bridgestone Press, 1990), p. 30.

Mill workers

In the second half of the century the Garnetts of Low Moor were Waddington's main employers. Initially there was some reluctance to work at the mill. Hours were long, discipline strict and mills were no places for the respectable. For many years the term 'factory girl' was regarded as an insult. Horsfall and Garnett, the mill owners, had to advertise for labour and about 1800 Jeremiah Garnett brought in 140 so-called 'apprentices' from London hospitals to meet their needs.[1]

As the prejudice against factory work decreased and hand-loom weavers could no longer complete with the machines, people sought work at Low Moor. Some moved to a cottage in the factory village; others walked two miles each day along the Low Moor road, crossing the Ribble by a wooden footbridge. According to the 1841 census there were five spinners, forty-one weavers and three others employed in the textile industry. Although no distinction is made between hand- and power-loom weavers the majority probably worked at the mill rather than in their own homes. The table gives further details of those working at Low Moor.

Workers at Low Moor

	Weavers		Others		
Date	Men	Women	Men	Women	Total
1851		14	14	23	51
1861	7	24	16	15	62
1871	5	13	11	17	46
1881	12	13	8	12	45
1981	27	25	7	14	73

These factory workers were spared the worst horrors of the factory system for in 1833 parliament had passed an Act forbidding the employment of children under nine and limiting the hours of employment for young people. Though inspectors were appointed to enforce the Act, their effectiveness, in view of their limited numbers, is debatable. A further Act in 1844 limited the working day of women to twelve hours and forbade the cleaning of machinery while it was in motion. Serious accidents, for which there was no compensation, still occurred, however. Three hours' education was introduced for the eight- to thirteen-year-olds (the age limit had been lowered to make their 6½-hour day acceptable to employers). The Ten Hour Act of 1847, though it did not apply to men, was considered a great victory. Workers still had to endure noise, humidity, temperatures of eighty degrees in summer and cold in winter. Strict discipline was maintained with fines for lateness and a variety of misdemeanours. Spinners and piecers worked barefoot so that their clogs would not strike sparks. Though Low Moor was fortunate in having its own fire engine, fire was a constant hazard increased by the installing of gas in 1827. On one occasion when fire did break

---

[1] A. Langshaw, *How Cotton came to Clitheroe* (Borough Printing Co., Clitheroe, 1953), p. 4.

out it was extinguished within ten minutes. Some factories had been known to burn down in that time.

In 1849 fifty years of Garnett–Horsfall management were celebrated at the mill. More than a month was spent in arranging the celebrations and in obtaining provisions so that five hundred tenants could consume 'a whole ox, quantities of beef, ham, veal, plum pudding, ale, punch, lemonade and raspberry liquor' at dinner. Teas were provided for the children and a grand ball for a thousand guests, factory operatives, gentlemen and ladies. The *Preston Guardian* reported enthusiastically 'We never saw such an assembly of healthy and handsome young women. We wish that those persons who draw their notions of factory people from fashionable novels had been there to see it.'

Further legislation led to a 10½-hour day for men except on Saturday, when they worked 7½ hours to complete a sixty-hour week. In spite of inspectors the hours were exceeded at times. Trade unions, with no legal status until 1871, held secret meetings in fields and barns and organised strikes to secure better pay. The only holidays were at Christmas and on Good Friday. Occasionally, when there was too much or too little water in the river, the mill was closed. In cases of illness there was no pay: if absence was prolonged the workers were liable to be dismissed. It was still common practice for a tenter to sweep machinery whilst it was in motion; even in 1892 a Waddington weaver had her hand trapped when sweeping looms.

Work began at six or seven o'clock and continued until breakfast at eight when there was a half-hour break and a further break for dinner. Those who did not live at Low Moor took their own meals with them and ate them beside their machines. At the end of the week, provided there were no deductions, the men had 12s. and the women 10s. to take home.

These were the conditions accepted by fifty-one factory workers from Waddington in 1851. Fourteen women, most of them in their thirties, worked at looms placed close together in the weaving sheds. Five of the women were married: three of them had children. (In two cases there was someone at home to care for them.) Four of the women had already worked at the mill for at least ten years: some were still working there twenty years later, and one was there in 1881. Three, even four, members of a family were employed: discipline, in these cases, was easier to enforce.

The other women and girls (twenty-three of them) were employed as sweepers, minders of boxes, weighers, carders, piecers, rovers, drawers, fluters and winders. Their work was similar to that being done at Feazer in the 'thirties though the machines were bigger. Some of the spinning frames had 1,200 spindles and the roving billies had 92 spindles. The youngest of these workers was eleven; all except six were under twenty. In time some could expect to be promoted to the weaving shed.

The fourteen male workers from the village included two experienced workers, a grinder and a stripper, who cleaned matted fibres from the cards and ground with emery paper parts of the carding machines. The others were much younger and worked mainly as piecers. The youngest, a nine-year-old, swept the floors.

In 1858 the Horsfalls were bought out of the company and a new partnership of Thomas Garnett and Sons (William and James) was formed. This marked the beginning of a period of expansion. 35,000 lbs. of yarn were produced weekly as compared with 14,000 lbs. in 1824. Work was begun in 1859 on the building of weaving sheds separate from the main spinning mill. New mules, carding machinery, blowing-room machinery replaced the old and a mechanic's shop was built. The use of more steam power and water turbines meant that production was no longer affected by the varying water supply of the Ribble. James Garnett might well enter into his diary for the last day of December 1859 'The year just closing has been one of almost unprecedented prosperity.'[1]

Another diary, that of John O'Neil, gives the workers' point of view. O'Neil, a former hand-loom weaver, had left Carlisle when it was no longer possible to make a living there. Eventually he became a power-loom weaver at Low Moor and settled with his daughter in one of the factory cottages in St Ann's Square. On 1 January 1856 he wrote, 'We have both of us plenty of work but little for working for, but as we cannot mend ourselves we must bear it as well as we can.'[2] Not all were prepared to accept 12s. for a sixty-hour week and a Power Loom Weavers' Union was formed to obtain higher wages, if necessary, by strikes. O'Neil joined and paid his twopence a week. Support was given to strikes at Padiham and Colne. In January 1861 there was a strike at Low Moor. Although it was settled in the next month the employers complained that the hands were almost unmanageable when trade was doing well.

O'Neil's diary refers to an operative who left his work without notice. He was brought before the magistrates and ordered to pay costs. Accidents occurred. O'Neil himself was almost killed by a falling beam. Another operative was less fortunate: he was killed between the carriage and frame of a self-actor. In December 1857 the manager sent word to O'Neil 'If I could not come to my work or find a weaver to work for me he would shop my looms.' (O'Neil had been absent for four days.) The union faced difficulties. On 27 January 1860, 'The Committee met this morning and their committee room was the open fields where we stood for an hour ankle deep in snow.' However, in December 1859 O'Neil was able to write, 'Upon the whole I think we are not badly off.' Neither man nor master knew that the Cotton Famine would soon change that.

The outbreak of the American Civil War meant that supplies of cotton from the blockaded southern states were cut off. Alternative supplies proved unsatisfactory as they were of poorer quality and dirty. The price of such cotton as was available rose from 8d. to 2s. 5d. a pound and led to the closing down of factories. By 1862, in Lancashire, a quarter of a million, over 8,000 of them in Blackburn, were unemployed. By the end of the year half a million were dependent upon relief. There were also the 'concealed paupers' who preferred to starve rather than claim relief. Low Moor suffered with the rest. On 11 July, three months after the outbreak of the civil war, James Garnett wrote in his diary: 'Notice was given to the weavers stopping a great portion of the narrow looms as we have 27,000 pieces in stock without the slightest prospect of any immediate sale except at very unremunerative prices;' and on 20 August, 'The state of trade is now in a worse way than it was been for a very long time. The rupture in America causes cotton to be dear.' Some of the cottages at Low Moor stood empty as people moved elsewhere in search of employment.

---

[1] O. Ashmore, *The Diary of James Garnett of Low Moor, Clitheroe, 1858–60, 1861–5.*
[2] M. Briggs (ed.), *A Lancashire Weaver's Journal 1856–64, 1872–5.*

To help meet the crisis the public made generous donations. At a meeting in Manchester addressed by Lord Derby, £130,000 was raised; 'a contribution of a single county at a single meeting, to a single object, it is certainly without a parallel in our history and without example in any other nation,' *The Times* declared. The queen made a donation. Money came from the Continent and from Australia. A cargo of food was sent by the New York Relief Committee; part of it reached Clitheroe where charitable organisations helped with the distribution.

Edwin Waugh, the special correspondent of the *Manchester Examiner and Times*, wrote of the distress; of the 'slow funeral' of a family of ten who had lived on 5s. during the last nine weeks. Faced with the final choice of starvation or relief, having sold all their possessions, some chose the former. Public supply works saved others.

From John O'Neil we learn of the effects upon the workers at Low Moor Mill.

August 1861: We got notice of our mill this morning to run four days per week until further notice.

12 September: We are stopped again this week.

16 November: There is great distress all through the manufacturing districts, they are all running short time through the scarcity of cotton.

1 January 1862: We are beginning the New Year under very poor prospects. Bad trade, short time and a prospect of war with America.

17 January: A great number of weavers have given up their looms as they cannot keep it on, the yarn is so bad.

He himself was unable to earn a shilling a day using Surat cotton which he described as 'rubbish'.

For the remainder of the year and for the next two years men worked very short hours at reduced wages and were often idle for weeks on end. The Garnetts gave money and goods, sold soup at ½d. per quart, opened a sewing school for girls and a school for young men and women.

The winter of 1862–3 was the hardest time. The mill was closed altogether and O'Neil had to rely on 3s. a week relief. For seventeen weeks there was no work for the card-room hands.

The Waddington operatives suffered the same hardships. From the relief fund of £294 which was started in the village, twenty-two people received money in 1863 and nearly as many accepted relief in the following year.![1]

By June 1865 the war was over and trade resumed. Looking back many would say 'A gradely plague it's bin to me.' A few could say 'It's bin a gradely blessing too.' These were the people who went to school for the first time and learnt to read.

Trade revived but Waddington's smaller population in the 1870s and '80s meant fewer factory workers and when new machinery was installed women were the first to be laid off; by 1891 almost as many men as women were employed.

Disputes concerning working conditions led to a nine-week strike in 1878. After the reading of the Riot Act the Lancers, brought from Leeds to Clitheroe, charged and broke up the demonstration, using swords and bayonets to clear the streets. At

---

[1] LRO, PR 2993/1/7.

least one Waddington man witnessed some of the events before taking the precaution of hiding up the chimney of the Calf's Head.[1]

However, hours were shortened, the number of bank holidays was increased and a week's holiday was allowed before the century ended.

Though famine in India had adverse effects upon trade and Thomas Garnett was alarmed at the prospect of the imposition of duties on cotton, the workers believed as they joined in the centenary celebrations of 1899 that their future was assured.

Craftsmen

In 1801 RATHER LESS THAN a third of the men in Waddington were craftsmen. They included carpenters, cabinetmakers, turners, shoemakers and cloggers, tailors, a tanner and blacksmiths. There were also masons, thatchers, slaters and pavers. By 1901, although the population had increased, their numbers had fallen.

The shoemakers—cordwainers as they were sometimes called—and the cloggers worked in their own homes. Young lads served an apprenticeship of seven years; then they might find employment as journeymen before setting up on their own.

For the clogs special bases were shaped. In Yorkshire, alder was generally preferred: it was light, easy to cut and would take a nail without splitting. Three kinds of long, sharp knife were used to shape and hollow the base and cut a groove for the upper. For the uppers, waxed kip with the flesh-side out was used. Thread made of six strands of cotton, tapered, twisted and waxed was used to join the upper. This was then attached to the sole with nails, longer ones being placed at the back. A welt was fixed all round with brass tacks and to finish the clog toe-tins and a clasp were added. An iron made by the blacksmith was attached to the bottom of the sole. At the beginning of the century a pair of shoes cost 4s. and a pair of clogs up to 2s., though cloggers and shoemakers were sometimes given produce as payment.

There was a big demand for clogs. Most labourers wore them and power-loom weavers wore them for protection against the damp flooring of the sheds. Slater's directory of 1858 gives the name of Henry Baldwin, clogger and patten maker, as a resident of Waddington. The iron frames or pattens which he made were attached to shoes to give protection from the mud and dirt of the unpaved roads.

The shoemaker prepared individual lasts for his customers. Hides were bought from Robert Walker, the tanner, as were the sheep and calf skins from which the shoemaker's apron was made. Calf skins, although much dearer, were preferred. In 1801 Thomas Boothman, William Smalley, Robert Turner, James Marsden and John Pinder were shoemakers as were Luke and John Smalley and Henry Turner a few years later. By mid-century another John Pinder was helped by his seventeen-year-old apprentice son and by a journeyman clogger from Bashall Eaves. Francis Alston had an apprentice and a journeyman working for him. There were then nine shoemakers altogether and Robert Fowler, farmer at Newy Nook, supplemented his income by

---

[1] S. Clarke, *Clitheroe in its Railway Days*, 2nd edn, p. 87.

shoemaking. Pinders continued to work as shoemakers until the end of the century by which time Alfred Dyson, the last of the village shoemakers, had begun to work at Spring Gardens as a boot, shoe and clog maker. The later shoemakers had to compete with the factory-made boots and shoes which shoe-dealers, one of whom was living in Waddington in 1881, tried to sell.

Skills were not only passed on from father to son; at busy times, journeymen seeking work might be paid to sole pairs of boots, and new methods, picked up by them in their travels, were in turn acquired by their employers. Journeymen, soling four pairs of boots a week, could earn 4s. a pair. From this their keep was deducted. Of necessity the shoemakers at times worked until eight or nine o'clock at night by the light of oil lamps or candles and in the company of village gossips.

Straps and reins were often repaired by shoemakers but in 1812 the inn-keeper at the Buck could also offer the services of a saddler. There is evidence of saddlers in the village in 1839 and in 1871. As apprentices they had learnt how to boil up pitch, oil and resin to make wax for waxing the ends of the thread. Next, using an awl and two needles, they learnt to sew straight and evenly with from five to fourteen stitches to the inch. They were shown which parts of hide were to be used for the different parts of the harness and finally they made the harness, saddle and collar. Collar-making was the hardest work. Saddlers, like the shoemakers, got material from the local tannery.

There were four tailors in 1801: Benjamin Frankland, John Howarth, Oliver Ormerod and James Wilson. A few years later they had been joined by George Howarth. They, like other craftsmen, served their apprenticeship. Working cross-legged on the sitting board they learnt to sew and were eventually entrusted with making a jacket. They provided their own tools which included bodkin, thimble, scissors, measure, needles and beeswax. Some tailors worked at home, others went to outlying farms to make new clothes and repair the old. Five yards of cloth for a coat and 'britches' cost 8s. 4d; buttons, bought at the village shop, thread and the making cost 4s. 2d. Waistcoats were the easiest garment to make: 1¼ yards of material were needed for a 'weskoat'; thread and the making came to 7d. These were the prices at the beginning of the century; they rose during the Napoleonic Wars as did the wages of craftsmen, most of whom earned 3s. a day.

As early as 1820 it was evident that a few people were looking beyond the village for their suits. The Hospital Trustees paid four guineas to J. Lofthouse, mercer and draper, Clitheroe, for a suit of black clothes for the Reader; 18s. for a hat, 12s. for leggings and, to complete the outfit, £5. 18s. 3d. for a greatcoat. Later, the wider choice offered by the town and the invention of the sewing machine (one could be bought for £3 18s. od. before the end of the century) reduced the number of village tailors: there were only two in Waddington in 1851 and one in 1881. More women, however, became dressmakers; some, like Mrs Foulds, employed apprentices for dressmaking and millinery.

A number of men worked with wood. The records refer to them as 'joiners or carpenters' for the rigid distinction maintained by guilds in cities did not exist in the village. In 1803 Richard Chaffer and John Coar were carpenters; William Dugdale was a cabinetmaker; William Morley, William Hanson and Edmund Chippendale were turners. Thomas Pye was a joiner who later became a wheelwright. In the 1820s

John Nowell and William Arkwright were joiners. Between them these men could supply most of the village requirements of tools, hay-rakes and other implements, ladders, furniture and coffins.

When in 1827 Thomas Pye paid the Hospital Trustees £5 for a tree, planks were made into boards with the framed saw, probably at the saw pit at the end of Katey Lane. There was ample work for the carpenters and joiners at this time, with old buildings being repaired or replaced. Items such as a gate and a wheelbarrow cost 5s. and £1.

In 1901 the big wood store at the end of Katey Lane was owned by the joiners Silverwood and Banks. The latter was responsible for much of the woodwork when the church was restored.

Turners are included in the 1803 Muster Roll and Thomas Hanson, 'artist in turning bobbins' is mentioned in 1814. An advertisement which appeared in 1835 claimed to be of interest to carpenters, cloggers, chairmakers and bobbin turners. It announced that, following winter storms, some timber—ash, alder, birch, poplar, beech, sycamore, larch and scotch fir—was to be sold by auction at Browsholme. A later advertisement for alder, ash and elm suitable for bobbin turners and cloggers appeared in Whewell's paper. (Bobbins were much in demand by weavers.)

The same skill required for turning bobbins was used in the making of spindles for chairs. Several members of the Southworth family from the Sun Inn were chairmakers as were John Cottam from West Bradford and his three children. In 1824 one of his chairs was sold to Grindleton Vestry for 6s. 6d. A small factory behind the Sun Inn for bobbin and chairmaking believed to be in existence in 1822,[1] appears on the 1850 Ordnance Survey map. There were then nine chairmakers, three of whom had moved into the village. William Wallbank, originally from Hurst Green, had lived for a few years in Chipping where there was a well-established chair works: Jonathon Speakman came from Preston and William Bradshaw from West Derby. They specialised in making rush-bottomed chairs with spindle backs. By 1869 Speakman was working on his own. His house with workshop attached formed part of the newly built West End Cottages (Ramsden Terrace). At his request the builder had left the floor of the workshop unflagged so that timber 'to set the benches to' could be set into the floor.[2]

John Hanson, chairmaking in 1826, became a master chairmaker and prospered during the 'fifties. After that, chairmaking in Waddington began to decline and by 1872 only two chairmakers were left, the others having transferred to Tabbin's Yard, Clitheroe. John Ormerod, last of the chairmakers, was also a cabinetmaker.

For most of the century the village wheelwrights came from two families, the Pyes and the Tomlinsons. In 1841, at the age of twenty-four, William Tomlinson from Bowland was employing an apprentice and was later joined by his three sons. One of them, Thurstan, was killed in an accident at the saw mill in 1895. Wheelwrights were considered to be among the most skilled, if not the master craftsmen, of the country-side. When making a wheel, mortices, accurately spaced, were chiselled in the hub for the spokes. The spokes, made of oak, were tenoned into the hub in a staggered

[1] M. Rothwell, *Guide to the Industrial Archaeology of the Ribble Valley* (Bridgestone Press, 1990).
[2] WYAS, Leeds, Ramsden papers, bundle 25.

The wheelwright's shop.

fashion to prevent weakening. The felloes, or rims, of ash, elm or beech, were made in sections and dowelled together when the spokes had been fitted. The wheel had to be 'dished'—made slightly concave—in order to resist the sideways thrust of a load swinging from side to side on the uneven roads. Wheels were made for gigs and dog-carts as well as for waggons.

When hooping wheels the blacksmith had to measure the length of iron, shape, pierce and heat it until red hot, place it on the wheel and slake it to make it contract. Having been hammered down on one side the wheel was turned over and the process repeated. The hooping of the wheel was often done by a blacksmith but present-day inhabitants remember the wheelwright fixing the heated band of iron to the wheel and taking it down from the shop to be cooled in the brook.

When building the body of the waggon, care had to be taken in fitting the floorboards which ran lengthwise. Nails, which would have worn and splintered the boards when anything was shovelled out, were avoided. In 1802 over £2 was paid for 'bottoming' a cart. Four-wheeled waggons and two-wheeled carts were in use on farms and were also used for carting stone. If well made they would last for fifty years or more.

John Masefield says of the waggon-maker:

> ... This man made
> Waggons of elm to last a hundred years;
> The blacksmith forged the rims and iron gear.
> His was the magic that the wood obeyed.

Old Smithy Cottages.

And of the waggon:

> Beautiful always as a work of art,
> Homing the bride, the harvest, and men dead.

For over half the century there were two smithies (one was replaced by the Wesleyan Sunday school) and four blacksmiths. Jonas Boothman was making nails and shoeing horses at the beginning of the nineteenth century; other members of the family carried on the work until well into the twentieth. Early summer, just before hay-making, was a busy time for them. Farmers brought in their horses to be shod and could expect two smiths to shoe four horses in a day. Scythes, sickles and shears had to be made or sharpened. There was competition in 1856 when a Clitheroe paper advertised a large supply of scythes for sale.

In winter, horseshoes were adapted to prevent slipping on icy roads. There were locks and bolts to be made for doors, snecks, hinges at 8d. a pair, handles at 8½d. each, clog-irons, hammer heads, crooks for gate posts and nails: spar nails at 3d. a pound. The highways surveyors brought chisels and picks to be sharpened and hammers to be repaired. There was no shortage of work for the smith, especially as the number of horses rose in the 1880s and 1890s.

Most of the remaining craftsmen were concerned with building. These were the masons, thatchers, slaters and pavers who were employed in work at the Hospital, the church and the chapel. Three generations of Hansons, Thomas Howarth, two Parkinsons and William Frankland worked as masons and trained others to follow them.

New Smithy Cottage and Smithy.

An indenture dated 25 October 1806 refers to Thomas Taylor of Clitheroe and William Hanson of Waddington. Taylor was bound apprentice 'until he shall attain the age of 21. He shall faithfully serve his master, his secrets keep, his lawful commands gladly obey and do; hurt to his said Master he shall not do.' In return William Hanson promised to

> teach, inform and instruct by the best ways and means he can in the Trade, Art, business and profession of a stone mason: to find and provide good wholesome and sufficient meat, drink, washing, lodging and also all sorts of clothing both linen and woollen suitable and fitting for the said apprentice at his sole cost during the whole term of the said apprenticeship.[1]

Another William Hanson was employed by the Mrs Ramsden in the ten years before she sold the manor (1879) when many of the old thatched cottages were falling down and needed to be replaced. Typical was the building of the two houses and workshop in Ramsden Terrace for £400. There was work for masons, slaters, glaziers and plasterers even though Clitheroe firms were called in for major undertakings such as the rebuilding of the almshouses. There was a departure from tradition in 1884 when the first brick houses in the village were built.

---

[1] LRO, DDX/19/89.

Until the 1870s there was work for thatchers who used straw and ling for their work. As late as 1873 £2. 18s. 9d. was paid for the thatching of some cottages and £5 17s. 7d. for the straw—straw was becoming increasingly difficult to obtain. Ling, gathered from the fell, lasted from twenty to fifty years. It was pulled up by the roots in the early part of the year and when used for roofing it was laid with the ends upwards. At the top of the steeply pitched roof the thatch might be a yard thick.

Gradually thatch was replaced by slate. New houses—Waddow Lodge built in 1824 and Carter Fold in 1839—were built with slate roofs. Henry Frankland had slate brought from Liverpool by canal to Enfield and then carted to Waddington.

Five members of the Read family were pavers. In the previous century Reads had earned 2s. a day road-making: one worked on the Burnley to Blackburn turnpike road. By the time the Napoleonic Wars ended they were earning from 3s. to 4s. a day and an apprentice was paid 1s. 6d. The family prospered and bought property in Back Fold. One of them, John Read of Whalley, became county 'pavior'.

Building materials were obtained locally. Felix Leach sold lime from his kiln at Brungerley for 10d. a windle or 1s. 6d. a load in 1816. Plasterers, earning from 3s. to 4s. a day in 1824, paid the tanner 3s. for a stone of hair, 4s. for white hair, to mix with the plaster. Much of the stone came from Waddington Fell where quarrying was a developing business. In 1855 at the sale of Delph Plant on the fell, forty-five cutting picks, 120 cutting wedges, two powerful cranes, drills, hammers, an anvil, a fire grate with hot hearth and one stone waggon were sold.[1] The industry appears to have been thriving. In 1881 Edward Chester, master stonemason, was employing fourteen men, most of whom were quarriers and masons. He used a traction engine to bring the stone down to the village.

There was a variety of minor crafts. Many villagers were able to make their own candles, besoms of ling, baskets and mats of straw: some became specialists. Two basket-makers from Arkholme were staying at the Moorcock in 1881. They were relations of the innkeeper and may have been itinerant workers. For over ten years there was also a ropemaker from Bury in the village. It was quite usual for such workers to travel round supplying the local demand for cow halters, leading reins and waggon ropes before moving on. In making rope, a rope walk such as the one which remains at Hawes was set up. This allowed the hemp to be warped between two points. A twist was put in when sufficient threads had been drawn out.

The Muster Roll of 1803 contained the names of twenty-two craftsmen, under fifty-five years of age. In 1891 when the population was slightly larger there were still over twenty craftsmen. Mechanisation and better transport, however, meant that they faced a continuing slow decline.

---

[1] LRO, DDX/28/286, *Whewell's Family Paper*, June 1855.

Innkeepers and others

The Roebuck Inn

The Roebuck Inn, built in 1760, possibly to replace the Bonny Bird Inn, was owned by the Parkers of Browsholme Hall. In 1820 Thomas Lister Parker sold it and the 33-acre farm for £3,000 to the Hospital. Its connection with the Hospital gave it an importance otherwise lacking, for in the early part of the century when John Pilling was landlord it was said that 'The premises are excellent and the accommodation everything that is required, but its position out of the direct route of traffic travelling from Slaidburn, Newton etc. to Clitheroe detracts from its legitimate custom and renders it comparatively a private house.' Travellers did call: there was stabling, a mounting block and a barn across from the inn. A bill of 1816 lists the drinks and services then available.

The Hospital Trustees, not altogether satisfied with the supply of drink, took steps to ensure that their requirements would be adequately met.

> The wine produced at the dinner of the Trustees on their day being rendered thick and undrinkable in consequence of its having been carried to the Buck from Mr Dent's house [up the fell road] it was unanimously carried that a subscription be entered into for the purpose of making a cellar at the Buck in which the wine belonging to them be placed.[1]

A cellar was built in 1841 and kept well stocked. In 1866 the trustees bought '3 doz. Port for £8 2s. and 3 doz. sherry for the same price'.[2] 'Their day', referred to above, was 13 June, Founder's Day, when the trustees went to church for a service and to the Buck for dinner. Tenants were provided with dinner when they paid their half-yearly rents and for those who helped built the new hospital there was a 'sumptuous repast'. It was the custom when building contracts were made and the work started, for the workmen to be supplied with drink. The entry made in the church accounts in 1825 'for liquor and rearing £1.0.0.' was not unusual. In this instance the Roebuck supplied the drink. In 1838 they also supplied the drinks for the bidders when the Hospital had an auction sale of timber at the inn.

Vestry meetings were held at the Roebuck and there, the cloth bought with the Ellen Wilkinson Charity money was distributed every third year.

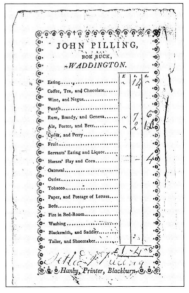

1816 bill, Roebuck Inn.

---

[1] Hospital Archives, Trustees' Minute Book.
[2] *Ibid.*

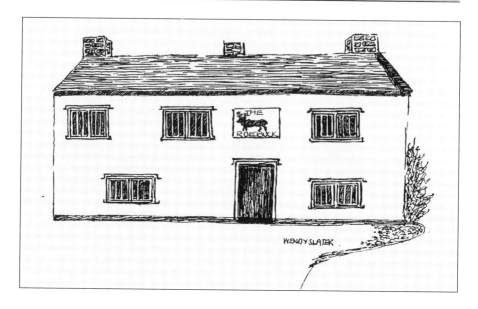

The Roebuck.

Later in the century when the electoral roll had to be checked the revision meeting was also held at the inn.

Several changes to the inn took place during the century. For a time it was 'quite in a ruinous state'. Ling, later slate, was used to repair the roof. The exterior was rough-cast in 1829. Wooden floors were put in and changes made to the bar and back sitting room. In 1868 the north-east gable was raised and extended; this with the re-roofing of the inn cost £305. A new sign had been put up in 1864. By this date the inn was usually referred to as the Lower Buck to distinguish it from the Buck i'th'Vine—the Higher Buck, as it had become known. Twenty years later water was laid on and the old pump was no longer needed.

The farm consisted of several fields along the Low Moor road and the tenant or a farm servant did most of the work. It was in a poor state in 1820 when the rent was £79 9s. The trustees declared that 'much land was run out by ploughing and a considerable part wants draining and cultivating. Some of it is very thin of soil and without drainage no improvement can be made.' In 1850 when John Garforth was tenant there were 3½ acres of arable, the rest was pasture and meadow. Thirty years later Margaret Altham agreed 'not to plough nor to set more than half an acre of potatoes'. The farm buildings, a large barn, shippon, stable, pig-cote remain; the milk-house on the north side of the inn no longer exists. In 1892, when there was not much demand for farms, Margaret Altham was paying £70 rent. Tenant for thirty-five years, in spite of an unblemished record she was fined for selling whisky nineteen degrees under proof.

The Sun Inn

The inn and 16-acre farm were part of the manor held in 1801 by the Clarkes and tenanted by Mary Tomlinson who paid £1 1s. 4d. land tax (as compared with the Roebuck's £1 16s. 1d.) There was not much profit to be made from such a small farm. A cow, calves, sheep, pigs, a mare and foal were kept. Some hay was stored in the barn/shippon in the close a short distance from the inn. The rest of the hay was kept in the stable-loft adjoining the inn. Butter and cheese were made.

In the early years of the century there were several short tenancies including that of John Sanderson. After only a year as landlord he was being threatened by creditors; he owed £25 to Thomas Clarke and £1 3s. 6d. to the overseer of the poor. As a result, his 'household goods, farming stock, husbandry gears, goods, cattle and chattels', 350 items in all, were sold in February 1808. Purchasers of goods at or under 40s. had to pay ready money; others had until 1 May to use promissory notes. There was a large attendance at the two-day sale with people coming from Mitton, Bashall, Grindleton as well as from the village. £137 12s. 9d. was raised; of this the auctioneer was paid 1s. in the pound.[1]

As not many details are available of house contents in Waddington at this period it may be worthwhile to mention some of the items at the Sun Inn sale. Most of the kitchen contents—the fire grate, boiler, bacstone, oven, fire irons, fender, tongs and bellows—were sold. Saucepans, dripping pans, frying pan, toaster, the knead tub and backboard, kettles, brass pans, iron dishes, ladles, plates, trenchers, soup pots, chop and knife, coffee mill, tea cannister, rolling pin, castor, tureen, spoons, tankards all went. Two smoothing irons and a maiden were sold.

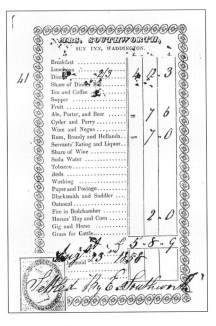

Sun Inn bill, 1858.

Furniture included a set of six chairs and the great chair which went for 10s. 6d., stools, forms, dressers, cupboards, clocks and candlesticks, pictures and books. Five bedsteads, a washstand, night chair, sheets, counterpane, feather and chaff beds, bolsters, quilt and 52 lbs. of feathers at 2s. per pound were included.

Some items such as pint and quart measures, barrels, tubs, a peck, a brewing pan (sold for £9 10s.), a peck of malt (£ 12s.) had been for use in the inn. The malt-kiln at the inn in 1782 was most likely still in use. John Leach of Fields House Farm bought 95 lbs. of hops at 1s. 3d. a pound for brewing his own ale.

---

[1] LRO, DDX/54/72.

The Sun Inn.

After Sanderson left there were three short tenancies before William Southworth became landlord in 1820. Though he himself had the misfortune to be killed in a local brawl, his wife ran the inn for over forty years with her son or an agricultural labourer to run the farm. Other members of the family worked in the chair and bobbin factory behind the inn. A bill dated 1858 was not so different from Pilling's bill at the Roebuck in 1816; things still changed slowly in the trade.

As well as the social gatherings at the inn, Vestry meetings were held there and charity money and material were distributed on St Thomas's Day. When the Foresters' connection with the Buck i'th'Vine ended they held their annual meetings at the Sun. There were occasional disturbances when the drink, some provided free of charge by the house, flowed freely and caused the local constable to break up the scuffle. An experiment conducted from an upper window to see whether a man wearing goose feathers could fly appears not to have been repeated.[1] Some interest was aroused when the old parish chest containing eighteenth-century documents was found in one of the attics and was presented by Mrs Duckworth to the newly formed parish council.

The Buck i'th'Vine

On the death of John Smith in 1807, his son-in-law Stephen Whalley, became the owner of the Buck i'th'Vine with its brewhouse, stable and coach house, a shippon and warehouse. Though there was no farm attached to the inn some land might have been rented. Whalley also became owner of the other property in the row and of some cottages in Back Fold.

While hand-loom weaving was carried on in the village Whalley acted as a putter-out of yarn, which he bought from the mill for the weavers, paying them when they returned their 'pieces'. Many such middle-men had a reputation for parsimony. His various business activities certainly helped him to prosper.

---

[1] J. H. W. Fishwick, *In and Around Waddington*, p. 10.

The Buck i'th'Vine.

In 1838 the Ancient Order of Foresters was started in Waddington. Henry Fishwick, schoolmaster and son of a weaver, was the first secretary. His grandson relates how the founding members with Robin Hood and Little John riding white horses, followed by their chief officials dressed in full regalia of the order and carrying bows and arrows, came to open a court lodge and enrol members at the inn. The secretary wrote out the rules of the order in fine copperplate handwriting using ink of his own making.[1] At the time, the wages of the weavers were falling and it is not surprising that they resorted to this measure of self-help.

When Whalley died in 1857 the inn was sold to Felix Grimshaw for £380. The Foresters maintained a connection with it until 1870. Then, Shaw and Rutherford, and in 1897 Shaw and Co. of Salford became owners. The Althams, John Herd and Richard Turner, auctioneer, were landlords. In 1891 Mary Hey was the 'licensed victualler' and had the assistance of her two daughters at what was by this time known as the Higher Buck.

Vestry meetings and distribution of charities took place here as at the Sun and Lower Buck. James Butterworth, schoolmaster was a 'visitor' in 1881, according to the census. This does give rise to queries as to the use of this term.

After 1888 the Bowland Rural District Council was responsible for issuing licences to publicans at a special session—the Brewster Session. Not surprisingly in view of the excessive drinking then taking place restrictions were being imposed on public houses. They could no longer remain open as long as the publican wished but had to close at 11.00p.m. The Temperance Society supported the bill to stop the sale of drink to children under sixteen. Checks were made on the alcohol content of drinks,

---

[1] J. H. W. Fishwick, *In and Around Waddington*, p. 10.

The Moorcock.

necessary perhaps as one Clitheroe landlord thought it advisable to assure his customers that his beer was 'arsenic free'. Bowland Council showed Victorian concern for
propriety in complaining about those public houses in their area where people used
a handy corner as a urinal, creating 'a public nuisance to passers-by on the road, there
being no proper drainage nor proper protection from view of persons'.

The Moorcock

When the Enclosure Act was passed in 1812, some of the common land was sold to
pay the commissioner's expenses. Joseph Whittle of Whalley bought just over 9 acres
for £125. He may have intended to let the land for grazing or have wished to qualify
to vote for Yorkshire's two county MPs. In 1835 his enclosure on Waddington Fell
passed to his brother Robert.[1] It was about this time that a small house with a vat in
the cellar was built. As the Beer Houses Act of 1830 had encouraged the setting up
of beerhouses in an attempt to counteract the increasing drinking of spirits, it may
well have been a farm/beerhouse combined. Certainly it was being used as such in
1853. In that year Robert Whittle died and 'that messuage, barn, stables and other
outbuildings erected by the said Robert Whittle and now used as a beer-house' were
sold to Thomas Proctor of Clitheroe.[2] In 1865 Frederick Leach bought 'the inn,
ale-house or victualling house known by the sign of the Moorcock.'

---

[1] WYAS, Wakefield, Land Registration, MB p. 4403/334 2.
[2] WYAS, Wakefield, Land Registration, RT p. 621/723 1.

New Hall, home of the Walkers, tanners.

John Chester remembered Tom Barker, John Higson, Thomas Proctor, Richard Seed and Thomas Wilkinson as landlords. There were others—Edward Pye, evicted when a new owner took possession, Robert Taylor and James Grimshaw. Chester also relates how a strange gentleman called and when chatting with old Dicky (Seed) asked 'Who attends to your spiritual affairs out here?' 'We get em fra Blegburn,' he was told.[1]

The amount of land farmed varied from 9 to 25 acres; in 1892 there was no reference to any land being farmed. Quarrymen, labourers and two ropemakers related to the inn-keeper stayed at the Moorcock. Farmers and cattle-dealers on their way to market stayed overnight. Even at the end of the century it was still a fairly primitive place with visitors sleeping three to a bed. There was grazing for the cattle; they were penned in at night.

The tanners

There was a tannery in Waddington in the eighteenth century on land owned by the Parkers of Browsholme Hall. In 1806 it was sold to Jonathon Wilson along with two cottages, the tan pits, tan yard, warehouse, buildings and adjoining croft.[2] In 1810 these were sold to Robert Walker along with 7 acres and New Hall.[3] Walker, who

---

[1] *Clitheroe Advertiser*, 7 December 1906.
[2] WYAS, Wakefield, Land Registration, FA p.311/416.
[3] WYAS, Wakefield, Land Registration, FM p.272/237.

came from a family of tanners in Bolton-by-Bowland, had settled in Waddington by 1797 and started to build up a successful tanning business combined with farming.

He sold cattle to the local butcher and cured the skins in Tan Pit Meadow, now Pinder Close. The skins were placed in vats and steeped in a solution of tannin made from oak bark. When the hair and grease had been removed the skins were hung in sheds to dry. The hides had to be soaked for months and the smell from them and from the drying hides was far from pleasant. When an Act was passed for the prevention of nuisances, the Waddington tanners, believing it to be 'centralising, oppressive, vague and indefinite' and a threat to their business, sent a petition in 1855 to Richard Cobden MP expressing their concern.[1]

Leather was sold locally to shoemakers and saddlers. Tannery waste was used for making size; hair was used by builders.

Walker's son, Robert, employed from three to six men and ran the business for some years after his father's death in 1868. When he himself died in 1879 the tannery passed to his nephew, James Walmsley. The public weighbridge in front of the entrance to the tannery remained until the late twentieth century although the tannery had ceased to operate long before this.

Brick and tile makers

By 1873 Caleb Bishop was manufacturing bricks and tiles (curved for use as drain pipes) in Waddington.

Bishop was born in Handborough, Oxfordshire, in 1839. His father, a labourer died in 1849 from cholera—there was a particularly severe outbreak in that year. Other members of the family were agricultural labourers who by the 'sixties were feeling the effects of increasing mechanisation and the importation of cheap corn. The agricultural depression in Oxfordshire may have been responsible for Caleb Bishop's move to the north. By 1866 he had married and for a few years lived at Padiham before moving to Whitewell, where he helped manufacture tiles. Tiles had been made in the district for some years. At the Bolton Hall yard 1-inch tiles sold at 12s. per thousand in 1855. There was also a yard near Dunsop Bridge.

On moving to Waddington the Bishops occupied a small cottage, The Healings, along the West Bradford road not far from the field where clay was obtainable. Evidence remains of the pits formed when the clay was dug. Tiles and bricks after drying out were fired in the kilns to which coal was carted from Clitheroe station. A brick-built shed with chimney remains on the site. George Berbridge was working for Bishop in 1874. Two sons, William and Richard, later joined their father and the two or three other labourers whom he employed.

In 1877 William Dewhurst of Brungerley was supplied with drain tiles at a cost of £4 7s. 3d. Twitter Bridge Farm and Carter Fold and others were also supplied. Five brick houses were built in the village before the end of the century.

---

[1] LRO, DDX/28/286, *Whewell's Family Paper.*

Brick and tile workers.

The business was small-scale and methods rather primitive. It was later bought out by the Accrington Brick Company.

Lime-burners

In 1851 there were two lime-burners in Waddington of whom one remained in 1861. They could have been working at Brungerley where there were two kilns or, along with fourteen lime-burners from West Bradford, at Pimlico. This district of Clitheroe had been important for the production of lime in the eighteenth century and in 1824 ten kilns existed.[1]

At the beginning of the nineteenth century Felix Leach was dealing in lime which, as fell land was being enclosed, was in great demand for reducing the acidity of the soil. When he moved to Brungerley in 1812 Leach had his own supply of lime which he continued to sell to farmers and to builders. Accounts show that at this time landowners supplied their tenants with lime; when there was competition for farms in the 'fifties tenants were prepared to buy their own. Newy Nook, near the fell, also had its own kiln.

The Brungerley kilns were of the field or running kiln type in which the lime was burnt by a continuous process. A field-kiln was described by Raistrick as

---

[1] Baines, *History, Directory and Gazetteer of the County Palatine of Lancaster*, 2 vols.

Lime-kiln at Brungerley.

a sturdy structure of dry limestone walling forming a circular or square tower about 15′ in diameter and about the same or greater height. The core is a circular bowl 18′ to 10′ in diameter lined with sandstone ... tapering to a bottom diameter of not more than 3′. At the bottom of the bowl a grate was inserted through which burnt lime and ashes could be raked out. The grate was at the end or top of a short tunnel the mouth of which is the arch which gives the kiln its unmistakable character. The kilns are usually found near the small scar or quarry from which its limestone supply could be wheeled with the greatest economy of labour.[1]

An ample supply of coal—poor quality was adequate—was required. The kiln was loaded with layers of limestone (stones cleared from the fields were sometimes used) and fuel; the lime was drawn out from its base at regular intervals.

---

[1] A. Raistrick, *Old Yorkshire Dales.* (David & Charles, Newton Abbot, 1967), p. 68.

4

Communications

IN THE EARLY PART of the century most of the villagers, if they left Waddington at all, did not go beyond Clitheroe, where such needs as could not be met in the village could usually be supplied. The state of the roads discouraged travel and, in any case, there were few opportunities for people to leave their work to visit relations and friends and little money to spare for the journey. If they had to make a journey most villagers walked.

Those who were obliged to travel included the poor law overseers and constables. The constable had to make returns and payments at Gisburn, Settle and Skipton. Church officials and the schoolmaster went to Skipton when the annual visitation was held. One of the churchwardens went to Mitton to pay dues to the mother church and communicants were expected to attend service there at Easter, though few did.

Robert Smith, vicar, regularly visited his literary friends at Blackburn and Whalley, Occasionally, he ventured across 'the Alps' to visit the Parkers at Newton Hall. Later vicars, involved in litigation, went to York. Until Waddington had its own Wesleyan chapel a few villagers attended the chapel at West Bradford and when the Clitheroe Circuit was formed there were journeys to Paythorne, Holden, Rimington and other villages for the quarterly meetings. Some local preachers walked impressive distances to take services.

The Hospital agents travelled to Hellifield to supervise property, to Wakefield to register sales of land, to Preston to bank money. To obtain an Act of Parliament, in 1824 some of the trustees went to Westminster.

Freeholders had to make the sixty-mile journey to York in order to vote. Few did so before 1832 as the election of the county members was seldom contested. The Great Reform Act of that year meant more voters and a shorter journey to the new polling centre at Settle.

Mrs Clarke, with a house and friends in York and many relations, was sometimes away from home travelling in her private carriage. The vicarage, Brungerley and Waddow Lodge also had stables and coach-houses but even for the wealthy travel was no easy matter, especially at night. Dining with friends usually meant an overnight stay. Most farmers had stables but these were for working horses. Though mention is made of a side-saddle at a sale in 1808, it is unlikely that many women in the village rode.

That few people came to Waddington is evident from the stir caused in 1842 when two travellers intent on seeing the Old Hall arrived by chaise. 'Half a dozen villagers soon gathered together and along both sides of the village, doors were opening, or eyes straining through casements as they chanced to wonder what sufficient reason there

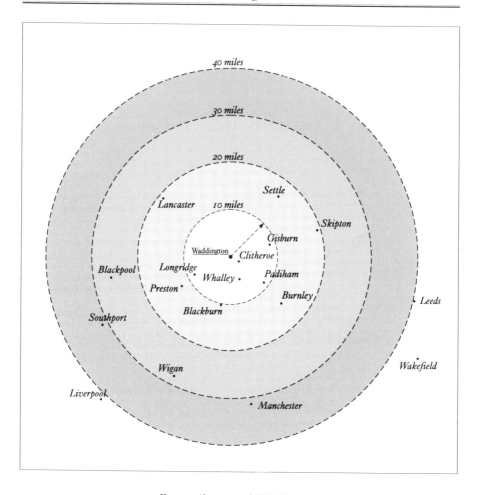

Forty miles around Waddington.

was for such a visit to their poor, humble and secluded spot.'[1] By this date a few children from the Lancashire cotton towns were attending Grimshaw's school. The Hospital Trustees came twice yearly, then quarterly, to deal with the accounts and celebrate the founder's birthday. The Parkers of Browsholme, although they some-times attended services at Whitewell, came to Waddington whenever they had com-pany, as the close carriage needed for their guests could not ascend and descend the hill at Whitewell.

At the time of the enclosure dispute John Walmsley rode over from Rochdale to judge the situation for himself and the commissioner appointed to make the enclosure

[1] C. Redding, *An Illustrated Itinerary of the County of Lancaster. England in the Nineteenth Century*, vi Lancashire (How and Parsons), p. 213.

award came from Samlesbury on a number of occasions between 1812 and 1819. Charity Commissioners came in 1824 to make enquiries about charities and the school.

Those who used the roads found that conditions were improving, thanks to the turnpike trusts. In Waddington, the Enclosure Act of 1812 resulted in the widening and general improvement of the old drovers' rode across the moors to Newton; the surveyors spent considerable sums on road repairs.

An important achievement was the construction of a wooden foot-bridge at Brungerley about 1800. This became necessary when the owners of Low Moor Mill constructed a weir which raised the water level. As the alternative crossing at Edisford meant a much longer journey to Clitheroe, the first bridge at Brungerley was built, to be replaced some twenty years later by a stone cart-bridge.

Travel usually involved the expenses of tolls and the hire of horse or carriage. The constable paid one shilling to hire a horse to Grindleton, two shillings for the journey to Slaidburn, and seven to Skipton, Gargrave or Settle. By 1839 the Skipton journey cost ten shillings. A Methodist preacher from Burnley was given nine shillings expenses in 1843 from the horse hire fund. The Hospital officials paid £1 1s. od. in 1802 for the hire of a horse to Wakefield, but generally they travelled by coach, chaise or gig. Gig and horse hire to York cost £2 15s. 5d. in 1825—'it being four days'. When some of the trustees went to London in 1824 each received £30 for fares and expenses.

The most uncomfortable journey might well have been that made by the trustees' agent to consult Thomas Lister Parker, then staying at Bala. The vicar's friend, the Revd Thomas Wilson, found the coach to be a 'travelling kitchen' in which 'the outside gentry fried and roasted and the inside passengers parboiled and stewed'.[1] Once, in winter when the roads were frosty, he suffered a two-hour delay while the horses' shoes were sharpened.

It was not until 1815 that the first stage coach came from Manchester to Clitheroe, 'drawn by four gaily bedecked and caparisoned horses' and reaching a speed of ten miles per hour.[2] Even without delays it was a four-hour journey for which the first-class passengers paid 7s. 6d. and those travelling outside 5s. From Clitheroe there were coaches to Skipton and Preston.

Longer journeys involved an overnight stay at an inn. A local traveller in 1812 paid 1s. 6d. for tea, 4s. for wine, 2s. for gin, 3s. for breakfast and 2s. for dinner. On a journey to Keighley in 1808 1s. 6d. was paid at the turnpike and later 2s. was paid to the waiter, 1s. to the barber, 4s. to the chambermaid and 7s. 6d. for hay and corn.

The coming of the railway, in the construction of which larch poles from the Hospital woods were used, brought revolutionary changes. In 1850 people from Waddington might have joined the schoolchildren as they watched the first train approach Clitheroe. Children from Blackburn, Wigan and other Lancashire towns attending Grimshaw's school in Waddington might well have been early users of the train. The novelty of travelling by train was such that people walked to Clitheroe, took

---

[1] F. R. Raines, *Miscellanies. Memoirs of the Life of Revd Thomas Wilson*, (Chetham Society, vol. 45, 1857–8), p. 172.

[2] S. Clarke, *Clitheroe in the Old Coaching Days* (2nd edn, 1929).

the train to Chatburn and then walked home after the excitement of the ride, during which 'there was not time to take a pinch of snuff'. Soon, eight trains a day were running from Clitheroe to Blackburn, Bolton, Darwen and Manchester. Although the carriages were far from comfortable and the shilling fare to Blackburn was the same as by coach, the journey took less time. The initial reluctance to travel by train was gradually overcome and improvements were made in the service. By the 'eighties over thirty trains a day were stopping at Clitheroe on weekdays and ten on Sundays. There were omnibuses to take people from the station to the Colthurst sale in 1855. Gigs and drags were available for hire. A 'conveyance' from Whalley to Waddington in 1868 cost the trustees 10s. 6d. In 1889 a Charity Commissioner arriving in Clitheroe expected to be able to hire a fly.

On bank holidays people used special excursion trains for 'trips'. One could go to Liverpool for 1s. 6d.; to Manchester, with admission to Belle Vue, for 2s. 6d. The Wesleyan choir went to Southport for the day in 1889 for £3. 10s. 6d. Factory workers, when they had their week's holiday, went to Blackpool; some ventured to North Wales.

Both groups and individuals made increasing use of trains. The school managers took the Manchester train when they went to examine heating apparatus at the Cheetham Hill exhibition in 1875. Preachers came from Manchester and Burnley to take anniversary services. The Garnetts, with their interest in cotton, also found the Manchester train convenient. Edward Parker, travelling from Eastbourne to attend meetings of the Hospital Trustees, received £5 for expenses; £8 1s. 6d. covered his return journey by train and steamer to Jersey. At the end of the century, Private Almond of Waddington, wounded in the Boer War, was accompanied to the station by the Clitheroe Band when returning to his regiment; a honeymoon couple caught a train to the south, and the vicar, Francis Parker, began his journey to Russia by train.

Two people who relied upon an efficient train service in the late 'eighties were William Wallbank and Richard Marsden. They travelled all over the country to exhibit their prize-winning poultry. Among the shows they attended were several in Yorkshire and Lancashire—Doncaster, Wakefield, Lancaster, Manchester—shows at Bath, Birmingham, Norwich and the Crystal Palace. At Strabane they won the Five Guinea Cup.

Census returns indicate that in the second half of the century people were coming from greater distances to live in Waddington. In 1851 only six people in the village had been born over forty miles away. Two of them came from the Liverpool area, the others from Doncaster, Rydal, Durham and Staffordshire. In 1881 there were thirty-three people whose birthplace was over forty miles from Waddington. Six came from Wales, Ireland or Scotland: others were from Lincolnshire, Shropshire, Cheshire, Derbyshire and Westmorland. As might be expected, by 1891 a still higher percentage had been born over forty miles from Waddington. Easier and cheaper travel by train in part explains this development. It also enabled people to leave the village in search of employment.

The horse continued to be used for both business and pleasure. In the early 'fifties, the Brocklehursts of Colthurst were occasionally seen driving in their new and very handsome landau. This was lined with drab cloth, figured silk, and lace and had full

Pony and trap: a common sight.

plated lamps, silver furniture, a hind rumble, drag shoe and chain complete. This and their drag had been bought in London.[1]

Soon after James Garnett moved to Waddow he repaired the coach-house and stables and bought a waggonette, a vehicle which made its appearance in the 'forties and was then in general use. Edward Parker at the vicarage had a waggonette which held four persons, and a dog-cart. The former was painted black and green, fitted with cushions and had a pair of lamps, all supplied by a Preston firm. The latter, painted in the same colours, was fitted with a sliding seat and india-rubber mat. With its high clearance it was useful over rough ground and had room for dogs, luggage and people.

Waggonettes holding eight people could be hired. Larger ones and lurries took parties of children on Sunday school outings. 'Eighteen old females able to stand the strain were taken from the workhouse on a lurry to Waddow for a picnic', and widows from the Hospital went to Browsholme by waggonette. A pony and trap was a common sight towards the end of the century. On Good Friday 1889 a trap containing three ladies and a gentleman from Blackburn overturned while passing through Waddington. The ladies—one of whom was driving—escaped with a shaking, but the gentleman was 'somewhat bruised'. Such accidents were not infrequent.

The increased traffic kept the surveyor and his assistant busy maintaining the roads. In 1863 £63 was spent on road works. £150 was spent in 1877 when a footpath

[1] LRO, DDX/28/286, *Whewell's Family and Clitheroe Monthly Advertiser*, May 1855.

had to be made alongside the road to Brungerley.[1] Because of the number of accidents which occurred, the Hospital was asked to prune and lop the trees which 'were excluding the sun and obstructing the traffic'.

When in 1899 the building of a new bridge at Brungerley was being considered, a survey of traffic was made. It was found that in seven days 309 carts with one horse, 60 with more than one horse, 70 carriages with four wheels, 331 carriages with two wheels, 5,460 passengers, in addition to cows, horses and sheep, had crossed the bridge.[2] There could be no doubt as to its importance.

The bicycle made its appearance towards the end of the century. Among the first in Waddington was a wood and iron model owned by the vicar, Edward Parker. Later, machines made at Whiteside's in Clitheroe, or in Coventry, cost ten guineas. In 1898 'The prettiest cycle for Ladies' cost eleven guineas. In the week's traffic survey 269 bicycles were recorded. There were certainly enough cyclists for the Foresters to arrange a bicycle race at their sports in 1900, and those who wished could join the Clitheroe Cycle Club.

The appearance of the first motor car was almost as startling as that of the first train. Dr Musson, the first person to own a car in Clitheroe, drove in it to Waddington in 1893. Villagers had for some time been accustomed to seeing a man with a red flag enforcing a speed limit of four miles an hour. Edward Chester had for a time used a traction engine for carting stone until the considerable damage it did to the road surface caused him to desist.

Though during the century dramatic changes had taken place in speed, cost, method of travel and distances covered, many people still had to rely on Shanks's pony. Mill workers walked along the Low Moor road, their clogs resounding as they crossed the foot-bridge to approach the mill. Low Moor teams walked to Waddington before they played their football matches. Schoolchildren, farm workers and church-goers kept the footpaths worn by constant use. A walk to Clitheroe or a country ramble was the main recreation for many at the end of the working week.

A few actually ventured overseas.[3] About 1846 Matthew Ellison, who had been brought up on Mitchells farm, left for America at the age of sixteen. He evidently did well there, bought a farm in Illinois and, when his wife died, came to England on his eighth visit in 1890, remarried and returned to the States. At the time of the agricultural depression *The Clitheroe Times* encouraged people to emigrate to Canada, Australia and New Zealand where they could expect wages of 6s. to 8s. a day. Agents ready to make arrangements, and the proximity of Liverpool, helped to promote emigration; would-be emigrants were warned against going to South Africa in 1900 (the Boer War was then in progress).

Before 1850 many goods were carried by waggon; those from a distance came by road and canal. The Hospital Trustees paid the Union Company carriage on a case of wine and on chimney pots from Leeds. Slate from Liverpool came by the Leeds & Liverpool canal to Enfield in 1824 at a cost of £2 and was then carted for 19s. 6d. Hampers of wine and sherry were brought from Lancaster. According to tradition,

---

[1] LRO, DDX/1889, Vestry Minute Book.
[2] *Clitheroe Times*, April 1900.
[3] 1841 census.

when Lancaster was still a port, cotton was brought through the Trough of Bowland to Feazer Mill.

In the later part of the century speed and cheapness gave the railways the advantage over canals in the transport of goods. In 1877 slate came by rail, as did coal for domestic and industrial use. A widening range of commodities for the home was brought by train. The grand piano at the vicarage came from London; the Garnetts bought their furniture from Kendal Milne and Faulkner's, Manchester; the flowers for Miss Burton's wedding were from the Riviera.

Locally, carriers' waggons and carts were still used. A carrier's cart left Clitheroe for Waddington every Wednesday, and tea and groceries from the town were brought by horse and trap to be delivered to customers in the village. The carrier's cart made a weekly journey from Slaidburn, passing through Waddington, to collect supplies from Clitheroe. Other carriers passed through on their way to Lancaster via the Trough of Bowland for supplies of fish. A few people in the village—Hansons, the chairmakers, and Jackson, the 'postboy'—kept a donkey. The farmers used pony and trap to take their milk kits to the station.

The introduction of penny postage had led to a big increase in letter-writing. Before 1840 letters had been paid for by the recipient, with charges varying according to weight and distance. In 1824, for example, 1s. 3d. had been paid on a letter from York. The penny post encouraged the sending of Valentine and Easter cards. It was not long before people were being urged in November to 'make their selection of Christmas cards for foreign parts'. The railway speeded up delivery: the Hospital Trustees were no longer obliged to send documents by coach first to Preston to be transferred to the Derby coach for their final destination.

When a main post office was established in Clitheroe in 1850 a mounted rural post began between Clitheroe, Waddington, Grindleton and Bolton-by-Bowland, with a branch foot post between Waddington and Slaidburn. John Jackson made the five-mile journey over the moors to Newton and Slaidburn and back to Clitheroe for some years before his death in 1875.

Robert Walker was post master in the 'fifties: he received the letters from Clitheroe at 9.30 a.m. and they were delivered at 3.30 p.m.[1] When James Leeming was post master, letters arrived earlier and residents had until six o'clock to catch the post.[2] In 1889 Waddington post office was opened as a telegraph office 'to the great convenience of the inhabitants'. The cost of sending a telegram had, by then, been reduced to sixpence for twenty words. Telegrams were sometimes sent to call the doctor, and on one occasion led to the arrest in Blackburn of a Waddington man wanted for receiving stolen goods. A further improvement in communications was imminent when, in 1900, the telephone company was given permission by the parish council to erect poles along the West Bradford—Waddington road on payment of one shilling per pole per year. Parcel post began in Clitheroe in 1882 and money orders were obtainable there. These services were later extended to Waddington. These developments in communication improved the standard of living and increased Waddington's contacts with the outside world.

---

[1] *Slater's Directory*, 1858.
[2] *Slater's Directory*, 1876.

5

Leisure Hours

FOR MUCH OF THE CENTURY only the wealthy had leisure and money to enjoy it. For the rest there were the holidays associated with the Church festivals of Christmas and Easter. People in the Waddington area by custom had a holiday on Whit Monday. Sheep-shearing and harvest brought ample supplies of food and drink and encouraged merrymaking. The four annual Clitheroe fairs, with their side-shows, wrestling matches and pedlars passing on news while selling their wares, provided a variety of cheap entertainment.

At the three inns home-brewed beer and ale, baccy and snuff, were consumed amidst congenial company. There, crops and the weather, births and deaths were inevitably discussed, along with the poor harvest of 1800, the war against France and the rise in prices.

Outside the Sun and the Buck i'th'Vine there was entertainment of a more violent kind when a bull was baited in the Square.[1] Those who relished such 'sport' could walk to Chatburn where bull-baiting was continued, despite the law, until 1834. Even towards the end of the century people talked of the Chatburn rushbearing celebrations when

> as in the fifteenth century a large waggon was thatched with rushes and all round hung silver and pewter jugs, cups and bracelets lent by gentry and common folk. Young girls with ribbons rode in the cart; there were morris dancers on foot. You might have walked on the heads of folk who thronged from the villages all about Pendle Hill to take part in the bull-baiting and watch Tom Chatburn and his dog Nell attack the bull. Tom was alleged to have seized the bull by the nose with his own teeth. The dog was so injured in the fight that it had to be held up in its kennel in slings.[2]

Threshing the hen—throwing sticks and stones at a hen tied to a stake—had died out, but interest in cock-fighting lingered on sufficiently for two lads to stage a mimic fight at a Whit Monday field day as late as 1892.

The few wealthy in the village had other entertainment. Letter-writing took up much of their time. The vicar enjoyed reading and discussing literary topics with friends and he delighted the Parkers with his ready wit. Major and Mrs Clarke dined at Browsholme, at Major Wright's and at Colonel Rigby's. The hospitality was

---

[1] J. Harland and T. T. Wilkinson, *Lancashire Traditions* (London, 1863), p. 149.
[2] *Clitheroe Times*, 1898.

returned: 'Mr Clarke begs the favour of Mr Parker's company to dinner on Wednesday next to meet Mr Lloyd, Mr Brocklehurst and some others and to take a bed. Dinner precisely at 3.'[1]

By the 1830s dinner had become a late afternoon meal and often involved an overnight stay. Invitations still concluded with words such as 'put your night-cap in your pocket'. The Clarkes visited friends in York and invited their relations to Waddow, where there was a good library and a well-stocked cellar. Conversation turned to such subjects as enclosure, the departure of the Tempests to Bath for the season and of others to Blackpool, taxes on servants and carriage horses, and the appointment of Major Clarke to be a trustee at the Hospital. Occasionally they attended functions in Clitheroe, at one of which—a lecture on philosophy and chemistry—they met the Revd Thomas Wilson, headmaster of the grammar school. The entertainment offered by the Brocklehursts of Colthurst included loo and bagatelle.

Their outdoor pursuits included fishing—there was an abundant supply of salmon in the Ribble—and shooting. William Parker, vicar, anticipated 'great sport on the fells Waddington particularly'. A neighbour wrote in September 1801 'It is now about the season the Manchester sportsmen make their annual visit. They ought to be well attended.'[2] Plans were made for one or two active young men to accompany them when they set out to shoot hares, rabbits, woodcock and pheasants. When Mrs Clarke let the Hall her tenants were allowed 'rights of hunting, coursing, shooting and fishing in and over the manor', but they were not to keep harriers. William Brocklehurst kept a pack of hounds at Colthurst and by 1846 there was enough hunting taking place in the area to provoke one reader of the *Clitheroe Monthly Advertiser* to condemn 'the cruel diversion of hunting'. In another item the hare was said to be 'a brute without reason'. Furthermore, it was claimed that 'the musical cry of the pack—so charming to the ear, so animating to the mind of man and so encouraging to the horses kept for the chase—affords a conclusive reason why the hound was designed to follow the hare.'[3]

For the poorer people conditions were changing. The August bank holiday was established in 1871; mill workers no longer worked on Saturday afternoons, and before the century ended they had an annual week's holiday. The coming of the railway to Clitheroe made new leisure pursuits available. Following the success of a trip to Preston Guild in 1862 further 'sensational' trips were organised. On Good Fridays there were excursions to Liverpool and to Manchester for the Belle Vue Gardens and the races. Some preferred to go to Whalley, where the gala proved a great attraction in the 'eighties. Outings to Settle and Giggleswick were arranged. The church choir and Sunday school teachers, not content with the annual visit to Southport and a tour of its Botanical Gardens, visited Windermere, rowed on the lake and drove to Grasmere. One year they left Chatburn late on Sunday evening for Glasgow, sailed down the Clyde and returned early on Tuesday. For their holidays mill workers went to Blackpool; their employers, the Garnetts, went to Lytham. Lady Holker went to Nice.

---

[1] LRO, DDB 22/928.
[2] LRO, DDB 22/928.
[3] LRO, DDX/28/316.

Festivities at church and chapel

Much of the social life of the village revolved round the church and the chapel: in both music was of vital importance. Methodism, with the great hymns of Charles Wesley, in some cases set to popular tunes, encouraged an interest in singing—an interest later maintained when the Moody and Sankey hymn book appeared. Both church and chapel had choirs accompanied by instruments: bass viol, bassoon, violin and cello, then by a harmonium and later still by an organ. Membership meant regular practices of hymns, anthems and, for special occasions, oratorios. There was carol singing, too. Singers from the chapel went through the village up to Cuttock Clough to sing and let in the New Year.

As a reward for their services the choir and officials of St Helen's had a goose supper followed by an entertainment, or they went to the vicarage for tea and afterwards sang glees and part songs at the pianoforte. The Wesleyans were treated to a 'sumptuous repast' at their choir supper. They had their annual outings to Whitewell or, later, went farther afield to Lytham.

There was a wealth of musical talent in the village: William Boothman was church organist for thirteen years and Tom Herd was an accomplished pianist. The church ringers rang carillons as well as the grandsire and Oxford treble changes.

By the 'seventies the Tea Festival was well established. There is an early reference to a Tea Feast in 1835 and to others in the 'fifties. Twenty years later it was taken for granted that on Christmas Day at the chapel there would be a tea party, free for the scholars and 6d. for ticket holders. If the teas were anything like those provided for a neighbouring Methodist Christmas party, over 30 lbs. of beef and nearly as much ham, over 100 lbs. of flour and 28 lbs. of lump sugar would have been consumed. At Waddington five different kinds of bread were provided along with all the other food. After tea there were recitations and dialogues from the scholars. The day school also had a Christmas party. In 1888 350 had tea and then listened to songs and roared with laughter at the dialogues. The entertainments became more and more popular, and the large schoolroom was at times 'densely crowded', even 'packed to suffocation' for a 'capital miscellaneous programme' of songs, recitations, drill and callisthenics provided by Willie Boothman, the choirboys and others.

Tea parties were provided on every possible occasion and they afforded a welcome opportunity for the exchange of news: 'a tea-party without a gossip was like a knife without a handle'. Not wishing to be behind the times, the unmarried men arranged a tea party at the chapel; six of them presided over tables, one of them carved the beef and ham, and afterwards the young men's choir sang glees. This, of course, had to be followed by a ladies' tea meeting: happy were those who were accorded the honour of presiding at a table.

The entertainments on such occasions included action songs and drill performed by the schoolchildren, items given by the girls of the Snowdrop band and solos from the headmaster, Mr Danson, whose repertoire included 'The Jovial Monk'. Mrs Jarley's waxworks, which included models of Her Majesty, Baden Powell and Madame Patti, made their appearance at the mothers' tea party. Madame Patti, when wound up, sang 'Home, Sweet Home'.

Whitsuntide celebrations were of equal importance to the Christmas ones, and by the 'sixties included processions. In 1889, according to the *Clitheroe Times*, about two hundred teachers and scholars met at the Old School. After a sermon they formed a procession headed by Chatburn Brass Band and, with a banner in front and other paintings and banners at intervals, they visited the vicarage and the Reader's House, then went to West Bradford where they sang a hymn. Mrs Burton of Eaves Hall provided tea and coffee, and the children were given oranges—a rare treat. They then 'repaired to the field in front of the Day school for a free tea and games till dusk'.

The Wesleyans had similar festivities. After singing hymns and the National Anthem at the chapel they proceeded with their banner through the village and had tea and buns at Brook Farm.

One of the important events in church life was the holding of a bazaar. Preparations began over a year before the event: goods were made and collected and a wide variety of items, even hens and chickens, were brought in for sale. To cover the initial expense of their 1889 bazaar, the chapel had three conversaziones—evenings of entertainment and refreshments. On each day of the bazaar itself the opening ceremonies included chairman's remarks, opener's speech and vote of thanks. Teas and an evening's entertainment—a different programme for each evening—followed the sale. A church bazaar held at the day school was on an even bigger scale and necessitated closing the school for the week. 'Sales of work' (small-scale bazaars) were held, with bran-tubs, 'draw-wells' and competitions as side attractions.

Concerts

Many concerts took place. At one given in the chapel in 1889 the instrumentalists included a first and second violin, viol, flute and pianoforte; there was a duet for piccolo and ocarina, and musical glasses and fairy bells were played. Among the visiting performers was Alonzo Jackson of Low Moor with a choir including several Waddington men. Tom Herd was their accompanist. Inevitably, there was tea afterwards—a knife-and-fork affair served at Mrs Speakman's. Jackson, who was noted for his telling of original jokes, later formed a troupe of 'Minstrels'. With blackened faces, they performed for the Reading Room Society and at many other functions.

Well patronised concerts were given in the wheelwright's shop before the Wesleyan schoolroom was built and permission given to use the day school. There was a 'Grand Dramatic Performance of The Duchess of Bayswater and Company' in 1900, and the cricket club organised a Shrove Tuesday concert with refreshments, followed by dancing to the accompaniment of a piano, violin, cornet and piccolo. Later in the year a Grand Social was held. For sixpence there was dinner at 6.30 and entertainment and dancing until 10.30—an advance on the ten o'clock finish of twenty years earlier. Visiting choirs and bands and a professional whistler from Nelson who gave bird imitations performed at some of the concerts. Popular songs included 'On the Banks of Allan Water' and 'Victoria, England's Queen', and there were humorous songs, according to the report, 'in the good old fashioned Lancashire'.

The Waddington Handbell Ringers were much in demand. In 1891 they bought the forty-five bells which the Low Moor team had used, and in the following year took part in a contest at Belle Vue, Manchester. 'We failed to get a prize,' the secretary confessed, 'nevertheless we learned something and came home in good spirits.'[1] Four years later they acquired a new set of fifty-six bells for £22 and gave their first concert in the Wesleyan school. In Clitheroe and district they gave many performances for charity.

Other entertainment

Dancing was becoming increasingly popular. In addition to the field dancing on Whit Monday and on Foresters' Day, occasional dances were held at the Buck Inn. Dancing was arranged for wedding guests and the Clitheroe Band provided the music when Miss Ramsome's Sunday school class had their social.

In the home, the well-to-do had pianos; even some of the middle class could afford them by the end of the century for, at £20, they were half their mid-century price. Edison's phonograph, 'that marvel of modern inventions', appeared in the village. At party time there were charades and the old favourites of hunt the thimble and pinning the tail on the donkey. Stations and postman's knock were coming into favour. Draughts, halma, card games, especially cribbage, patience and whist, were played.

A certain interest was shown in reading. The Garnetts read *The Times*, the *Manchester Guardian* and the *Preston Guardian* and, in 1861, took the first *Illustrated News*. As early as 1846 the *Clitheroe Monthly Advertiser* had appeared, price one penny. Although it was on sale in Waddington, Sabden and several other villages, the 'depression of the times' led to its early demise. In 1855 *Whewell's Family Paper and Clitheroe Monthly Advertiser* began a rather longer run. By this time the Hospital had organised a lending library for the widows and a circulating library was later considered by the Reading Room Society.

This society, founded in 1882, was soon broadening its interests and activities by providing dominoes and billiards as well as papers. Eleven of its members formed a team and played matches against West Bradford and Low Moor. When they lost to the latter, some concern was shown, for 'the Yorkshire men took a deep interest in sport'. Sufficient interest developed in the village for them to consider having a billiards club (in 1904 an architect actually prepared plans, and a site below the smithy was chosen), but nothing came of the scheme. Meanwhile, they organised social evenings and enjoyed their first Potato Pie Supper in 1893.

---

[1] S. Clarke, *Clitheroe in its Railway Days*, p. 250.

Organised sports

In the last decades of the century young men in the village took part in organised sport. By 1888 there were enough of them with free Saturday afternoons to be able to form a football team. With Rushton in goal, Hayhurst as captain, three Lunds and two Wallbanks among the players, they had matches against Clitheroe Gymnasium and West Bradford. Home matches were played at Cross Lane.

The cricket club was formed in March 1892 with the new schoolmaster as secretary. In May they played Low Moor. 'Just short of 1,000 witnessed a very interesting game' in which Waddington scored thirty-two and Low Moor fifty-two. The following month Low Moor won by one run. 'The spectators were rather wild towards the finish and I hear some shed tears. With such a close finish the umpires came in for a fair share of hard criticism.'[1] Judging by some of the scores, the teams played with rather more enthusiasm than skill: in one match, which lasted only an hour and a half, no-one reached double figures. After a few years, however, Waddington were able to enter the Blackburn League. Under the captaincy of Richard Lund they played matches against Barrow, Bolton-by-Bowland and Hyndburn. Matches were played on Altham's field along Low Moor Road. Adults who came to watch paid 2d., children 1d. In 1899, of their fourteen matches they won ten, lost three and drew one.

Although according to Waddington rules no bad language was to be used on the field, not all was 'cricket': the 'sodding' of victorious teams and of umpires was not unknown. Golf may not have attracted many players, though the game was played on Lillands in 1892.

The big sporting event of the summer was organised by the Ancient Order of Foresters. Typical were the activities in 1900. Early in the year they advertised for a brass band to play for their anniversary and sports from 10 a.m. to 9 p.m. (their own Excelsior Band had only just been formed). On the day itself, 23 June, there was a procession in the morning when the great banner was carried forth and the officials appeared wearing their green sashes and full regalia. The sports, held on the cricket field, included races of 100 yards, one mile and hurdles; high jump, tug of war, bicycle race, walking and wrestling matches. The weather was 'on its best behaviour' and 1,200 people paid for admission. Prizes to the value of £26 were awarded. On a previous occasion a silver watch, a walnut writing desk and a clock were among the prizes. Afterwards, there was dancing to the Clitheroe Band until dusk.

Although some still took pleasure in a country drive, cycling and rambling became increasing popular, and as early as 1856 the gatekeeper of Sawley Abbey was offering tourists and visitors to the ruins 'a comfortable cup of tea and other refreshments upon very reasonable terms'. A Clitheroe shopkeeper bought in a special consignment of walking sticks for the Whit holiday. When a rambling party came to Waddington in 1887 they were shown the cinerary urns which James Walmsley had found at Pinder Hill. Two years later a great storm which brought down an oak tree in Waddow Park

---

[1] *Clitheroe Times*, 8 July 1892.

led many to Waddow where some collected pieces of the oak as souvenirs. Waddington ramblers went to Wensleydale, others went up to Feazer to see the marigolds, primroses and cowslips. There were cuckoos on Cuckoo Hill and corncrakes and curlews could be seen and heard. Had any ramblers walked to Paythorne in October 1898 they might have seen 'the greatest rush of salmon for twenty-one years'.

The Ribble provided many opportunities for recreation. The Garnetts had the fishing rights and James Garnett enjoyed many a good catch of salmon and grayling. As a magistrate he tried to stop pollution by imposing a fine on the owners of the Primrose Factory who allowed chloride of lime to enter the river. It was kept well stocked with trout brought from Loch Leven—necessary, as forty-four of them were caught in one day. Poachers, too, sometimes had a good catch despite the efforts of water-bailiffs.

There had been otter hunting since the 1830s. James Lomax of Clayton Hall, Great Harwood, according to his diary, often hunted the Ribble and Hodder, as these extracts show.

> *27 March 1830.* Took the trail of an otter at Hacking, and found him at a root beneath Waddow Call [the Caul]. Venture and the otter came from beneath the root fast hold of each other, and went overhead together. We swam him for about two hours in a strong black water. We caught him just below Eastford Bridge; let the hounds fight him into the water again and called off. This otter seemed to be 21 or 22 lbs. weight.

> *25 March 1835.* Had a trail down Calder and up Little Ribble to Waddow; got a glass of wine at Mr Garnett's and then crossed over to Hodder above Bashall Lodge. No hunt. Messrs Barker, Keeling and the Parkers were out.

The following month a twenty-one-pound otter which they had trailed from High Hodder Bridge to a drain in a meadow above Waddow Deep was killed in front of Waddow. In 1847 they were again near Waddow and in 1852, having trailed an otter down Calder through Mitton Wood to Waddow Deep, killed it at Henthorn lime-kilns. One of the later entries for October 1866 records a hunt above Gisburn Park, where for a time the hounds followed a salmon which 'performed just like an otter'. 'We had a capital trail to Waddow Deep where we called off ... lunched at Stanley House. A rail broke as I was getting over it, just below Grindleton, and I got a proper ducking in the Ribble, but was no worse for it.'[1] Lomax was then over sixty-three.

Five years later rabies broke out in the kennels at Clayton Hall and all except three hounds and six terriers were destroyed. 'The most perfect pack of otter hounds ever formed by one man ceased to exist.' The sport was still being pursued in the late 'eighties, however. On a September morning in 1889 Captain Yates' hounds entered the Ribble at Brungerley and proceeded upstream towards Chatburn. 'A large company followed but although several otters were seen at Bottom there was no sport that day.'

In the first week of December 1879 the river was frozen to a depth of seven inches. In the winters of 1890 and 1895 the skaters were again having a lively time and some found Waddington Road made an excellent skating rink.

---

[1] J. Lomax, unpublished diary 1828–71.

In summer there was boating. Below the bridge on the Clitheroe side, Eli Tucker had by 1876 provided swing boats, pleasure and rowing boats. He brought the old ferry boat from Grindleton and another from Caledonian Lake, Blackburn. Refreshments were on sale. Given fine weather on Good Friday, when the season began, crowds would come from the Lancashire towns and nearby villages: as many as three thousand arrived at Clitheroe by train. Those who came found that 'it was almost impossible to get a pull on the river without waiting an hour or more for a disengaged boat'. There was the occasional accident, as when six people from Burnley, against Tucker's advice, took out a boat and, disregarding his instructions, went through the centre arch instead of keeping to the side. When turning they were swept against a pillar, the boat was upset and three of the party were carried downstream. Fortunately, all were rescued.

Occasionally, on Sunday afternoons the Clitheroe Band played at Brungerley. When some young men and boys were romping about there were fears that the privilege might be withdrawn and, with hundreds frequenting the river banks, there were objections to the Sunday afternoon bathing which took place. By 1898 two wooden huts had been provided as changing rooms for bathers, and a diving platform. There was also the warning notice: 'All persons bathing at the new bathing houses at Brungerley without bathing drawers to be prosecuted.'

Annual events

There were special attractions to look forward to throughout the year. In Clitheroe there was the Great Saturday Fair at Michaelmas, fairs in December, March and August and, after 1883, the Horse Fair in May. As well as the buying and selling of produce there were roundabouts, side-shows of a dwarf's head in a box, of a fat woman and a skeleton man, of a drum-performing pony; sweets and liquorice were for sale and sometimes there was a Punch and Judy show. So many children attended the Agricultural Show in August that a school holiday was eventually granted. When the show became a Whit Monday event many attended to see the horse-jumping, the collie dogs and pigeons.

In April 1890 Barnum's 'The Greatest Show on Earth' with swings and shooting galleries came to Clitheroe. Later in the year came 'The Largest Exhibition that ever moved upon the surface of the earth'. Mr Sanders from America had arrived with his zoological collection. Waddington people flocked with the rest to see the quaggas, sacred camels, leopards, elephants and the circus. This, too, became an annual event. Some years later people were assured that it was worth coming a hundred miles to witness the performance of 'With Kitchener at Khartoum'.

In 1856 Edward Parker expressed the belief that interest in bonfire night would soon diminish following the omission of reference to the Gunpowder Plot from the prayer book. He was wrong. Bonfire night continued to be observed with preparations beginning in September. Fireworks were on sale at registered shops in Clitheroe twenty years later. Collop Monday, with gifts of money rather than collops of bacon, was followed by pancake parties on Shrove Tuesday and 'pace' egging when children went round begging for eggs at Easter. Another favourite activity at Easter was the climbing of Pendle Hill. Mischief-making on the eve of May Day had almost died out, much to the relief of farmers. Bolton-by-Bowland was one place where, as late as 1891, the custom of bringing gates, implements and carts from the fields and leaving them in the centre of the village was still observed.

Women had little leisure time. For those who had, the *Clitheroe Times* recommended gardening as 'a very healthful pursuit' so long as they left the hard and rough work alone. 'With a little tuition and experience they can become quite as successful as men in planting and raising flowers.' Probably some women had taken up gardening before this, as the first Flower Show for the cottagers of Waddington and West Bradford was held in the day school in 1881. The village had a reputation for growing rambler roses, and Mrs Mitchell at Ivy Cottage was one of a number of greenhouse owners. At Colthurst people could sit on the wrought-iron seats round the rustic table and admire the lawns cared for by the gardener with his patent mowing machine and iron garden rollers.

On a fine summer's day it was not unknown for mothers to take their children up the fell for a picnic—all the more enjoyable for its being in school time. Outings to gather nuts, blackberries, cranberries and herbs combined work and pleasure. That women should take part in sporting activities was accepted by the end of the century: the Foresters' sports programme included races for unmarried and married women.

Children's games

Children devised their own games. Those with skipping ropes and hoops knew the season when these should appear. Parents who could afford to give presents could, in the later part of the century, buy unbreakable dolls complete with skipping rope for 1s., painting and crayoning books for a few pence, and paintboxes from 1s. to 2s. 6d. Toys for boys included metal soldiers, horses and carts, trumpets and Noah's arks. Some of these items cost as much as 4s. 6d. Most boys, however, had to be content with bird-nesting, tickling trout in Bashall Brook, or a game of marbles or knur and spell.[1] James Fishwick as a boy played cricket, single wicket and five-a-side, in Th'old Thack garden.[2] Others, like John Bright during his schooldays in Newton, enjoyed country walks, fishing and swimming. Some of those learning to swim used corks.

Pastimes for the wealthy

Again, the better off had other pursuits. The young ladies at the vicarage had their sketching and painting in the studio, and tennis and cucumber sandwiches on the lawn. They entertained their Parker relations and friends and showed their accomplishments as pianists; they rode; they may even have enjoyed a bicycle ride.

---

[1] J. Harland and T. T. Wilkinson, *Lancashire Legends, Traditions*, p. 149.

[2] J. H. W. Fishwick, *In and Around Waddington* (*Clitheroe Advertiser and Times*), p. 12.

The Garnett children had music lessons, and ponies which they raced from Brungerley Bridge past the ha-ha to Peg o'Nell's Well while their elders played croquet. The family enjoyed birthday parties when their relations came for dinner and dancing. In 1864 they had their first Christmas tree to add to the celebrations.

When Lady Holker remarried in 1894 there was a rumour that the estate would be sold. 'It was hoped that her husband would dissuade her.' If he succeeded 'he would have at hand either hunting, fishing, shooting, riding or driving or good society'.[1] In fact, far from selling the estate, Lady Holker rented part of the fell from the Hospital so that the guests at Colthurst could have additional land for shooting. The grouse there were 'numerous and healthy'. Pheasant shooters expected to have the birds driven rather than have to approach them, as in the past.

As the power of the landowners in parliament diminished, so did the severity of the Game Laws. The Ground Game Act of 1888 allowed tenants to destroy hares and rabbits on their own holdings. Some went after hares and rabbits even without such rights. Tom Hayhurst, farm servant, was charged in 1900 with trespassing in search of game. He had been seen by a gamekeeper to shoot at a hare in the Tan Pit Meadow where the Garnetts had the shooting rights. The case was dismissed as Hayhurst was not actually in the field: had he been found guilty a sentence of two months' hard labour might have been imposed. Sixty years earlier Edward Parker had, as a youth, helped break up a gang of poachers on the Browsholme estate. Three of the five had been captured and were sentenced on the following day to three months' hard labour at Wakefield, a penalty which Parker thought 'rather severe', especially as punishment did not end there. Their wives and daughters who were working at Low Moor were 'turned off'.

The Pendle Forest Hunt, too, rented land from the Hospital. In 1881 there were kennels and a house for the kennelman near Carter Fold. The huntsman lived in the village in one of Colonel Starkie's cottages. According to the *Clitheroe Times* in 1881

> a visitor to the kennels of this pack of crack harriers situate in Waddington under the control of Col. Starkie of Huntroyd, cannot fail to observe the order and cleanliness that exist under the able management of Messrs Brock and Fairclough, the hunt and whip respectively.

The Colonel kept between twenty and thirty hunters, some of which he stabled in Waddington. From October until November, when the first of the monthly meets was held, the young hounds were to be seen being trained 'in the wilds of Tosside and district'.

A memorable hunt took place on 25 February 1899. A red hind brought from Surrey was uncarted near Gisburn. After the five-minute start to which it was entitled the pursuit began. The scent was lost for a time when the hind crossed the canal and then the railway line. After a seventeen-mile chase the animal was taken and was later returned to Gisburn and freed. Among the six hundred who followed were Mr and Mrs William Garnett, he on horse and she on foot. Because of illness the Master was unable to attend and ride as he had done on 24 February 1863, when the last deer

---

[1] *Clitheroe Times*, 25 April 1894.

hunt at Gisburn had taken place, but 'a finer horseman or a better sportsman never rode across Craven'.

Only a few fox hunts took place in the district. Badgers, said to be killing geese, were sometimes hunted.

Social events were special occasions, even for spectators, and weddings, particularly Miss Mary Burton's early in 1900, drew admiring crowds. In the evening, tenants and servants were treated to a display of fireworks at Eaves Hall. Funerals were sombre occasions, but the ham teas and reminiscences which followed were consolation to some.

Throughout the century royal marriages, jubilees and the conclusion of peace were celebrated with all the enthusiasm inspired by longed-for breaks from hard and monotonous work. After the Crimean War there was a great procession from Clitheroe to Waddow Park, with evening fireworks to conclude the event. Ten tons of material were used for a bonfire on Coplow to celebrate a Boer War victory.

When the Duke of York married Princess May of Teck in 1893, there was a procession in Clitheroe a mile in length, lit from end to end by hundreds of flaming torches. Along with horsemen and cyclists the Waddington Snowdrops took part. For the Queen's Golden Jubilee in 1887 the children had a holiday and, having enjoyed celebrations provided in the village, took another day off school to attend the games and festivities organised in Clitheroe. At night the beacon on Pendle was seen for miles around: it had taken a week to carry up the material. William Dewhurst of Waddington and his committee organised an ox-roast for the festivities.

Ten years later, celebrations were again on a lavish scale for the Diamond Jubilee. Though there was no bonfire on Pendle, cannon, fired in Blackburn Park, could be heard and rockets and bonfires seen. Balloon ascents were made, and one balloon came down at Gannies Farm. Once again there was a procession and ox-roast.

These rare events were reported in detail in the local paper. Minor events did not escape notice. Felix Leach became Captain of the 2nd Lancashire Rifle Volunteers, and William Dewhurst presented a cup for their shooting competition. Captain Yates carried off prizes at a local canary-singing contest; others were content to spend their leisure time at the Lower Buck, the Sun and Higher Buck, much as their ancestors had done a hundred years earlier.

6

Church and Chapel

THE NINETEENTH CENTURY was a time of some religious fervour: the building of new churches and the rebuilding of old ones was its outward expression. On the other hand strong anti-religious feeling was expressed by sceptics and some scientists in both the written and the spoken word.

The Anglican Church, richly endowed and privileged, enjoyed the support of most of the upper class and the greater part of the rural population at the beginning of the century. Towards the end there was fear of disestablishment, already effected in Ireland and Wales. The Methodist movement continued to gain adherents until, eventually, with the older Nonconformists—Baptists, Congregationalists and Presbyterians— dissenters outnumbered Anglicans.

The Roman Catholics also increased their numbers after 1829 when the Catholic Emancipation Act gave them full civic rights. They were further strengthened by an influx of Irish during the famine years of the 'forties and by Newman's conversion. Rivalries, especially over educational matters, developed between Anglicans, Roman Catholics and Nonconformists.

Within the established Church the evangelicals were the first to realise the need for reform if the Church was to maintain its position. They helped to bring about a revival during the 'thirties and, with the help of parliamentary legislation, were responsible for such measures as the creation in 1836 of the new diocese of Ripon (it included Waddington), the prohibition of the holding of more than two livings, and the curbing of non-residency. The interest taken in education was not only to promote learning, but to weaken Nonconformity. From the evangelicals developed the Broad Church Party opposed to the ritualist High Church Party of Newman and the Tractarians.

As well as divisions within the Anglican Church there were, as John Wesley had predicted, withdrawals from the Wesleyan Church. Independents and Primitives organised their own churches. New sects, including the Latter Day Saints, appeared. The Salvation Army was formed to combine religion with social work, and the Temperance Movement, with its Bands of Hope, had widespread support at a time when excessive drinking created social problems.

Whether people went to church or not, Sunday observance was generally accepted. Work in field and factory ceased; many went to church either once or twice during the day. A few, like Mr Gladstone, were 'thricers'. The urban poor, however, were not churchgoers: people in working clothes were not made welcome and churches still remained to be built in the expanding towns.

Though much work needed to be done by home missions, a great interest was shown in foreign missions, largely as a result of David Livingstone's work in Africa. Missionary meetings were well attended, especially if lantern lectures were given.

What was writ large in the religious history of England was reflected on a small scale in Waddington.

The parish church

The parish church of St Helen, built in the fifteenth century in the Perpendicular style, was a plain, well-proportioned building. The etchings of J. C. Buckler show that along the nave were three square-headed windows and in the chancel a window of five lights, flanked by aisle windows of three lights.[1] There was a small porch over the south door, and on the same side of the church, nearer to the east end, was another door.

Whitaker, who gained much of his information from the vicar, Robert Smith, states that the tower and choir had been rebuilt in the reign of Henry VIII. The tower still bears the coat of arms of the Tempest family who had helped build the church, and a beam in the choir is dated MDXI. Although the tower, battlemented and buttressed, had been 'built of local stone of excellent masonry'[2] it had by 1801 lost its pinnacles. The roof, probably lowered during sixteenth-century alterations and repairs, was of the same height along the nave and chancel, and extended in unbroken line over nave and aisles.

There appears to have been a very beautiful Perpendicular roof 'enriched with carving'.[3] There was a nave arcade of four bays and steps up to the chancel. The flagged floor was covered with rushes brought in at rushbearing time—a custom which survived locally until well into the nineteenth century. The woodwork was of oak: oak timbers rich with carvings in the roof, an oak pulpit, communion table and rails. By the early nineteenth century, however, the table was in a ruinous state, with loose boards on top.

A few people had their own pews. One with the letters T.P. and the date 1692 carved on it belonged to the Parkers of Browsholme Hall, holders of the advowson. This pew, curtained on three sides, stood to the left of the communion table in front of the chancel arches. Opposite were the Waddow pews and one belonging to Mr John Taylor of Bashall Hall. Even with these pews encroaching into the chancel there was still room for some forty people to stand there during a marriage service. The churchwardens' pew was to the left of the small oak door which gave the six bell-ringers access to the belfry tower; the Hospital pew was to the right. Most parishioners had to be content with benches.

The vicar received a donation towards an organ in the early nineteenth century. In 1805 he wrote to the donor, 'I hope our organ will soon be erected and that we shall

---

[1] T. L. Parker and T. D. Whitaker. *Description of the Parish of Waddington with Etchings by J. C. Buckler*, p. 18.

[2] *Ibid.*, p. 19.

[3] Church Archives, Leach *v* Parker 1865, p. 21.

St Helen's Church before rebuilding, 1824.

praise the Lord with gladness and come before his presence, as the Psalmist says, with a Song. I have no Doubt of this Instrument having a good effect upon the congregation in general.'[1]

There was a cup dating from 1725 and the Parkers had made gifts of a chalice and paten in 1809 and of an alms-dish, flagon and paten in the following year.

Among the memorials were seventeenth-century brasses to Edward and Mary Parker bearing their coat of arms: 'Vert a chevron between three stags heads caboshed or (Parker) per pale three lions passant countercharged (Sunderland)'. The crest was a hand and an antelope's head erased.[2] There was a memorial to Christopher Wilkinson of Waddow Hall, MP for Clitheroe at the time of the Glorious Revolution, and two hatchments in the chancel along with the late eighteenth-century memorial urns to Edward Parker and his son, John.

The chancel window was as Dodsworth saw it when he had visited the church in 1618 and noted the kneeling figures of a knight and lady. On the knight's surcoat were the Tempest arms and on the lady's those of Bowling. Beneath were the words *Orate pro anima Ricardi Tempest, Ar. et Rosarnae uxoris suae, necnon omnium filiorum et filiarum praedicti Ricardi et Rosarnae qui istam fenestram fecerunt* A.D. *MDXIII.* [3] (Pray for the soul of Richard Tempest Armiger and his wife Rosamund also of all the sons and daughters of the aforesaid Richard and Rosamund who made this window A.D. 1513).

[1] LRO, DDX/118/149/14.
[2] T. D. Whitaker, *History and Antiquities of the Deanery of Craven*, 3rd edn, ed. A. W. Morant (London, 1878), p. 29.
[3] T. D. Whitaker, *ibid.*

St Helen's Church interior before 1824.

Above the communion table was a picture of *The Good Shepherd* painted by James Northcote, RA in 1807 and presented by Thomas Lister Parker in the following year. There were commandment tables on either side of this, and elsewhere in the church a benefaction board with details of the Wilkinson and Chapman charities, and a royal coat of arms.

In the small churchyard were the remains of an old sundial bearing the date 1686 and the initials of the vicar, William Calverley, and those of the vicar's churchwarden and churchwardens from the townships of Waddington, West Bradford and Grindleton. Calverley's tombstone of 1690 could still be seen in 1801, as could that of Robert Parker, founder of the Hospital.

1824 rebuilding

As the century advanced, repair work to the church became increasingly necessary. Old age and illness may have deterred Robert Smith from dealing with the problem, and when William Parker became vicar in 1809 more attention was paid to the extension of the Georgian vicarage than to the repair of the church. However, the matter was discussed at a Vestry meeting held in September 1824 and presided over by William's successor, his elder brother John Fleming Parker. Among those present were Robert Walker and James Hoyle, churchwardens, Thomas Taylor of Waddow Lodge, and many craftsmen who were to take part in the rebuilding of the church which was eventually decided upon. Initially the intention was to restore the roof and north wall, but when these and the south wall were examined they were found to be in such a ruinous state that they had to be pulled down.

In November another Vestry meeting was held to consider the costs and how they were to be met. Grindleton, although it had its own church, was called on as the largest of the three townships in the parish to pay half the expense; Waddington and West Bradford were to pay the rest. In January 1825 a rate of 7d. in the pound was fixed as 'we consider money to be wanting'. This brought in £115 8s. 3d. Grindleton at first refused to pay, but, as a result of a suit in the ecclesiastical court, had to pay both the rate and costs. By 1826, when £313 17s. 8¼d. had been collected, it was estimated that some £400 would be needed to complete the work. According to custom, the Parker family paid for half the chancel repairs and Mrs Clarke of Waddow and John

Taylor of Bashall Hall the remainder. Financial problems remained, however, throughout the rebuilding. Times were hard and the church accounts contain several entries such as that made in July 1825: 'Please send or bring your proportion without faile, so as the workmen can be paid.' Some of the old material, including glass, was sold to raise money.

When the roof and old walls had been cleared away, foundations were dug, the earth wheeled away out of the churchyard by order of Robert Walker, senior church-warden, and scattered, along with some bones, on his farm. Coffins which were exposed while the new foundations were being dug were not moved.

Next, the masons started their work. The old church had been built of random or rubble walling which was re-used where possible and then faced with new stone obtained from Weston Cliff, Waddington. The new walls were built to a greater height and the east wall was extended. Though the sanctuary itself was not pulled down, the rest of the chancel was rebuilt with a vestry, complete with chimney, on the north side.

According to Charles Toft Newstead, a London architect writing some forty years after the rebuilding, 'The windows are modern, not Gothic, of no particular merit whatever and constructed entirely at variance to every principle of Gothic architec-ture.' [1] Walls and windows were completed by January 1825 and the roof and slate were expected to be put on in early spring. Inside, the arches and pillars had been pulled down, the benches removed, the flags taken up and some of the brasses carried away. Betty Dugdale, one of the parishioners, later said that 'all was desecrated and destroyed. This sad state of things went on for months, nay a year or more'. She knew the brasses well, having gone down on her knees 'to clean and read them in the old church before it was pulled down'. These brasses, belonging to Robert Smith's family, had been in the chancel. 'Now, only one inscription is left,' she lamented.

Much inconvenience was suffered at the time of the rebuilding. Luke Smalley, and others, were married 'near the steeple' as they could not get near to the communion rails. Sarah Leach, married in May 1826, later recalled 'looking up and seeing the sky overhead'. In July, Ann Hanson at her wedding had to walk over planks, sand and lime and found the roof scarcely covered in. Not surprisingly, some attended services at Grindleton.

The woodwork, flags and glazing were almost entirely new. Two joiners, John Nowell and William Arkwright, were paid £47 18s. for ten weeks' work. Most of the workmen, glaziers, plasterers and slaters were paid from 3s. to 4s. a day. Some Baltic timber was used, though the pews, with doors, were of 'good American pine' painted in grained oak and varnished. Oak was used for the pulpit which, with soundboard, cost £9 2s. 7½d. A cheap deal top costing 6s. 8d. was put on the communion table.

Surviving accounts show the cost of some of the materials used. Five tons of slate brought from Preston cost £15 8s. 3d.; carriage was £3 2s. 6d. Some was brought by canal to Enfield. Hair, to be mixed with plaster, cost 3s. a stone; white hair cost 4s. According to custom, supplies of drink were provided when contracts were arranged: 15s. 6d. was paid for liquor when the contract about the pews was made, and a quart of gin was provided when the pulpit was moved.

---

[1] Church Archives, Leach *v* Parker 1865, p. 22.

The church as it was 1824–1901.

The new pews varied in size and some were assigned to particular families. John Fenton of Eaves House had a pew; there was also the New House or Colthurst pew. The door which had given access to the tower having been blocked up, the widows' pew was placed in front. In the chancel the Browsholme pew was brought forward, as were Taylor's pew and the Waddow pews with their thirty sittings. As a result, it was no longer possible to 'turn all corpses at funerals opposite the Lord's table'—this was to give rise to controversy later. Moreover, as pillars with cornices and rails were put on top of two of the pews, the chancel was now screened from the body of the church as well as being separated from it by rails. The pulpit itself, the reading desk and the clerk's desk were placed along the north wall of the nave near to the minister's pew. When Stephen Glynne wrote his notes on *Yorkshire Churches* he dismissed Waddington's as:

> An uninteresting church for the most part, rebuilt in poor style. It has a wide nave and chancel without distinction; a west tower. The nave has a flat ceiling and wretched Gothic windows. The east end presents the original three gables and marks the local type to which this church belonged. It must have had aisles, but the arcades are gone; the three gables at the east end are unaltered; the centre has a plain Perpendicular window of five lights, trefoiled and without tracery the two lateral ones still plainer and of three lights. There are fragments of old stained glass.[1]

Some of the parishioners were equally unimpressed by the church in its rebuilt state and thought it to be 'barn-!ike'.

---

[1] *Yorkshire Archaeological Journal*, vol. 24, 1861, p. 202.

Finance 1830–31

With the work completed, normal church life could be resumed. The churchwardens' accounts for 1830–31, a typical year, throw light on this:

	£	s	d
Whitewashing church by Norcross	2	0	0
Cloth for surpless	2	4	1½
Surpless making		7	0
Ould surpless repairing		3	0
Base vial strings		5	0
Miss Whitaker wine for sacrament	1	7	0
Bred ditto		2	0
Coales for Vestry		4	0
Pd. for 2 letters		1	4
Regesters riting		6	0
Clarke's dewes	3	3	0
Saxton's ditto		6	0
Bill for ringers	3	14	0
Singers		10	0
Scru nails for pewes		2	9
Miss Wittaker's bill, eating and liker	1	6	0
Two brushis for church		4	11
Mitton dewes	6	19	1
Collected one rate at 6d. in the pound	41	17	2½

Other items during the 'twenties and 'thirties included:

	£	s	d
Parchment and ink		13	0
Dog whipper		6	0
Measuring and mapping churchyard	1	2	0
Walling churchyard	32	19	3½
Allowed to Grindleton for wine		2	6
Court fees at Visitation		14	8
Straw for mats	1	8	0
To John Boothman for making	1	11	6
Richard Pye bill for repairing bier		2	0
For notice publishing at separate times		1	0
Paid to Post Office for briefs			8
Expenses to York and back being 4 days	2	15	5
To bones removing out of charnel house		10	6
Paid one half of Faculty	7	6	4
Postage of plan and Faculty from York		4	0
Clark and sexton 2 journeys to Clitheroe before the magistrates		5	0
Serving six summons		5	0
Spent at Vestry meetings		6	8

Payments were still being made at Easter time to Mitton, the mother church. At the annual visitations held at Skipton the churchwardens made a report on church affairs to the Bishop of Ripon or, more usually, to his representative. The journey by horse to Skipton cost 10s.; court fees were 6s., and on one occasion 2s. 3d. had to be paid to a farrier.

From the late sixteenth century onwards, copies of the entries made in registers of christenings, marriages and funerals had to be sent each year to York. These were made by the clerk, although some, in the nineteenth century, were made by the schoolmaster, James Grimshaw. Ten sheets of parchment cost £1. Postage was paid on receipt of the faculties, which permitted alterations to be made to the church, and on letters.

The singers or choristers, who received a small payment for their services, occupied the gallery at the west end of the church and were accompanied by the musicians, not unlike those in Hardy's *Under the Greenwood Tree*. Thomas Pye said that he was one of the choir and played the clarinet. As well as the bass viol there were a bassoon, cello, and possibly other instruments. By the 'fifties there was an organ on the north side of the nave, and Betty Dugdale was organist for some years.

Weekly collections were not the custom at this time. If someone or some other church was in need, a brief allowing an appeal to be made after morning service could be applied for.

The dog-whipper, usually the sexton, had the task of keeping in order the dogs which the farmers brought with them to church; payment continued to be made until 1840. (A dog-whipper's whip is to be seen at Slaidburn, a few miles north of Waddington.)

Notices of Vestry meetings and of other matters of general concern were posted on the church door or in the church. One such notice published in church in 1815 gave details of certain payments to be made to the minister and clerk. Marriage by licence meant a payment of 13s. 6d. to the minister and 4s. to the clerk: by banns the payments were 6s. 6d. and 1s. 6d. Churching cost 1s. Payments of 3s. 6d. and 1s. 6d. were made to minister and clerk for burials in the churchyard, £5 5s. for burials inside the church, 6d. for the passing bell and 1s. for the tolling bell.

Money for church maintenance was obtained from the church rate which was levied on property owners. In 1835 a rate of 4½d. in the pound brought in £30 19s. 8d. Five years later a farthing rate was levied for the repairing of the bells. (Twenty-six people attended the meeting which fixed that rate.) During the next twenty years the rate fluctuated, but was never more than three-halfpence. In 1868 compulsory church rates were abolished, but pew rents brought in some money, and in later years there were weekly collections producing some 13s. in 1874 and rising to £2 by the end of the century.

Vicars

Robert Smith 1764–1809

The nineteenth-century vicars, with the exception of Robert Smith, were all members of the Parker family. Details about Smith are contained in the biography of Wilson, headmaster of Clitheroe Grammar School; and his portrait, considered by Wilson to be one of Romney's best works, is to be seen at Browsholme.

Born near Amesbury in Wiltshire, educated at Winchester College, afterwards of St Albans Hall, Oxon. M.A. 1752; was licensed to the Perpetual Curacy of Waddington on the presentation of Edward Parker of Browsholme Esq. 23rd. March 1764, and subsequently instituted to the Vicarage of Almondbury in the West Riding of Yorkshire on the nomination of the trustees of Clitheroe School. He resided at Waddington where he had a small thatched house and a large family.[1]

Robert Smith, vicar in 1801.

The Georgian vicarage in which he lived, although small, was an improvement upon 'The Olde Vicarage' near Bonny Bar Gate.

His wife Elizabeth was eighteen years his junior. Anna, their eldest child, 'the fairest Bird of Hope', died in 1789 at the age of fifteen. Their son Thomas Lamplugh died in 1802, and shortly afterwards 'two of his daughters sickened about the same time, gradually declined in health and strength, and died within three days of each other. He bore the losses with the spirit of a Christian.'[2]

Another son, Robert, born in 1778, helped his father as curate before being presented to the incumbency of Honley in the parish of Almondbury, near Huddersfield. In 1802 the vicar was anxious to see his son, 'a novice in the affairs of the world', properly settled in 'his Bishopric of Honley' and was prepared to pay from five to ten guineas to secure a professional man to help with the collection of rent. (With only a small income, a vicar had to farm the glebe or let it out and make sure that rents were collected.)

---

[1] F. R. Raines, *Miscellanies: Memories of the Life of Revd Thomas Wilson*, (Chetham Society, vol. 45, 1857–8), p. 179. (Henceforth F. R. Raines, *Miscellanies*.)

[2] F. R. Raines, *Miscellanies*, p. 180.

Parochial work was 'little known and less practised' at that time and there are few records of Smith's work as a parish priest. His sobriquet 'Gaffer' suggests that he was regarded with affection and respect: certainly he had the interests of the freeholders at heart and was ready to defend their rights when Mrs Clarke and her relations, 'the blood-sucking leeches', began to enclose the common land. He appears to have spent most of his time in Waddington and paid a curate to look after his Almondbury parish—the usual arrangement when pluralism existed. His last curate, Walter Smith, 'a very worthy man', was paid £45 a year.

His dry and caustic wit caused Wilson, whom he 'loved as a brother', to compare his good sayings, which followed each other in rapid succession, to 'the cataracts of the Nile'. Throughout his life he cultivated the Classics and when Watson, Bishop of Llandaff, stayed at Browsholme he called Smith 'the living Juvenal'. Though Smith himself made light of 'his grating reed' some of his Latin poems and translations were considered by Wilson as 'above mediocrity'. 'His temper was cheerful (notwithstanding his gout), his disposition kind, his conversation playful, and the liveliest sallies of his wit, even when amongst those whom he termed the "commilitones Clitheronienses", were always devoid of offence.'[1] He and a small group of friends, including Wilson, Whitaker and the Vicar of Blackburn, were accustomed to dine monthly at each other's houses for 'pleasurable conversation and quiet enjoyment'. He died in April 1809, aged eighty-four, and was buried at Waddington.

William Parker 1809–1819

William Parker, the first of the Parker vicars.

Following Smith's death, Thomas Lister Parker appointed William, his youngest brother, to be vicar; he was also Vicar of Almondbury. A letter written by William Parker while vicar reads like one from a squire—but then, in the early nineteenth century there was not much difference between squire and vicar.

After mentioning a poor widow whom he had recommended to his brother, Thomas Lister, for admission to the Hospital, he recounts that he

left Browsholme this morning after having spent an agreeable time. Lady Diane and Lady Fleming in high force, also their lap Dogs ... very many invitations to Rydal [the home of the Fleming relations].

---

[1] F. R. Raines, *Miscellanies*, p. 179.

The Vicarage, 1816.

Mr Wilson left Browsholme with his wig well whitewashed and a span new hat for this agreeable rainy weather—as spruce as a bottle of Soda Water.

I am still lame and have had Leeches to my ancle, and I assure you it is a great misfortune to me and has prevented me enjoying many a pleasant day among my friends. Great sport expected on the fells Waddington particularly and I understand the fell will exhibit a grand field day. [On one occasion he killed three geese at a shot.]

I got my Hay well housed and a very good crop—this weather keeps all moist and in a perspiration. I find my cheese is benefitted by it. Have you been to Malham water yet? What say you to a jaunt into the upper regions I will not add of Bliss but of mountains.[1]

In 1819 family connections and influence enabled him to become Vicar of Skipworth in the East Riding, chaplain to Lord Howe, and a county magistrate. An older brother, John Fleming, became Vicar of Waddington.

John Fleming Parker 1819–62

John Fleming Parker, third son of John Parker, was born at Marshfield in 1782. He was educated at Clitheroe, and Brasenose College, Oxford, gaining his BA in 1801 and his MA in 1807. He held the two livings of Almondbury and Waddington and remained in Waddington until his death in November 1862. During his early years in the parish he was assisted by Thomas Dent, Curate, and Reader at the Hospital,

---

[1] LRO, Parker letters.

and others, to the extent that in 1841, a typical year, the vicar christened none of the fifty-one children brought for christening. In the previous year he had christened three. John Chester said of him, 'Mr Parker only preached occasionally and read the lessons now and again. He was a bit of a sportsman.'[1]

Shortly before coming to Waddington, Parker married his cousin, Catherine Lister, daughter of Thomas, Lord Ribblesdale of Gisburn. Of their two eldest children the vicar's cousin, Edward Parker of Alkincoats, wrote in 1831, 'I fear John Parker of Waddington will have sad plague with his two boys, from report they are very unpromising but he has much to blame himself for.' All their four children predeceased them, Catherine and Frederick dying within three days of each other in 1841, John at the age of twenty-three in 1845, and Thomas, the eldest, in 1851, leaving the vicar and his wife with four servants to care for them.

Admittedly, Edward Parker was not particularly well disposed towards the vicar. In 1833 he upbraided him for making some addition to the chancel without first asking permission: 'It cannot be permitted to remain,' he told the vicar, accusing him of a lack of consultation.

And if John Parker was remiss about church matters, he also failed to attend meetings of the Hospital Trustees for some ten years. As Edward Parker observed, 'We are not on these occasions favoured with the company of the Revd J. F. Parker tho' he is one of our body.' When he did eventually attend, he safeguarded his own rights: 'No tracts or papers were to be introduced into the Hospital without the approbation of the Incumbent. The Reader was not in anywise whatsoever to interfere or intermeddle with any of the parochial duties discharged by Incumbent or curate unless authorised.' It was the vicar who nominated his relation, Richard Parker, a layman, to be the next Reader.

The vicar had an average net income of £122 from a permanent yearly payment of £135. He held other ecclesiastical preferments, being Prebend in the Cathedral of Llandaff and Rector of Bentham, Yorkshire.[2] For the latter appointment, as for Waddington itself, he was indebted to his Parker relations. In addition to his stipend and dues there were 49 acres of glebe, 16 acres of which were being farmed by him at the time of the Tithe Award, 1850. The award arranged that he was to pay £1 18s. 11d. in lieu of grain and corn tithe, and 10s. 6d. in lieu of small tithe.[3] He himself received no tithe, but an annual payment of £1 6s. 8d. from the manor.

Evidently the vicar was not without money. As a Hospital trustee he favoured the purchase of land in Waddington and lent money to buy the Buck Inn and farm.

It was during his ministry that the church was rebuilt. When dampness appeared along the north wall not long after the completion of the work, the vicar had this attended to at his own expense. He also wished to provide more seating, as the church had seats for only 205—less than a third of Waddington's population. When Browsholme Hall categorically refused to allow changes in the chancel—the Parker pew was not to be interfered with—the vicar in 1834 gave notice of a public Vestry 'for

---

[1] *Clitheroe Advertiser*, 7 December 1906.
[2] Report of Commissioners of Ecclesiastical Revenues of England and Wales, 1835, p. 974.
[3] LRO, PR 3031/4/6, Tithe Award, 1850.

the purpose of obtaining their consent for the erection of a gallery on the south side entirely free of expense to the inhabitants'. The church records contain an account of the proceedings. At the meeting the vicar was 'fully authorised by the churchwarden of Grindleton and the major part of the inhabitants of the chapelry of Waddington in Vestry assembled to cause a gallery to be erected'. Parker duly applied to the Ecclesiastical Court at York for the necessary faculty. On the second court day 'this was opposed by the very chapel wardens of Waddington who had not only signed the notice of Vestry without any scruple, but had also expressed their full consent for the erection of the gallery'. In addition, the two Grindleton churchwardens appeared at York and opposed the faculty. However, 'under such duplicity and in the absence of all well-founded objection, the opposition giving way the faculty was granted'.[1]

As a result, a gallery 35 feet long and 6 feet 6 inches wide, supported on cast-iron pillars, was put up along the south wall of the church. A letter written by the curate to the people of Grindleton to allay possible objections had explained the vicar's plan of increasing the number of free seatings in the nave by selling pews in the gallery 'to such people of the chapelry as had expressed their desire to have one'. William Brocklehurst bought one for £18 19s. 10d. as a second pew for Colthurst; the vicar also had a pew in the gallery and the Sunday school children used it for a time. According to the ecclesiastical census of 1851, 200 free sittings and 70 others were available. Morning and evening attendances were given as 156, and Sunday school attendances as 100. The same figures were given for average attendances during the previous twelve months. However, as the vicar had completed his return in advance, no more reliability may be attached to his figures than to most others in that census.

A terrier dated 1838 lists the furnishings of the church as:

six excellent bells, an altar table with crimson velvet cover, 2 service books, 2 crimson velvet cushions, 2 buffets covered with velvet (given by T. L. Parker) for use at the altar, 1 Bible, 2 Common Prayer Books for the use of the Minister and Clerk, 1 Book of Homilies, 1 crimson velvet pulpit cushion, the tables of the commandments.

During the 'thirties the churchyard was extended. 'Realising that the churchyard was now full and fearing lest we shall be burdened with the expenses of a public cemetery,' the parishioners requested the calling of a meeting 'to consider enlargement so that we and our descendants may be buried with our forefathers'. In 1834 an extension was made when the Bradshaw family agreed to exchange their land adjoining the churchyard for Church Croft. Previous to this, remains had been taken from graves and placed in the charnel house so that the graves could be re-used. From time to time the charnel house itself had to be emptied—hence the 1824 entry by the churchwarden, 'to bones removing out of charnel house 10s. 6d.' The charnel house was now no longer needed. Various types of tombstone appeared in the churchyard in the later part of the century—flat stones, stones on pillars, and box tombstones necessitating payments of 10s., £1 10s. or £2 respectively. If a monument was erected a charge of five guineas was made. When an inscription was added to Robert Parker's tombstone in 1812, 1½d. was paid for each of

---

[1] Church Archives.

the 195 letters, and 4s. 6d. for the polishing of the stone. Most of the inscriptions were prosaic and the tombstones plain. Towards the end of the century glass domes placed over artificial flowers appeared on some of the graves, despite the disapproval of the vicar, who thought them 'ostentatious and un-English'.

When a funeral took place, bearers carried the dead to the church where the csoffin, covered by a pall (black for an adult and white for an infant) was placed on the bier. The sexton tolled the bell twelve, nine or six times for man, woman or child, followed by 'the minute bell', tolled for an hour. (The superstitious believed that evil spirits were terrified of bells and were driven out by the tolling.) A hearse brought the dead from Grindleton. Towards the end of the century it was the custom for the clerk, accompanied by Betty Dugdale and Ellen Wilkinson, to meet the funeral party on its entrance to the village and sing a solemn dirge.

In addition to the clerk, who took part in the services, the vicar could look to the sexton and churchwardens for help. The sexton kept the church clean, wound up the clock, lit the vestry fire and rang the morning bell on Sundays. In 1838 he received three guineas for this. Though the amount was considered small, it was an increase on the 32s. paid in 1810. The clerk received rather less. The churchwardens were responsible for looking after the fabric of the church and the churchyard, and for appearing at the annual visitation to report on the state of affairs in the parish. After 1838 they were responsible for keeping all records, except the registers, in an iron chest.

One of the last things John Fleming Parker attempted to do for his parishioners was to improve the heating system in the church. Writing to Edward Parker at Browsholme he explained that £15 was needed to renew the boiler and heating apparatus: 'the old widows of the Hospital receive great comfort and advantage from it.' He asked if money might be granted by the Hospital Trustees, since it could not be obtained on the rate.

Edward Parker 1863–95

Following the death of John Fleming Parker in 1862, Edward Parker became vicar. The third son of Edward Parker of Alkincoats and Selby, he was born in 1821 and educated at Leeds Grammar School and Peterhouse, where he gained his MA. An incident which occurred at Cambridge gives some indication of his character. According to a letter home, he was

> greeted by a man when coming out of chapel who introduced himself. I should not have cared if he had been a respectable looking man but he was exactly like a shop boy dressed out for Sunday with a velvet waistcoat, gold chain and long hair. I did not ask him up to my rooms but asked him when he was leaving Cambridge and said good day.

When he lived in Waddington he showed similar disdain for Waddow Hall, dismissing it as 'just an ordinary house of moderate dimension'. It would appear that he had been destined for the Church before going up to Cambridge. His eldest brother was in the army and Thomas Goulborne, the second son, had inherited Browsholme. To provide for his third son, Edward Parker paid £500 in 1840 for the right of making one appointment to the living in Waddington, a right he duly exercised in 1862.

Edward Parker, vicar, and his wife came to Waddington early the following year with their four sons and two daughters. Two more sons and a daughter were born in Waddington. Previously, Edward had been Vicar of Kilham, of Everingham near York, and of Holy Trinity, Blackburn. While there he married Catherine, daughter of James Neville of Beardwood. Of the vicar's sons, the three eldest became solicitors and three entered the Church. His daughter Phoebe became an accomplished artist who exhibited at the Royal Academy.

The house in which they lived was old, rambling, ill-arranged and suffering from dry rot. William Parker had largely rebuilt it in 1809 and had added rooms and a slate roof. The thatch on the brew-house, coach-house, cow-house, stable and barn had been replaced by slate, but since then few improvements had been made. Edward Parker proceeded to spend £140 on repairs. Downstairs, where there was a drawing room, dining room, library, parlour, kitchen, scullery, larder, butler's pantry, earth closet, dairy and cellar, some of the rooms still had flagged floors. Front and back stairs led to the five bedrooms and two dressing rooms. There were day and night nurseries; one room was used as a studio.

According to the sale catalogue of 1896,[1] the bedrooms were mostly furnished with mahogany wardrobes, dressing tables and washstands complete with toilet sets. As there was no bathroom, a hip bath was used. There were mirrors, swing dressing mirrors, bedside tables, chairs—arm, reclining and devotional—bookcases and towel-airers in most rooms. Among other items were a hat rail and a medicine chest, brass-bound, with thirteen compartments and ten bottles. The old nursery still had its fireguard, rocking chair and ottoman box. The beds had hair or flock mattresses and feather beds. The bed linen included bed ticks, some twill sheets, bolster slips and counterpanes. In the servants' room there was a kidder carpet, iron bedsteads, painted furniture and a rush-seated chair. The family bedrooms had Axminster rugs, Brussels and tapestry carpets, cretonne curtains and valances. The Kidderminster stair carpet was held in place by brass rods set in eyes.

In the hall was a hat and umbrella stand with a large octagonal water receiver. On the side table was a gold and ebonised card tray. There was a mahogany-cased clock, several hall chairs, an ormolu 'hang-up' lamp, numerous pot stands and a cocoa doormat. The dining room was occupied by a large extending mahogany dining table set on four massive legs on castors. There was a butler's tray and a brush and crumb-tray, white damask floral table covers, a quantity of cut glass, china and silver, napkin rings, Wedgwood and Spode dinner services, decanters, an embossed cruet with seven cut-glass bottles with stoppers and plated tops. The rooms were heated with coal fires and lit by candles and oil lamps, one of which had a fireproof globe. Candlesticks and tray snuffers were much in evidence. Among the other items of furniture were a chiffonnier with bookcase, a reading desk and pianoforte. The variety of smaller items—such as three pistols in a mahogany case, a wicker dove cage, and a unique collection of 174 Russian medals—gave some indication of the family's interests. All the main rooms contained many pictures and engravings, about a hundred in all, as well as portfolios of engravings. Among them were engravings after Rembrandt,

---

[1] Church Archives.

an oil painting after Landseer, old proof engravings of *The Blind Musician*, *The Rent Day* by David Wilkie, *Fruit*, *Dog*, *Wild Roses*, *Ducklings*, *The Wreck* and *Elijah*.

The contents of the boot room, housemaid's pantry, store parlour, larder, kitchen and scullery give some idea of servants' work for a large family in a Victorian vicarage. A cook, housemaid and two servants, all unmarried, lived in and spent much time in the kitchen, which was furnished with a dresser, rush-seated chairs, a rocking chair, two tables and a clock. Their work was heavy as it involved lifting iron kettles, brass preserving pans and a fish kettle, and using meat choppers, cleaver and saw. A vast amount of cooking was done; bread, pies, puddings and custards had to be made. In addition there was butter-making and laundry work; box and flat irons were used for the ironing. Before piped water was laid on, rainwater was carried from water tubs to the wash house, where an 'improved patent wringing and washing machine' was supposed to make the work easier. The coalplace, stick-house and ashpit in the yard were reminders of all the arduous work involved in having open fires. The old brew-house remained near the coach-house. Even when Edward Parker moved to the vicarage the racks and mangers of the stable were antiquated and had not been replaced. Beyond the stables were the cow-house, calf-house, piggery and hen-house.

The front garden had a high stone wall around it. There was also a tennis court (later used as a hen-run), a kitchen garden, a greenhouse with oil stove and a cucumber frame. A vast assortment of tools, including a lawn mower, was in use. The location of the privy and servants' privy was unmistakable.

Nearby were the orchard, a fold, a croft and barn. The glebe was much as it had been when first given to the Church in 1438. At the time of the tithe award (1850) it included the Great West Field; Little West Field (arable); Church Riddings; Great Field; Pitt Field; Little Field; The Holme; Great South Field (arable); Little South Field (arable); South Field End; The Nook; Lillands; Hammond Hey, and an allotment on the fell made in the enclosure award. At the 1896 sale 'sixty yards of well-seasoned hay and seventy yards of well got hay' were sold. Also included in the sale were two scythes, a hay chopper, grindstone and chain-harrow.

In addition to the land in Waddington there was a farm at Copy Nook for which Edward Parker built a new house in 1865, and a few acres in Clitheroe. The old vicarage in Dobson Close with adjoining cow-house was in a poor state. It consisted of two ground-floor rooms and one chamber above. The house, garden and croft had been let for many years to the Hanson family, but shortly after 1881 it ceased to be occupied, the house was pulled down and the stone used for building a boundary wall. 'The little house' remains.

Within two years of Edward Parker's arrival in the village there was trouble. The cause and results are suggested in certain lines which originally appeared in a local paper in April 1865 under the heading 'Supposed Conversation between the Revd E. Parker and Mr R. Walker'.

Vicar: You can't do as you like, my friend Robert Walker
         Because I'm the Vicar, a reverend Parker.
         Don't you know I'm the parson, a great Sunday talker?
         Just vote for the rate. Support me in this
         And I'll give you a passport to sepulchral bliss.

Walker: First one leaves the flock, then goes another
            Why don't you cease this priestly bother ...
            Prove a gentler shepherd, O Parson Parker.[1]

There seems to have been a dispute as to where Walker's father was to be buried and, early in 1865, the Vestry had refused to sanction a church rate of one penny. Some thirty years later a parishioner commented that Parker was conscientious, but he had alienated his followers and emptied his church by his intolerance, caused families to split up, and was partly responsible for the closing down of the old day school. When the new day school was built, his domineering manner led to protests from some of the managers and their resignation. Even a few months before his death his son wrote: 'if he ever became strong enough to get about again the first thing he would do would be to involve himself in a dispute with the managers of Waddington School. As a result of his feeling a little stronger he has a slight return of his old bellicosity.'[2] Others complained that he acted in an 'underneath' sort of way. In 1866 there was trouble with the Hospital when Edward Parker wished to be appointed a trustee. He made it clear that, unless appointed, he would stop the Reader from taking services. The threat was carried out and for a time the Hospital chapel was closed. In this matter, however, the vicar did not get all his own way. After recourse to the bishop, the services were resumed and it was not until 1882 that he became a trustee.

The 'supposed conversation' may have referred to a dispute arising from 'the perturbation of seat or pew in the church' and involved the vicar, the lady of the manor and a former churchwarden, Felix Leach. Leach eventually brought a case against the vicar and the matter was referred to the Chancery Court, York.

For some fifty years Leach had used the Waddow pew, with the authorisation first of his aunt, Mrs Clarke, and then of Isabella Ramsden. As he later stated,

the style in which the Defendant, Edward Parker, read the lessons and preached did not suit me as the tone in which he read was such that I could not follow him nor understand what he said in his sermon, being rather deaf. I told him I was unable to hear or understand and wished he would read and preach in his natural tone of voice. The defendant appeared to be offended at me.

The two never met on friendly terms again and, as the vicar did not modify his delivery, Leach began to attend St Mary's Church, Clitheroe, and seldom appeared in Waddington Church after June 1863. This gave the vicar an opportunity to deal with the chancel pews which, he believed, 'had encroached upon the space in front of the rails during the rebuilding of the church to the detriment of the offices of Holy Communion and matrimony'.

In June 1863 a Vestry, assembled 'by call of bell', agreed to the removal of the reading desk to allow the number of sittings to be increased. The re-arrangement and lowering of the chancel pews was also discussed but not settled. However, claiming support of 'seventy male and female inhabitants, ratepayers, renters and communi-

[1] *Clitheroe Times*, 22 April 1898.
[2] Church Archives, letter to John Parker.

cants', the vicar wrote to the Bishop of Ripon. He informed him that 'Waddington from its Hospital containing 30 aged widows and from its general salubriousness is singular for the number of persons of advanced years and afflicted with deafness'. As the lofty pews in the chancel meant that many could neither see nor hear, he sought the bishop's advice about the chancel pews and also about some high ones in the nave.

In reply, the bishop declared that the pews 'situated within the body of the church and objectionable in point of height' should be re-arranged. He hoped that a peaceful settlement concerning the chancel pews could be arrived at, otherwise legal action would be likely.

Counting on the bishop's support and having found a faculty forbidding pews in the chancel, the vicar had some of the offending pews removed. Though he used the threat of *mandamus*, the churchwardens refused to sanction the removal of the Waddow pew; they, too, believed that this would lead to legal action. Disregarding them, the vicar let the choir use the Waddow pew, and Leach soon heard that his books and pew furniture were being thrown about the church. He therefore asked Mrs Carter to remove his carpet, cushions, hassock and books. When she attempted to do so, the vicar, determined to have his own way, told her that they did not belong to Mr Leach but to the Lord. On reflection, however, he said, 'You can tell Mr Leach that I will make him a present of them,' adding, 'It's very well that you have come for them, for if you had not I should have thrown them out.'[1]

In December 1863 he went so far as to order the local wheelwright to cut down the Waddow pew. Predictably, Isabella Ramsden was soon seeking legal advice about the 'violence done by the clergyman in pulling down her pew'. In August her advisers told her that 'the removal of the pew by the incumbent was an illegal act and we understand the Archdeacon informed him so at the visitation.' They talked matters over with the vicar's father, 'hoping to place matters on a better footing between the Incumbent and the parishioners'. It was of no avail. In November 1864 Parker was 'required immediately to restore the Waddow pew'. When he made no attempt to do so, Leach, on behalf of Isabella Ramsden, brought the action against him. The case began in York in June 1865 and ended in February the following year. Many villagers, among them one 'a deal to seventy years old though he could not speak to a year or two', gave evidence. Their affidavits are a valuable source of information about the rebuilding and alterations previously made in the church. Though many held that, as Parker, Taylor and Mrs Ramsden kept the chancel in repair, they rightfully had their pews there, 'the Parson conquered old Felix Leach' in that the chancel remained clear of pews. Mrs Ramsden did not readily accept defeat: in 1869 she was writing to the proctor in York about the possibility of obtaining a faculty for the re-erection of her pew. In the event, however, no further action was taken.

Yet further changes were proposed by Edward Parker at a Vestry meeting some twenty years later. It was agreed that

the present seats be taken out of the nave and replaced with new benches: that the organ be removed to the north side of the chancel now occupied by the

---

[1] Church Archives, Leach *v* Parker, 1865, p. 30.

vestry: that the font be removed to the centre of the west end of the church under the gallery and a vestry made on each side of the font under the gallery, one for the minister and one for the choir: the west gallery occupied by the school children be fitted up with new forms.

A committee was formed to carry out the resolution and the necessary faculty applied for, but as Edward Parker of Browsholme would have nothing to do with the reseating and William Garnett refused to allow part of his pew to be used as a vestry, the plan failed.

The vicar's years in Waddington were not happy ones. As well as the dispute about the pews, there was trouble about the old school which involved the vicar's being taken to court for non-payment of debt. Years later the vicar expressed the hope that 'there will be no more of this wretched petty squabbling in this unfortunate place'. By that time he had created considerable ill-feeling by refusing to allow a corpse to be brought into the church and, on changing the wording of the service, was greeted with cries of 'Shame'. Even the neighbour's dog proved unfriendly. The vicar stunned it with the decanter he was carrying when it attacked his own dog. When it ventured into the vicarage garden he called for his gun. The dog, growing bold, launched an attack against the vicar. In court the vicar stated that 'he chased the dog because he wanted to kill it. The animal looked astonished'.[1] That some partisan feeling existed in the village was evident: Wesleyans spoke on behalf of the dog, stating it to be 'quiet and companionable'.

As early as 1869 the vicar wrote to Sir John Ramsden,

After many years of persecution I appeal directly to yourself ... especially as a fresh dispute seems to be growing up—an alleged encroachment upon the High Road by one of Isabella Ramsden's tenants. I write at once to you in order that a simple matter of dispute may not be so distorted as to afford an opportunity of asserting that I wished to act in a spirit of hostility or opposition to Mrs Ramsden. I cannot express to you the misery and desolation which have been caused in this village by misrepresentation. I can only conclude by hoping that through your intervention the idea may be discouraged that in persecuting their clergymen they meet with Mrs Ramsden's or your approval. Thus further mischief might be prevented tho' the past be absolutely irreparable.[2]

Things did not improve during the next twenty years, and the vicar's health became worse. He was never strong: for this reason he had given up rowing as an undergraduate. In 1886 he was seriously ill from shock after a carriage accident. Then, in 1891, after 'a life of sacrifice', his wife died. Her coffin was carried to the churchyard by eight members of the congregation, Mrs Parker having always approved of simplicity in these matters. Many in the village attended her funeral, and the ringers gave a muffled half-peal.

Alone in the old vicarage, apart from two loyal servants, there were times when 'his hands were so numbed with cold he could hardly hold his pen'. He was nearly

---

[1] *Clitheroe Times*, 27 May 1892.
[2] WYAS, Ramsden Papers, 64/16.

blind, and on one occasion set fire to the letter he was writing. He lost none of his determination, however. In compliance with the Archbishop of Canterbury's wish that the proposed disestablishment of the Episcopal Church in Wales should be brought to the notice of his parishioners, he joined in the protest against disestablishment, taking for his text 'I would they were even cut off which trouble you'. When his nephew, Edward of Browsholme Hall, died in 1894 he made it quite clear that

> there is no objection to the selection of Hymns on Wednesday next but to any person, save myself, officiating on that sorrowful occasion I give an unalterable refusal. For thirty-three years of bitter persecution and neglect I have endeavoured to do my duty as the Minister of this parish and tho' an old man, I am perfectly able to conduct unassisted the funeral.

He saw that nothing marred the quietude, order and solemn dignity of the scene.

The vicar, suffering from heart trouble, became increasingly ill and nervous. His sons, Arthur and Francis, tried in vain to persuade him to give up his position. They realised that he was too poor to pay a curate to help and, in any case, as Francis pointed out, a curate, if appointed, would not stay long unless he were a man of great patience and forbearance. When the Reader, Thomas Parnell, was about to resign Francis wrote to his cousin, the chairman of the Hospital Trustees, to say that he was prepared to leave Mirfield to become Reader and help his father as curate. He thought that 'some well-to-do people would contribute £50 to his curacy'. Francis was made Reader and for a few months gave what help he was allowed to give to his father.

By July 1895 the vicar was writing 'Dropsy, heart disease, asthma and rupture are all at once assailing the old frame of mine and yet I look so well. I must do the duty tho' it terminates if God so please in my death.' And so he did. In his obituary he is described as

> a staunch son of the Church of England of the old-fashioned high church school and in politics a strong Tory. He was wholly devoted to his work and lived a retired life happy in the society of his Greek and Latin books. Of venerable appearance he was one of the last of the old clergy, a gentleman and a scholar.

This was perhaps a case of *de mortuis*, for not everyone had forgotten the unpleasant incidents which had caused some of his parishioners to leave the church.

Francis Parker 1895–1922

On Edward's death his son Francis became vicar. One of the first things he did was to write to his cousin asking for a Reader capable of acting as his curate, as West Bradford was in need of services: 'the place has a bad reputation for heathenism and immorality and I intend to make it a special care.' He wanted someone 'capable of sympathising with me and understanding my methods of work, a young man and not a venerable Evangelical fossil if I may so speak'.

His brother Ernest was appointed. The choice was not a happy one and after a short time Ernest left, some believed, for Rome. Indeed, in 1899 Francis was surprised to see a letter written by his brother in the *Daily Chronicle* announcing that 'the Church of England as an establishment is doomed. The Anglican Church tomorrow will lose one of her ministers in the person of your humble servant Ernest Neville Parker'. Having telegraphed his brother about this, Francis was able to assure the *Clitheroe Times* that 'My brother has not joined the Church of Rome; he does believe in disestablishment'. He attributed Ernest's letter to his impulsive nature.

When, after Ernest's departure, a new Reader was needed Francis wrote yet again to his cousin and patron, Major Parker, expressing concern lest his brother Arthur should be appointed to the vacancy.

> You have a saying 'Two Parkers can never agree'. This is true. After Ernest I do not wish to have another brother here as Reader and Curate of the parish, especially not an older brother. I have decided objection to men of this extreme ritualist school. Ernest led me a dance and finally ended in Rome. Arthur preaches certain doctrines in a somewhat extreme form and if he came here would upset my simple old-fashioned congregation of church people. I want to avoid rows and for this the fewer Parkers in the neighbourhood the better.

His wish was granted.

Francis had broken with family tradition by taking his degree at King's College, London. He favoured Low Church ideas and, as a supporter of the Christian Socialist Movement, wished to bring, not politics into religion, but religion into politics. Ordained deacon in 1887 and priest in 1888, his first curacy was in Leicestershire, his second in Manchester. He was Vicar of Mirfield before being appointed Reader to the Hospital in 1895. As Reader he quickly gained the esteem and affection of many, so much so that nearly three hundred people in Waddington, believing him to be

'pre-eminently fitted to supply the spiritual wants of this parish', petitioned Major Parker asking that Francis Parker should be the new vicar. After the sale of his father's furniture at the vicarage in 1896, Francis Parker left the comforts of the Reader's House (Oatlands) to return to the vicarage where he had been brought up. His net income was £115; the Easter offerings and other receipts raised it to £140.

The first few years were exceptionally busy ones for the new vicar. Like his father, he showed a great interest in the day school, which he frequently visited to hold catechism classes. As a trustee of the Hospital he became largely responsible for its supervision during his cousin's absence in South Africa. He wrote to him, 'I have done nothing else but build since coming here six years ago: 2 churches, 2 Sunday Schools and a Day School Master's

Francis Parker, the last of the Parker vicars.

House is a very fair amount of building for six years.' He referred to the rebuilding of Waddington Church and Sunday school and to new buildings at West Bradford. Even allowing the schoolhouse to have been Edward Burton's achievement, the vicar himself had accomplished much.

Typically, despite the pressing need for a new vicarage, he ignored his own comfort to give priority to the rebuilding of the church, again in a poor state. At a Vestry meeting in 1897 a building committee was elected. In the following year the necessary faculty for 'taking down part of the church, rebuilding the same, enlarging the chancel, erecting new clergy and choir vestries, removing the galleries' was applied for. Lady Holker of Colthurst queried the faculty, as she would lose one pew. She was allowed two pews, at her expense, on the south side of the nave and was assured that the window in memory of her husband, Lord Justice Holker, would be carefully replaced. The last service in the old church was held at the end of January 1900.

The church was rebuilt on the lines of the pre-1824 church, with an extension of the chancel. The architects were Austin and Paley of Lancaster, and Major Parker approved the plans before departing to fight in the Boer War. In a series of letters, the vicar kept him informed of the progress being made.

By September the walls were seven feet high.

November. The work goes on slowly but surely—very slowly. The stonework is nearly finished. Veevers has begun to put the roof on the south aisle.

In December the vicar gave details of the appeal made in the magazine for the items needed in the church and their probable cost: reredos £400; lectern £60; altar candlesticks £10; standard lights for chancel £20; font cover £20; eight pinnacles for the tower (as shown in old drawings) £4 each; clock £180; new stained glass window in tower £300. He expressed the hope that his cousin would shortly be home and the re-opening take place.

The vicar found 'the people here are really very generous' and was soon able to report that many of the required items had been given. The Burtons, in particular, had given generously and unostentatiously: '£500 from the old gentlemen and £200 from the younger Burtons'. Mrs Burton gave the lamps and Edward Burton, Reader, the carpet. £800 came from the Society for the Building of Churches and Schools which had been founded by Miss Sykes, a relation of the Burtons. A new organ, vestments and cloths for the altar, an altar cross and sanctuary carpet were donated; choir stalls had been obtained in 1895 from Bury Church by James Walmsley.

August 1901. The church is very nearly finished. The blocks are to be laid for the floor. The Parker monuments and brasses have been cleaned and put back as you wished.

William Banks of Waddington was paid for his work on the benches.

It was arranged that the Bishop of Ripon should consecrate the church and the 1834 extension of the churchyard.

We have a very fine chiming clock in the Tower. The chimes are the St Mary's, Cambridge, chimes. It rather disturbed our sleep at first but we are getting accustomed to hearing the chimes every quarter of an hour.

The rebuilding of the church, 1900–1901.

The clock had been given by Mrs Walmsley in memory of her husband. The lectern, referred to by the vicar as 'one of those fowls of the air that I believe you have no great love for', was, nonetheless, 'a real work of art'. The vicar, who had a strong aesthetic sense, kept everything inartistic out of the church—was this why he failed to replace the charity and commandment boards? In September he was able to write, 'The opening of the church passed off very successfully and we had a beautiful day for the function. The church is very much admired by everyone.'

The rebuilding cost between £7,000 and £8,000. To raise this money, social evenings, tea parties and a jumble sale had been held to buy materials for a bazaar which took place at the day school. For a week people flocked there to buy goods, with the result that most of the debt was paid off.

During the rebuilding, although services had to be held in the Sunday school, church activities were not curtailed. At the beginning of 1900 there was a mission service with a talk given on the slave trade, illustrated with 'numerous slides, thrown on the screen by a magnificent lantern manipulated by the Revd J. Burton'. Miss Ramsey, a governess in the Burton household before becoming a missionary, returned from Peking after being besieged there. She spoke of her work, and of a fellow missionary who was killed during the Boxer Rising. The bells of St Helen's rang out a merry peal for the marriage of Miss Mary Burton. Eastertide was duly observed with communion in the morning and well-attended services; on Whit Monday there was a procession and tea at Eaves Hall, followed by games.

The annual Vestry meeting was held in May. As the *Clitheroe Times* somewhat ineptly reported, 'There was only a poor attendance the vicar being in the chair. The accounts were passed and the wardens Edward Burton and Christopher Calvert and sidesmen John Herd and A. Tomlinson were thanked and re-elected.'

The organist, George Waddington, gained the Advanced Senior Grade Certificate for pedal organ playing, and the surpliced choir of some thirty men and boys had already established a reputation for fine singing.

In late September, Harvest Thanksgiving services were held. 'Harvest emblems adorned every available corner a pleasing effect being thus rendered.' There were good congregations at the Christmas services, and on New Year's Eve a Watch Night service was held. Details of these services were given in the parish magazine, which had first appeared in 1896, and there was mention of some of the five funeral services, thirteen baptisms and seven marriages which took place during the year.

Though with Francis Parker the religious activities of the church came first, there were other activities such as concerts, Whit Monday celebrations and outings, which served to enrich the social life of the members of the congregation. The mothers had a weekly meeting with tea provided by Mrs Parker or Mrs Burton. There was a sewing meeting for the young women, who organised entertainments and dances for themselves. The Mutual Improvement Society was open to all men and offered a programme of talks and outings to local places of interest. For the youngsters there was the Band of Hope, formed primarily to support teetotalism but, with the vicar's encouragement, it was widening its scope to include cane- and basket-work for the girls and fretwork and carving for the boys. Others joined the Snowdrop band, the handbell ringers, bell-ringers or the choir.

The Sunday school was another concern of Francis Parker's. A Sunday school had been in existence in the early part of the century. When witnesses made their statements during the Leach v Parker case some of them said that when they were scholars they sat in a recess of the chancel near the communion table; later they used the day school. With its closing in 1866 there was no Sunday school until 1873 when Edward Parker took over the old school, repaired it and re-opened it as a Sunday school.

James Grimshaw, schoolmaster, had taught in the Sunday school and masters of the new day school were expected to do likewise. When Harry Danson was superintendent, the Sunday school met at 9.30 a.m. and 2.15 p.m.

In 1895 the physical condition of the school was a matter of concern to the Charity Commissioners, who noted that the whole building (two rooms, one above the other) was damp and a constant source of danger to the children. Its ownership was a cause of dispute. One villager told the commissioners that the school belonged to the parish. James Garnett, speaking on behalf of his brother, said that William Garnett did not claim it, but would not allow anyone else to do so.

The matter rested there until Francis Parker decided to build a new Sunday school. He persuaded his fellow Trustees of the Hospital to give land at the back of the old school for 'sanitary accommodation'. For this the school committee was to pay a shilling a year rent.[1] One of the Trustees volunteered to interview William Garnett

---

[1] Hospital Trustees' Minute Book.

and settle the dispute about the ownership of the old Sunday school and site. Presumably this was settled, and eventually the building and land were presented to the minister and churchwardens 'for use as a Sunday school and for other purposes in connection with the parish church'.[1] By raising money at a sale of work, Francis Parker managed to build the present one-storey building with 'petties' in the yard. The work was completed by 1897 at a cost of £500.

Although morning attendance was poor, in the afternoon classes of twenty to thirty caused the vicar to plan to 'double our teachers and divide our classes'.[2] Within a short time he had established a library, started a teachers' training class and encouraged people to come forward to take classes for the young men and the young women. Prizes were given to regular attenders; they also gained honourable mention in the parish magazine. At the Catechism Festival prizes were given to those who answered well or wrote essays. The vicar believed that this not only helped provide a strong religious foundation, but consolidated 'the bit of knowledge' acquired at the day school. No mean scholar himself, he encouraged those who were prepared to 'sacrifice ease and pleasure' to attend the Evening Continuation School in order to benefit themselves.

Though determined, he had a gentler character than his father; he was also an exemplary visitor. Chaucer's words describing the Poor Parson were later applied to him:

> Wide was his parish and houses far asunder
> But he neglected not for rain nor thunder,
> In sickness nor in mischief to visit
> The farthest in his parish great and small.

As the parish magazine pointed out, 'The clergy of the present day are not farmers. They have no need of barns and cow-houses and calf-houses and pig styes and accommodation for half a dozen horses, together with park-like grounds. They are not like the old clergy.' Of Francis Parker, the last of the nineteenth-century vicars, it could not be said that 'Parochial work was little known and less practised in Waddington.'

The Wesleyan chapel

John Wesley is said to have travelled 250,000 miles and to have preached 40,000 sermons between his conversion in 1738 and his death in 1791. On forty-two occasions he was in the north of England preaching to people, some of whom knew nothing of God. He came within ten miles of Waddington when he preached at Gisburn and Padiham—nearer still if, as alleged, he came to West Bradford.

His influence was certainly felt there, for in 1797 a chapel with stable and burial ground was opened. In the same year another chapel was opened in Clitheroe.

---

[1] Charity Commission Report, 1896, p. 26.
[2] Parish Magazine, August 1900.

The Wesleyan Meeting House, Back Fold.

Waddington soon had connections with both places of worship; in 1800 the Fishwicks had their son baptised at Wesley Chapel, Clitheroe, and among those who attended West Bradford Chapel were families from Waddington. Soon there was talk of having a Dissenters' Meeting Place in Waddington itself.

In August 1802 the vicar was writing to Thomas Parker at Newton Hall to say that 'a horrid ill spelt Petition had been sent to the Bishop of York as they call'd him to Licence a House at the Bottom of the Town for a Conventicle. It was sign'd by Thos. Clarke, John Smith, James Wilson & Saml. Smalley' and was 'deliver'd in' at the Skipton Visitation. The answer was 'We do not licence dissenting Houses.'

The Mitton Parish Returns of 1811 show that John Whalley registered his house (formerly owned by his father-in-law, John Smith) as a meeting place for Protestant dissenters. The licence was signed by Jonathon Wood, John Barnes, Edmund Chippendale, James Hargreaves, Henry Battersby and Thomas Fletcher (Minister of the Skipton Circuit). The house was at the far end of Back Fold.

In 1812 it was proposed that the Clitheroe Circuit, with its own superintendent minister, should be formed from the Skipton Circuit. When this was done two years later, Waddington was one of fifteen churches to be included. Its quarterly contributions to circuit funds of £1 14s. od. were exceeded only by those from West Bradford and Clitheroe itself.

When the circuit was formed there were twenty-five Waddington members. They included Jonathon Wood, leader, formerly of Grindleton, six members of the Ireland family, Robert and Christopher Foulds, Mary Fishwick and Betty Shepherd (whose husbands joined soon afterwards), Betty Boothman, Jenny Turner and Betty Herd. Another class was formed with Henry Battersby as its leader and James Hargreaves, Samuel Smalley and Richard Pye among the members. Several members were recent settlers in Waddington and, with farmers, weavers and craftsmen among them, they were a cross-section of the village population. In 1823, as the society had continued to gain adherents, they decided to build a chapel.

A history of the chapel written by Edward Chester to mark its centenary gives details of this. A plot of land facing the Square and containing three cottages and a garden was bought for £150. The chapel was built to adjoin the first cottage. The total cost was £473 3s. 9d.—a considerable sum in the early nineteenth century and not easily raised at a time of economic depression. Eighty-five people, including the Boothman, Pye and Smalley families, subscribed to the building fund.

The local schoolmaster, James Grimshaw, and Felix Leach of Brungerley, although not Wesleyans, also contributed. Support came from neighbouring chapels and a further £20 was given when the chapel was opened in April 1824. Even so, £360 had to be borrowed.

The chapel was a plain building about 40 feet long and nearly as wide. In front was a small paved area, walled and gated. There were windows on each side of the door, with windows above to light the gallery. Inside, the whitewashed walls, flagged floors, benches without backs, and desks, lamps and candles for lighting and a stove for heating, emphasised the functional nature of the building which was to serve as both church and Sunday school.

At first, services were held at seven in the evening and occasionally during the week, but by 1832 there were also afternoon services. With fifteen churches to attend to, the superintendent minister was planned to preach only twice at Waddington during the half year, visiting preachers taking the other services. By 1837 Richard Foulds had become a local preacher, and in 1861 there were three local preachers living in the village: Robert Foulds, farmer and shoemaker; Henry Baldwin, an apprentice shoemaker from Grindleton living with him; and Robert Hanson, a chairmaker. Membership fluctuated. In 1825 there were forty-six members as compared with ninety-five at West Bradford, but in 1827 there were twenty-nine members, sixteen two years later, and twenty-six in 1849. The decrease is explained in part by the declining population but there were also 'backsliders'. However, at the time of the ecclesiastical census in 1851 the congregation was stated to be fifty-two in the afternoon, sixty-two in the evening, with sixty-five the average over the past year. On special occasions all the 163 free sittings and 63 other sittings were taken. The members were divided into two classes, with a third class formed later at Moorside. Each class had a leader who gave moral and spiritual guidance, kept an attendance record of class meetings and collected the class pence.

'Methodism was born in song' and music played an important part in the life of the chapel throughout the century. The singing of Charles Wesley's hymns was invaluable in helping those who were illiterate to learn something of divine love and forgiveness. At first, the hymns had to be 'lined'—one or two lines were read out and were then sung by the congregation. Several instrumentalists accompanied the singing. In 1866 when Luke Smalley, the cellist, was the only player left, a small harmonium was bought and was played by his daughter. In 1875 it was sold for £5 and a replacement was bought for £45. Soon after the purchase of the harmonium a choir was formed and occupied the 'singing pew'. £1 9s. 9d. was spent on a music book and a new hymn book for their use. As literacy increased, hymn books were bought for the congregation and for the use of visitors. Special services, such as the Billy Bray Song Service, were arranged and a performance of Guest's cantata *The Pentecost* given by an augmented choir and string band was 'considered to be probably

The Wesleyan Chapel.

the most successful service ever given from the point of view of numbers and enthusiasm.'[1]

In the early years the chapel had an annual income of some £20 obtained from the rents of the three cottages, seat rents, a contribution made by the Sunday school, quarterly collections and collections at the anniversary services. From this the trustees paid for heating, lighting, cleaning and repairs. They made donations to missionaries, Kingswood School, circuit funds and paid the interest, usually at 4 per cent, on the loans. Yet, far from being able to pay off the debt, the trustees were sometimes obliged to borrow more.

Gradually, as a result of donations from members and trustees, the sale of property and special efforts, the debt was reduced. An appeal for money for the harmonium fund met with a good response and, finally, with help from the Chapel Relief Fund and the Sunday school, after fifty years of faith and finance, the chapel was free from debt.

Details of finances can be obtained from account and collection books. On the first page of the 1867 account book are entries for five lots of paraffin at 1s. 7d. a quart, lamp burner, lamp wicks, eight lots of candles, matches, chips, coals and two new brass candlesticks bought for 2s 9d. A fire and stove which William Boothman, blacksmith, repaired from time to time, supplied heating. Thomas Hoyle made out his bill to the Church Masters in 1873 'for liten fires and boiler fire 14 times at 2s. per time will cum £1 8s. 0d.' Fire-lighting was not an easy job, judging by the amount

---

[1] E. Chester, *History of the Wesleyan Chapel, Waddington* (1924).

of money spent on wood shavings or chips bought from the clog-makers, and on threepenny firelighters. Coal was cheap. A hundredweight cost 1s. 1d. or, when bought in bulk, less than 1s. a bag in 1874.

Lighting needed constant attention. New lamps and covers had to be bought, the pulpit lamp altered and snuffless dips purchased. Even so, lighting costs in one year were only 10s. 4d.

Cleaning costs were rather more, the trustees evidently believing that cleanliness came very near, if not next, to godliness. There was a special cleaning to be done at Christmas and several major operations during the year. In 1869 Mary Jane Speakman received £1 6s. 0d. for six months' cleaning. A variety of brushes, floorcloths bought by the yard, sweet soap for the windows, soda and black lead were the cleaner's stock in trade. Most years when the chapel was whitewashed a few pence were paid for the lime and from 5s. to 18s. for labour. Window-cleaning, chimney-sweeping and painting were also carried out.

The trustees were responsible for arranging maintenance work such as the pointing of the slate roof and the reboarding of the gallery and, in 1861, for boarding the chapel floor. Even minor matters such as a new cord for the clock, repair of the pulpit board and clearing the area in front of the chapel with threepence-worth of salt 'to discourage further weeds' did not escape their attention.

Expenses in addition to those already referred to included insurance—this remained at 6s. a year for over twenty years—and an annual payment of 1s. for a right of way. Incidental expenses included the purchase of a pair of scissors for trimming wicks, ink, rat poison, printing of anniversary posters by John Cowgill, prayer books and Bibles. The trustees kept meticulous accounts and well deserved tea at 8d. a head after their meetings. When, in 1887, they decided to build a separate Sunday school, they become involved in a big money-raising effort.

Not a great deal is known of the early Sunday school. Possibly it was not unlike that which Samuel Bamford attended towards the end of the eighteenth century, of which he wrote:

> The Methodists of Middleton kept a Sunday School in their chapel and this school we young folk attended. Every Sunday morning at half-past eight o'clock was this old Methodist school open for the instructing of whatever child crossed its threshold. A hymn was first led out and sung by scholars and teachers. An extempore prayer followed, all the scholars and teachers kneeling in their places. The classes, ranging from those of the spelling book to those of the Bible, then commenced their lessons, girls in the gallery above, and boys below. Desks, which could be moved up or down, like the leaf of a table, were arranged all round the schools, against the walls of the gallery, as well as against those below, and at measured distances the walls were numbered. Whilst the Bible and Testament classes were reading their first lesson the desks were got ready, inkstands and copy-books numbered, copies and pens were placed opposite corresponding numbers on the wall; and when the reading lesson was concluded the writers took their places, each at his own number, and so continued their instruction. When the copy was finished, the book was shut and left on the desk, a lesson of spelling was gone through, and at twelve o'clock singing and prayer

again took place, and the scholars were dismissed. At one o'clock there was a service in the chapel, and soon after two the school reassembled, girls now occupying the writing desks, as boys had done in the forenoon, and at four o'clock or half-past the scholars were sent home for the week.[1]

The Sunday school in Waddington was well established by the early 'thirties, and by 1851 scholars were expected to attend morning and afternoon school. Henry Ireland of Page Fold was then superintendent. In 1861 the teachers' report 'of the state of the School together with our receipts and expenses for the last year' gives these details:

At present there are on the books	boys	30
	girls	35
Average attendance including teachers		63
Number of scholars who attend a day school		17
Number of scholars members of society		9
Number of teachers		19
Number of teachers members of society		15
Number of scholars and teachers who left school during the year		13
Number of scholars and teachers who have entered during the past year		8

The report continued, 'We are happy to state that we have belonging to our Sunday school a choice library of 163 volumes comprising Divinity, History, Biography and general literature which are lent gratuitously to the scholars and teachers.' (Of these, a book of Wesley's sermons remains.)

Expenditure for 1861 was £18 5s. 6d. The collection at the annual sermons was £8 2s. od., only one-third the amount given in previous years. In the following year there were five fewer scholars and collections were again down, with a further fall in 1863, possibly the result of the Cotton Famine.

When the village school closed in 1866 the educational importance of the Sunday school during the next ten years was considerable, and numbers rapidly increased. The vicar, Edward Parker, observed later that 'had it not been for John Dugdale (Superintendent) the children of Waddington might have grown up heathen.'[2]

In 1867 there were 112 scholars who came from 43 families, and 25 teachers, including 3 superintendents. The 56 girls were divided into 6 classes and there were 5 classes of boys. They and the teachers were gradually promoted. Some of the children began to attend when they were four; some stayed until they were in their twenties. There were two alphabet teachers, and the ABC continued to be taught until 1878. There were double and single spelling classes, as well as Bible and Testament classes. Judging by the quantity of slates, paper, inkstands and reading books that were bought, reading and writing must have occupied much of the time.

Morning school began at 9.30. In the afternoon there were readings from the Conference Catechisms and other lessons; twice a quarter the scholars repeated the

---

[1] S. Bamford, *Passages in the Life of a Radical*, vol. 1 (ed. Henry Dunckley, 1893), pp. 100–1.
[2] Revd J. Passmore, *Clitheroe Times*, 1906.

catechism to the minister. The class boards which had been hung up before school began were taken down before chapel service. Sometimes, instead of classes, one or more teachers spoke to the whole school after the opening hymns, prayers and collection. On two occasions some of the collection money was laid on the foundation stones of Wesleyan buildings in Clitheroe.

The library was well used by scholars and teachers. As early as 1837 *The Teachers' Magazine* and *The Child's Magazine* were being ordered. *The Shilling Magazine*, *The Youth's Instructor* and *Cottager's Friend* were bought by teachers and local preachers. Old books were sold off and from time to time £5 or more was spent on new ones, such as Ashworth's *Strange Tales* and Farrer's *Biblical and Theological Dictionary*, available at special rates. In 1886 the two librarians were given a day's wage so that they could set the library in order, catalogue the books and see to the binding of periodicals.

For a time numbers continued to increase. There were 127 scholars in 1870. With 20 new scholars joining in one year, four classes had to be taught in the gallery, and with limited space for the rest, conditions for teaching were not ideal. Not all the scholars were keen to learn, and not all were well behaved. A set of rules was drawn up in 1869 and copies given to each teacher and family. Unruly scholars and their parents were interviewed; absentees were visited. Scholars using bad language were reproved, and if the offence was repeated their names were crossed off the class list until a promise of good behaviour was made. Meanwhile, they lost their library privileges and the chance of joining in the Christmas and Whit Monday festivities. Teachers, too, were disciplined: if absent for four times in a quarter without sufficient reason they were excluded.

Christmas and Whitsun were occasions eagerly awaited. The Christmas tea was an established event by 1867, as was the Whit Monday procession. At Christmas there was a tree—bought for 1s.—and catering on a lavish scale. The prospect of a free tea may have induced five members of one family to join the Sunday school in November 1868. Tables were set up in the chapel and in the gallery, and tea began at 3.30 p.m. with a second sitting an hour later for ticket-holders. As many as two hundred tickets were sold, and sometimes an additional tea had to be arranged on another day.

After tea an entertainment was provided by the scholars. There was no reluctance on their part to participate; in fact, some had to be restrained. One piece only, and that to last not more than ten minutes, was allowed. The annual report followed, and there was much singing.

On Whit Monday children and parents gathered at the chapel at 12.30 p.m. and, after singing a few hymns and the National Anthem, formed a procession complete with banner and band. The Salvation Army Band from Clitheroe accompanied them on one occasion. There was further singing in the Square and at the Town Gate, then, having walked down Katey Lane, they adjourned to Brook Farm. There were buns for the scholars, provided they were not 'Runaways or Stayaways', tea and coffee. Some years later a more elaborate meat tea with carvers, bread–cutters and tea-urn carriers was organised. Swings were put up and games arranged, and the procession was held in the morning to allow more time for the field treat. In 1890, when a trip to Whitwell was arranged, scholars piled on lurries and set off over the fells for a picnic. There were also trips to Southport and, for a July party, meat, pop and botanic beer.

COPY OF CIRCUIT PLAN [IN THE POSSESSION OF E. CHESTER.]

Sunday Plan of the Clithero Circuit, 1824.

PLACES.	TIME. M. A. E.	FEBRUARY. 1 8 15 22 29	MARCH. 7 14 21 28	APRIL. 4 11 18 25	MAY. 2 9 16 23 30	References.
CLITHERO	10½ 2½ 6	7 18 3 21 2 17 1 16 2 2 1 1 2 2 1	14 11 3 4 1 11 2 4 1 2 c2 1	15 1 16 10 L1 1 2 10 1 2 s2 1	8 12 19 2 5 1 12 2 2 1 1 2 2 1 1	1 CRABTREE. 2 WATERHOUSE
BRADFORD	10½ 2	1 2 1 1 3 2 4 1	2 1 5 2 6 c1	L2 1 7 2 26 1	s2 1 19 2 10 1 20	3 BARNES. 4 BROXUP. 5 WHIPP.
DOWNHAM	2 6	10 13 15 6 7 10 2 15 1 2	8 14 18 11 2 14 c1 11	4 17 3 L5 2 17 1 5	6 16 21 12 4 2 16 1 s2 2	6 PARKER. 7 DEAN. 8 BOOTHMAN
STOPPER-LANE	10¼ 2	4 2 5 1 6 4 2 5 1 6	2 7 1 8 2 7 c1 8	2 9 1 17 s2 9 1 17	2 10 L1 11 2 2 10 1 11 2	9 PATTISON 10 CHIPPENDALL 11 THORNBER.
SLAIDBURN	2 6½	2 19 1 16 12 2 20 1 16 12	3 1 4 2 3 1 4 c2	5 6 24 2 5 6 24 s2	11 L1 8 10 7 11 1 8 10 2	12 GREENHALGH. 13 WILSON. 14 COX.
BASHAL-EAVES	10 2	15 1 4 2 14 15 10 4 8 14	1 12 c2 13 9 12 22 13	1 18 2 20 17 18 19 20	1 26 2 16 1 21 26 L5 16 10	15 LAWTON. 16 ARKWRIGHT. 17 BULCOCK, senr.
HARRAP	10¼ 2	2 1 6 7 8 9 11	1 c2 10 3 17 18	2 16 5 4 21	1 20 22 13 19 L12	18 HAWORTH. 19 FLETCHER 20 BROWN.
WHALLEY	6	18 16 17 15 22	12 8 c10 5	25 26 9 14	10 21 25 26 8	21 BULCOCK, jun.
SAWLEY	1½	9 11 10 12 3	L4 c5 7 6	8 15 22 18	17 19 20 21 11	22 ROBINSON (On trial).
BARLEY	2½	11 21 16	17 c10	L12 4	5 7	23 NUNICK.
PAYTHORN	10	8 6 22 7 4	11 18 9 c16	6 24 7 11	9 17 24 20 19	24 HOLGATE. 25 MOON
GISBURN	2	8 22 4	18 c16	24 11	17 20	26 SWAIN 27 MOLYNEUX
WADDINGTON	7	3 10 13 5 8	10 9 c16 17	15 21 3 13	19 18 12 14 10	28 PRESTON 29 THOS. LOFT-HOUSE.
CHATBURN	7	9 13 10 12 7	4 5 c18 22	8 15 21 18	17 4 9 12 5	
NEWHURST	2	12 7 19	L10 c20	11 6	3 13	
PENDLETON	2	18 17 22	8 c5	10 14	21 15	
WORSTON	3	4 17	16 c15	21 18	8 9 14	
NEWTON	10¼	9 3	19 c20	10 8	13 3 16	
DUNSUP-BRIDGE	2	9 3	19 c20	10 8	13 3 16	
GRINDLETON	6	16 8 11	13 c18	5 21	22 3	
CHIPPING	6	19 20 10	15 c12	28 8	27 29	
TWISTON	6	11 16	7	4	9	

The Quarterly Meeting at Clithero, March 29th. The Local Preachers meet that day, at Ten o'Clock in the Forenoon.
S. SACRAMENT.——L. LOVEFEAST.——C. COLLECTION.

HENRY WHALLEY, PRINTER, CLITHERO.

Schedule of services and preachers for the Clitheroe Circuit, 1824.

There were special celebrations—for example, when the Prince of Wales was married in 1863. The lady of the manor arranged a treat for the Anglican and Wesleyan Sunday schools who, in return, sang *God Bless the Prince of Wales* and *Sabbath Schools are England's Glory* and processed round the village. On the last Sunday in 1880 the Wesleyan scholars from Waddington, led by Mr Grime and Mr Dugdale, joined a grand procession in Clitheroe to celebrate the centenary of Sunday schools. Over 2,300 children took part and, after walking through the town, they assembled in the weaving shed in Brook Mill. The singing in praise of their schools was followed by a prayer, ten hymns and various addresses. Mr Grime gave a short account of the life of Robert Raikes, the founder of the movement.

Not surprisingly, once the day school opened in 1875 numbers in the Sunday school began to decline. In 1879 fifty-four scholars and one teacher left, and only seven new scholars were admitted. To encourage attendance, reward books were given to the best attenders and to those of good behaviour—those who lived in the village were expected to attend at least ninety times, and the others seventy, to qualify for a prize. After a few years it became the custom to award the prizes early in January and to give the teachers a tea party.

In 1888 plans were made to build a separate Sunday school. There were still nineteen teachers, but the number of scholars had continued to fall. This may be why the decision to build was carried by only a small majority. Having made the decision, however, no time was lost in drawing up the plans and in raising money. When James Boothman of Newchurch, a former scholar, sold his two cottages south of the chapel for £130, he donated £10 to the building of a hall and two classrooms on the site of the cottages. A building committee organised fund-raising activities. These included a concert by the Clitheroe choir, said to have been 'the best ever rendered in the village'. Alonzo Jackson and his company entertained with glees, recitations and violin solos. Subscriptions brought in £159 4s. 6d. and a bazaar raised over £166. This ready response meant that building began earlier than anticipated. Four foundation stones were laid, one by Alderman James Garnett JP of Waddow Hall, in January 1889. The school, complete with parquet floor, platform, a twelve-gallon boiler and hanging lamps, was opened on Good Friday. Following these proceedings there was tea, and afterwards an address in the crowded chapel. On each Sunday in April special services were held at which gold, silver, notes and cheques were generously given, and at the May bazaar £153 was raised on the first day. By the end of the year only £11 9s. 3d. of the total cost of over £623 was owing. This, and a further £40 for a new piano, was soon raised.

When the anniversary services were held in the following year, the chapel was full and 'a considerable number at each service had to be seated in the Sunday school'. The anniversaries continued to prove great occasions, with a lecture on the Saturday and special services on the Sunday and Monday, when the choir was sometimes accompanied by violins, viols and double bass.

The new schoolroom, said to be one of the warmest rooms in the village, was used for a variety of purposes. The Waddington Handbell Ringers gave their first concert there after acquiring a new set of bells. There was a concert to raise money for the West Bradford cart bridge. Miss Greenwood of the Society of Friends preached there, the Salvation Army held a service, and the Reading Room Committee and the Parish Council met there. A Mutual Improvement Society was using it in 1892, and the Band of Hope, first formed in the 'sixties, re-started there in 1896. There were also missionary meetings, bazaars and sales of work.

After the building of the school, improvements were made to the chapel, which Stephen Clarke described as a 'dingy old whitewashed building wherein some of the younger portion of the congregation proved troublesome through lack of reverence'.[1] It was now refurnished and beautified, and acetylene gas lighting was installed. In 1891 it was registered for the solemnisation of marriages, and when the first marriage was celebrated later in the year a Bible and hymn book were presented to the couple.

---

[1] *Clitheroe Advertiser and Times*, 30 May 1924.

Morning services, held at first once a month, began in 1891. Two years later morning Sunday school, already shortened, was discontinued and scholars attended chapel service.

Typical Wesleyan stalwarts who played a major part in the activities of school and chapel were John Dugdale and Edward Chester. The former died in 1893 after nearly fifty years as society steward, class leader, Sunday school treasurer, teacher and superintendent. Edward Chester, choirmaster for twenty-six years, trained the choir and arranged choral services and the music for the choir sermons and other anniversaries. He started a music class and introduced Sankey's music. On New Year's Eve there was carol singing at the Town Gate. On one occasion the singers went up the Fell Road as far as Cuttock Clough. After many falls on the ice and getting lost several times in the fog, they let the New Year in 'with a little harmony and plenty of Christmas cheer' before returning to the village at three in the morning. Soon after Chester retired, an organ was installed in 1898. Special recitals and services with preachers from Leeds and Manchester were arranged for the opening occasion. Some of the £150 needed for the organ was raised when the Stackstead Choir gave a 'capital programme of songs, glees, duets and quartettes' in Clitheroe.[1]

Although special money-raising efforts were needed from time to time, weekly collections, augmented by collections on anniversary days and at choir sermons, class pence and pew rents, were generally sufficient to meet all needs. In 1860 pew rents, including some of £2 a year, were being paid by twenty people. Some money went to particular causes such as horse hire, 'Worn-Out Ministers' and their widows, the Band of Hope, the children's home, home missions and local preachers.

The following activities reported in the *Clitheroe Times* in 1900 give an idea of chapel life at the close of the century. Special services were held on the first Sunday of the year:

> There was a good attendance in the morning and this was improved upon in the evening when the Chapel was crowded almost to excess. In the afternoon the annual distribution of prizes took place: 22 girls and 14 boys received prizes. Mrs Dewhurst had the honour of seeing seven of her children carry off first prizes: they had not been absent or late on one single occasion.

In April there were three evenings of conversaziones to cover the expenses of a bazaar: 'On the first evening Mr Chester was Chairman; the entertainment included recitations and songs including, by special request, "Soldiers of the Queen".' (The Boer War was still going on.) In March came the choir supper when, 'as was customary, a sumptuous repast was provided by Mr William Ireland who took a great interest in the musical part of the services.' At Easter special services were held and good congregations attended. In the evening there was a lantern service on 'The Crucifixion of Christ', with a collection in aid of the India Famine Fund.

The anniversary services, as usual, drew large congregations. 'Two most invigorating and uplifting sermons were preached. The collection of £7 12s. 6d. was two pounds in advance of last year.'

---

[1] *Clitheroe Times*, 1898.

A three-day bazaar was held in May. Many children stayed away from school to attend and on the opening day £76 6s. 5d. was received. 'On the Saturday the bazaar was opened by four girls of the Sunday school. Each made a neat little speech and then simultaneously declared the bazaar open.' A box-making competition took place and, as well as the stalls, there was a museum and phonograph. The debts, including that on the organ, were cleared. On Whit Monday, members went to Lytham on the annual Sunday school excursion. Revd J. Hind of Blackpool preached at the Sunday school anniversary when there was a special programme of music by the choir.

The choir sermons were held in August. There followed the decoration of the chapel with flowers and fruit for the Harvest Festival service in September. The Christmas Tea Festival was well supported, and the New Year's Eve social, with games and an entertainment, brought the year's activities to an end.

After the unpretentious beginning in Back Fold, the Wesleyan chapel was, at the end of the century, firmly established in the religious and social life of the village.

Other denominations

Other denominations were thinly represented. There were a few Roman Catholics who attended services in Clitheroe. A priest took part in a burial service in 1845. Curiously, the small tithe was paid to Thomas Weld who, after his conversion to Roman Catholicism, had been made a cardinal some years before Newman's appointment.

Though there is no mention of them in the ecclesiastical census, Latter Day Saints had a house in Waddington in 1842 which was certified as a place of worship.[1] The census does, however, refer to a meeting house in Chatburn, so they may have moved there by 1851.

When Edward Chester, a Congregationalist, moved from Easington to Mitchells Farm he held a service there every month for some thirty years. In the 1840s this was conducted by Bulcock Booth, the Congregationalist minister at Newton. According to John Chester, Edward's son,

> It was no uncommon thing for the congregation to fill two rooms in the house. The 'pulpit' consisted of a board fixed across the top of an old-fashioned arm-chair with sides. Sometimes a portion of the choir from the Waddington Wesleyan Chapel would take part in the service and afterwards would stay until a late hour rehearsing the old tunes so familiar to the countryside. The late Mr William Pye was a regular attender at the 'cottage meeting'.[2]

Members of the Chester family later joined the Wesleyan chapel.

If the figures given in the ecclesiastical census (1851) are accepted, two hundred of Waddington's population were regular worshippers. Later, the Anglican church was seldom half full. There was one memorable exception following the occasion when

---

[1] *Parliamentary Gazetteer of England and Wales, 1840–3*, vol. IV (London), p. 393.
[2] *Clitheroe Advertiser*, 7 December 1906.

the vicar, Edward Parker, donned his vestments in full view of the congregation. This caused such surprise that, in hope of a repeat performance, the church was filled on the following Sunday. Even Wesleyans attended.

Whatever the number of church attenders, throughout the century Sunday observance remained the rule. Mid-century, the Hospital Trustees, concerned at the possibility of holding their Founder's Day meeting on a Sunday, declared 'It is not decent for us to do so.' At the end of the century a Waddington churchman stated his views concerning Good Friday in the *Clitheroe Times*: 'I am not against people taking a walk on this day but as to running headlong into pleasure I think it is most unbecoming of us Christians.' To give Francis Parker, the Vicar, the last word: 'Good Friday throughout the land is now becoming a day which is observed both more devoutly and less devoutly than of old.' He may well have thought that of the rest of the year.

7

Education

THE NINETEENTH century saw the beginning of a national system of education to the age of thirteen. Until 1833 such education as existed was provided by grammar schools, church schools and dame schools. In that year the first government aid was given when £20,000—rather less than was spent on repairing the Royal stables—was given to the National Society and to the British and Foreign Schools Society to help them provide schools. When the grant was increased in 1839 the first government inspectors were appointed to supervise the spending of the money.

These two societies had been organised by Anglicans and Non-conformists to further the work of Bell and Lancaster who had introduced 'a new mechanical system for the use of schools'. This was the monitorial system whereby the master instructed some of the older children who then taught the lessons to the younger ones. Religious rivalry and the dull factory-line production methods were the undesirable results of a system whose only recommendation was cheapness.

In 1846 apprenticed pupil-teachers began to replace the monitors. At eighteen they were eligible for a Queen's Scholarship at a training college. Teaching, however, continued to be dull and factual as payment of grants to schools was largely determined by achievements in the three Rs. The realisation that 'upon the speedy provision of elementary education depends our industrial prosperity' led in 1870 to the passing of Forster's Education Act aimed at supplementing the church schools by 'filling in the gaps' with non-sectarian schools. In 1880 attendance was made compulsory for all to the age of ten; later to thirteen. Since the 'fifties more attention had been paid to secondary education, and commissions had been set up to enquire into conditions at public and grammar schools. Their findings had led to the Endowed Schools Act of 1869 and the introduction of much needed reforms. The higher education of girls was also considered although generally their education was regarded as of little importance.

University education developed with the foundation of new universities in London and Durham and the reform of the old. The universities were mainly for the wealthy; for others there were mechanics' institutes and evening classes. Publications such as the *Penny Encyclopaedia* and *Cassell's Popular Educator* helped those who strove to educate themselves.

Waddington's first school

Waddington, less fortunate than such nearby townships as Newton and Grindleton, had no old foundation school. In 1801 there was neither day nor Sunday school in the village. The first school, built by public subscription in 1812 on the site of the old tithe barn was a two-storey building. The Hospital donated £6 in 1813 and Mrs Clarke, Lady of the Manor and owner of the barn, also contributed to the building fund and allowed the yard to be enclosed by a wall. 'There is no satisfactory evidence as to the original purpose of the school but it may be conjectured that it was intended for the education of poor children in the township.'[1]

Grimshaw's 'famous' school

James Grimshaw was appointed Master of the school by the incumbent. Eventually he conducted it as a 'private adventure school, exacting fees from all alike, and continued in possession for forty years or more'.[2]

Grimshaw (1791–1860) came from Haslingden. In 1826 he married the great-niece of the lady of the manor, made his home at Belle Vue (now Beechthorpe) and bought the adjoining close. By 1833 'at the one daily school in the village forty-five males were being educated at the expense of their parents.'[3]

By 1841 the school had further developed and there were ten boarders living at Belle Vue.[4] Ten years later when Mrs Grimshaw was helping with the teaching there were thirty-two boarders, nineteen of whom were boys, with ages ranging from six to seventeen.[5] The children came from the cotton towns of Lancashire: eight from Blackburn and others from Accrington, Ramsbottom, Wigan, Haslingden, Darwen and Rawtenstall. They could travel to Clitheroe by train but, for those who preferred, there was still the Blackburn coach.

Nineteen other boys and eleven girls were also scholars.[6] Amongst them was a seventeen-year-old boy from Bailey who was in lodgings. He and some village children may have paid fees and attended Grimshaw's school, as did at least one boy from Clitheroe. The school seems to have had a good reputation—a local writer described it as 'famous'[7]—and judging by the amount of property Grimshaw bought it was evidently a financial success. Even so, a few Waddington children attended the school at Newton and the British School at Low Moor.

The 1833 Report on Education [8] stated that there was one Sunday school 'wherein fifty-five males and fifty-eight females are taught gratuitously'. It is not certain whether this was the Anglican or the Wesleyan school. The Anglican Sunday school is known to have been in existence by 1821 when the Hospital Trustees made a donation to it, but few of its records survive. The Wesleyan school began in 1824 when the chapel, built also to serve as a Sunday school, was opened. Reading and writing were taught as well as the scriptures, and the school

---

[1] Charity Commission Report, 1896. p. 25
[2] Charity Commission Report, 1896, p. 25
[3] Report on Education of the Poorer Classes. British Parliamentary Papers vol. 3 (1835).
[4] 1841 Census.
[5] 1851 Census.
[6] *Ibid.*
[7] S. Clarke, *Clitheroe in the Old Coaching Days* p. 51.
[8] Report on Education of the Poorer Classes.

was well attended. By 1860 there were thirty boys and thirty-five girls, seventeen of whom attended a day school, 'on the Books'. There were nineteen teachers, and a well-stocked library (see pages 118–19).

Closure of the school

Meanwhile changes were taking place at Grimshaw's school. Grimshaw was still in charge in 1858[1] and possibly until his death in 1860. Soon after this 'the incumbency being vacant ... the township asserted its right to the school' and four leading residents on the recommendation of a local clergyman appointed a schoolmaster. Within a short time, however, disputes occurred which eventually led to the closure of the school. The Charity Commissioners imply that the schoolmaster, Mattinson, was supported by the township against Mrs Ramsden.[2] Their report was based on evidence given thirty years after the event: the Ramsden papers, which include letters written during the dispute, and other sources, notably the *Preston Guardian*, give a different version.

According to the newspaper, the 'Waddington Slander Case Mattinson *v* Leach' began when the plaintiff, a former soldier and weaver, was said by the residents to be unsuitable as schoolmaster. Leach, their leader, told the clergyman 'You ought not to have given a testimonial to Mattinson: he is not a fit person for the situation he holds'. Mattinson then brought an action against Leach to recover damages for slander. When the case was heard at Liverpool the jury found for the plaintiff and awarded him damages of £5.[3]

Leach asked for a retrial on the grounds of misdirection of jury. He claimed that as the plaintiff held a public position no action could be taken for words spoken against him. In April of the following year the case was heard at Leeds Assizes. By that time further developments had taken place in Waddington. 'The principal inhabitants of the place' persuaded Mrs Ramsden, on whose land the school was built, to eject Mattinson whereupon the schoolmaster proceeded to bring an action against Mrs Ramsden and others.

The vicar, Edward Parker, gave his support to Mattinson who was by this time churchwarden and clerk, and installed a man at the school to prevent the opposition from taking it over. The latter broke into the building and a show of violence with 'men throwing each other over the walls' ensued. Already there was much ill-feeling against the vicar, and the opportunity of showing further animosity was not lost.

Mrs Ramsden, whose pew had recently been removed from the church by order of the vicar, was certainly not one of his supporters. Even so, she may have regretted her intervention on the behalf of Leach when she was subpoenaed to attend trial at Leeds on a charge of trespass and eviction. 'It is perfectly well known that I am not wanted ... this is done with the intention of giving trouble and annoyance' she complained. Her physician saved her from 'the terrible bore'

[1] Slater, *Directory of Lancashire*, 1858.
[2] Charity Commission Report, 1896, p. 25
[3] *Preston Guardian*, April 1865.

of the journey from her London home to Leeds by declaring her 'unfit to travel'—she was, after all, over seventy.[1]

In the end the court directed that trustees should be appointed and the school conveyed to them to be 'for ever used as a school in connection with the Church of England'. Though 'the horrid trial' was over, it had indeed proved 'profitless alike to all parties'. The school was 'a ruinous place' and the vicar was not being particularly generous in saying that, 'as far as he was concerned, the Ramsdens could have it'. The keys were handed over to a Mr Hulton, a County Court Judge in Preston, but, as no trustees were appointed, for seven years the school 'stood empty and disused'. In 1873, the court order still being unsatisfied, the vicar took possession of the building, repaired it at his own expense and opened it as a Church of England Sunday school.[2]

With the closing of the day school, the only education available in the village was that provided by the two Sunday schools and by a small sewing school for girls held in a cottage said to have been at the end of Masker Row. Many of the seventy-two listed scholars in the 1871 census were attending the Wesleyan Sunday school, whose numbers had doubled since 1860. The vicar's younger children were taught by a governess. Tom and Mary Garnett also had a governess and had learned to read before they were five; when they were six their father examined them in grammar, history and geography; when they were eight he examined them in astronomy and French. [3] The organist of St Mary's, Clitheroe, taught them music. Tom continued his education at Clitheroe Grammar school which a few other boys from the village also attended. David Leach at the age of twelve went to the school in 1837. Two years later his eight-year-old brother Frederick 'a well educated boy and a fair scholar'[4] joined him and had his name on the honours board when he left at fourteen. The school was still enjoying the reputation established by Thomas Wilson, headmaster from 1775 to 1813. A hundred boys were attending what was then recognised as one of the best schools in the north.

Very different was the education received by an eleven-year-old winder at Low Moor school. Like most factory workers she was often too tired to benefit from the three hours schooling a day required by law.

Whether educated in Waddington or elsewhere the local population steadily became more literate. Whereas at the beginning of the century most of the women and many of the men, being unable to write, had to 'make their mark' in the marriage register, after 1840 the number of signatures increased. In the 'fifties eighteen men and seventeen women made their mark; in the 'sixties only three men and seven women did so. By the end of the century only one out of three hundred petitioners was unable to sign her name.

---

[1] WYAS, Leeds, Ramsden Papers 64/15.
[2] Charity Commission Report, 1896, p. 25.
[3] O. Ashmore, *Diary of James Garnett 1858–65*.
[4] LRO, Register of Queen Mary's Grammar School, 1836–54, DDX/28/287.

The 1870 Act

Though the villagers may have been prepared to do without a school, the government was not disposed to tolerate such a situation. In 1870, Parliament, considering the time had come to 'educate our masters'—the newly enfranchised—proceeded to pass Forster's Education Act. This accepted the sectarian schools which already existed and allowed six months for the building of more church schools. Where they did not exist, school boards were to provide non-sectarian schools paid for by the rate-payers. Even so, four years after the passing of the Act, Waddington was still without a school.

A letter written in 1889 to the Charity Commissioners stated that 'to avoid a School Board the inhabitants of the two villages, Waddington and West Bradford, built a voluntary Church of England School'.[1] If this were so, it is somewhat surprising that they had not accepted the offer of a grant and built in 1870. Edward Chester later stated that no decision had been reached at that time because 'the whole of the two townships [Waddington and West Bradford] was in a state of turmoil and unrest'.[2] He held the vicar responsible for this. 'His conscientious views led him so far as to alienate his followers, empty his church, engender a spirit of uncharitableness' ... producing 'a seething mass of unrest and litigation'.

Certainly the vicar, Edward Parker, was not popular. He himself in 1869 referred to the 'many years of persecution' which he had suffered and, in a court case the judge expressed the opinion that the claims against him arose out of ill-feeling.[3] In both townships, children were attending nonconformist Sunday schools: some parents favoured a board school. The lady of the manor, still trying to get the Waddow pew restored,[4] far from supporting the vicar and a church school, planned to give land and money to a board school.

On 21 November 1870, Mrs Ramsden wrote to her son:

> You will see that the Bible is not to be taught in the Government School. [She had just been reading a pamphlet which—incorrectly—stated this.] Think about this school question before we consider if we ought or ought not to bestir ourselves. I was to have given a site and £200 towards a new one.[5]

Because of her misgivings about Bible teaching she gave neither site nor money for a board school; nor did she support a Church of England school. Though in 1872 Sir Ralph Assheton was asked for his advice, still no action was taken. Finally, in April 1874 the Education Department sent an ultimatum: the village had to build a school or one would be built and charged to them.

---

[1] Church Archives, School Managers' Minute Book.
[2] *Clitheroe Times*, 22 April 1898.
[3] *Preston Guardian*, 15 May 1869.
[4] WYAS Leeds, Ramsden Papers 64/15.
[5] WYAS Leeds, Ramsden Papers 64/16.

The Waddington West Bradford School

A meeting of ratepayers was speedily called. Thirty-three ratepayers of the townships of Waddington and West Bradford attended. Robert Walker took the chair and two resolutions were carried: 'That a school be built for the two townships by voluntary subscriptions' and 'That in each township, a committee of four be appointed to collect subscriptions.' In Waddington Robert Walker, William Redmayne, William Dewhurst and Felix Grimshaw were appointed. In June all ratepayers were invited to meet at the Lower Buck Inn to 'consider the kind offer made by John Burton, Esq. of a site for the proposed new school' and 'to consider the propriety of preparing plans.' The site, near the boundary between the two villages was accepted, as was Burton's donation of £200. In Waddington £499 1s. od. was collected and £336 in West Bradford, from 173 subscribers who donated sums from 2s. 6d to £200.

Amongst the Waddington subscribers were Adam Sykes, Colthurst, £100; Robert Walker £50; Revd E. Parker £50; Sir John Holker £30; Major Parker, Browsholme, £30; Thomas Garnett and Sons, £20; Mrs Grimshaw £10; F.W. Grimshaw, £10; Mrs Susannah Foulds, £5; Jonathan Speakman £1; James Fishwick £1. The Hospital Trustees with the approval of the Charity Commissioners gave £50 to the school which 'will be a public elementary school in conformity with the provisions of the Elementary Education Act of 1870.'

Both Anglicans and Wesleyans subscribed to the fund. Later, some parishioners insisted that when subscriptions had been solicited 'in every case it was particularly stated that the school should be undenominational.'[1] Others, equally adamant, maintained that 'this was not so and the Minute Book bore this out.' What the minute book does show is that it was not until 6 August 1875, when the school was about to be opened that, at a meeting attended by five of the eight committee members, a resolution was carried 'that this school be called the Waddington and West Bradford Church of England School'. Certainly correspondence with the Department of Education before this date and the subscriptions lists contain no such reference. This controversy flared up at the time of the Charity Commissioners' Enquiry in 1895 and again when Edward Chester claimed that nonconformity had a legitimate grievance and that the school should be handed over by the Church of England to the ratepayers.[2]

The dispute was by no means unique. At Kettlewell at about the same time when funds had been raised and a school built, the vicar and churchwardens assumed control. The outcome there was different; the infuriated villagers, many of whom were nonconformists, pulled the school down. [3]

Meanwhile, in Waddington, the ratepayers accepted the plan submitted by William Hargreaves of Clitheroe. The eight collectors formed themselves into a building committee and put out tenders for the school.

---

[1] *Clitheroe Times*, 26 April 1895.
[2] *Clitheroe Times*, 11 March 1898.
[3] E. Raistrick, *Village Schools* (Dalesman Publishing Co., 1971).

The Waddington West Bradford Day School.

There was to be a main schoolroom 66 feet long, 21 feet wide and 15 feet high with a room for the infants leading from it. Some help was given by ratepayers who carted gravel for the yard. The school was built at a cost of £1,060 and four pence. In 1876 the first school inspector reported that 'excellent new buildings and premises have been provided by the creditable voluntary efforts of the ratepayers and have been suitably furnished and supplied with apparatus.' Desks for the older pupils, cupboards, sewing table and clock were purchased. The infants, as one of them later recorded, sat on steps arranged in tiers[1]

Although a further ratepayers' meeting had been promised for the election of school managers, none was called. The building committee took this further role upon themselves and in July 1875, as the school approached completion, advertised in the *Preston Guardian* and other papers for a 'certified Master for the Waddington and West Bradford School.' Applicants were asked to state the salary required but there was no mention of religion as in later advertisements: the resolution about the school being Church of England had not yet been carried. When the appointment was being considered, one of the fifteen short listed candidates, Mr Osborne, was asked to state what certificates he held and what religion he professed. Although Osborne had the advantage of a wife who was prepared to help with the teaching, it was George Turner of St Paul's School, Middleton-on-Tees, who was appointed at a salary of £104 a year, to be paid quarterly. His letter of appointment dated 31 July referred to the 'discharge of duties appertaining to the office of schoolmaster and to keeping a correct account of school pence.'

---

[1] J. H. W. Fishwick, *In and around Waddington*, p. 17.

Attendance

The school opened on 31 August 1875. Fifty-five boys and forty-three girls were enrolled and twelve more pupils in the following week. Until 1880 attendance was not compulsory and then only from five to ten. As well as enrolling throughout the year, children left at intervals for a variety of reasons. There were 'part-timers' who applied for a labour certificate at the age of twelve and at thirteen began full time work at the mill. Others went into service on farms. Some parents, particularly if the father was 'off-drinking', could not afford to send their children. In the case of one boy who sent for his books and later said that he was 'not coming anymore' the master simply commented 'He does not like to come to school and wants to stop at home and play.'

The Master did what he could to maintain attendance as the number of pupils and their successes determined the government grant. 'Unless the attendance improves by some means the standard of the school must fall very perceptibly next year' William Hitchin wrote in 1885. Inspectors took care to examine the registers and reminded the managers of their duty to check them at least once a quarter. Absentees, like the girl who attended sixteen times out of a possible 130, were reported to the Attendance Officer but, as was regretfully noted, 'his threats are evidently of no avail.' In 1886 one girl was nearly eight before she began school, though her name had frequently been sent to the officer. Even in 1894 a child who did not know a letter or a figure, or even her name, was six before she began school. At times a pupil teacher was sent to the homes to round up absentees. Truants were punished: two boys were severely thrashed at their mother's request for playing truant. Not surprisingly the log book contains entries such as 'This kind of attendance is very discouraging for the teachers' and 'Very poor school all week: impossible to do much work.'

Towards the end of the century attendance was almost the lowest in the Clitheroe Union: on average thirty children were absent every day and after the annual examination half the school stayed away. It was reckoned that in 1895 absences lost the school £50 which would have provided another teacher.[1] Nor did things improve. The vicar reported that 'Attendance at our school is the lowest in the district and one of the lowest in the whole country.'

In 1898 when there were 151 'on the books' the average attendance was 100. Attendance was particularly poor on Monday mornings and Friday afternoons. Whenever there was a show, fair or menagerie in Clitheroe half the school took the day off: the rest were given a holiday in the afternoon. On 2 December 1885, 'The school was thinner being polling day for the district of Waddington.' That same year many children took the morning off to watch a wedding. Funerals, especially those of the school managers, Edward Burton and, on the following day, James Walmsley, were well attended. There were happier occasions which led to absence. The Wesleyan children stayed away to attend their Bazaar in 1900 and there was a whole week's holiday while the Anglicans held theirs at the school. One summer day when only seventy-four children were present, it was found that the mothers from Waddington had taken almost half the children for a picnic up the Fell.

---

[1] Parish Magazine, 1896.

As many children had to walk several miles to school, their attendance was often affected by the weather: 'More than half the children have been obliged to stay at home during the greater part of the week because of stormy, wet weather and the dirty condition of the roads. Weather quite unfit for children from a distance, very few present: some were quite drenched and had to be sent home. Only 5 of the 17 infants and 6 of the 36 children in Standard 1 were able to attend.' At times the roads were completely covered with ice, or, even in June, 'had water to the depth of several inches.' From November to March heavy falls of snow occurred: in March 1886 twenty-three children were present. In January 1895, 'it was bitterly cold; a great depth of snow.' In school the temperature was only 35°F., and the children had to be sent home. The following day only twenty-one children turned up and they found one room to be cold and smoky. By February the cold was more intense than ever. When the inside temperature was down to 24 degrees the children were sent home for the rest of the week. It was soon after this that a new heating system was installed. Spells of fine weather came as welcome relief: 'Delightful weather, attendance up.' In May 1886 'The weather has been fine during the week and a rapid stride has been made: the average 14.2 up on the previous week.' Only once was reference made to excessive heat—it made the children 'somewhat drowsy'.

Farmers as well as head teachers kept an eye on the weather. Entries such as 'very small attendance, many boys staying at home to help at sheep-washing' and 'poor school this week on account of many children being employed in the hay field' appeared almost every June in the log book. When the hay harvest was 'backward' children were absent in August. In October they were sometimes required to 'carry dinners'. In the later part of the century children over the age of eight were exempt from 1 July to 12 August from the restrictions concerning employment.

Illness

Illness also affected attendance. In 1877 many children were suffering from fever; when another outbreak occurred some years later the Medical Officer sent some 'disinfecting powder' to be sprinkled in the school. Later that year (1885) there were fifty cases of measles in West Bradford and fifty-six cases in Waddington. Ten years later the Medical Officer closed the school for a week in February because of an epidemic of measles. In March there was an outbreak of scarlet fever. The inspector later noted that the school had only opened a few times above the required minimum for the year. In 1887 all the girls in the top standards were suffering from mumps; in 1894 thirty children were away with scarletina. Whooping cough, scurvy and influenza were reported. The teachers suffered too. When twenty-five children were absent because of throat and chest complaints in November 1893, the pupil-teacher, unable to speak, had permission to stay away. The head teacher was unable to take singing because of a sore throat. When the infant teacher also had to stay away, two older girls were appointed to act as monitors in her place. During these years a number of the scholars died and many children were absent to attend their funerals. The inspectors appreciated the effects of so much illness: the report of 1889, although generally favourable, concluded 'not quite so good as last year because of illness.'

Holidays

Official holidays, fixed by the managers, included three weeks at Christmas and four weeks in the summer, usually in July. Towards the end of the century the local mills stopped for a week and the school holiday was extended to include this. Two days were allowed at Easter and two at Whitsuntide. Sometimes there was a half holiday on Shrove Tuesday and on special occasions such as the Queen's Golden Jubilee. There was a half holiday when the master and several children were singing at the wedding of a manager's daughter.

When the school first opened the Master for a short time taught all the children. Then, after a probationary period, one of the older pupils, only twelve years of age, was engaged as a pupil teacher for five years. Joseph Oddie became the second pupil-teacher. Each received £10 a year with an annual increase of £2 10s. 0d.

Curriculum

With the appointment of pupil-teachers, it was possible for the infants to be taught in their own room and for the older children, of whom there were over eighty, to be divided into six standards and taught in the main room. The emphasis was upon reading, writing and arithmetic, subjects in which the children were examined at the end of the year. There was much learning by rote as success meant a larger government grant. Those who were unable to do the work were put on the 'exception schedule'.

Inspection

At the end of the first year fifty-nine pupils were presented for examination; fifty passed in reading, forty-six in writing and thirty-two in arithmetic. The report concluded, 'The School has in all respects made a highly promising start, discipline being excellent and attainments, except for the Arithmetic of a part of the first Standard, good and intelligent. The master has only been seven months and deserves great credit.' The following year seventy-six children were examined. Seventy, sixty-eight and sixty-one were successful in the three Rs and the school was duly commended. It was 'much affected' when Turner left at Christmas after helping the school make this promising start.

The work of the infants was also inspected. The four-year-olds were taught the alphabet and were expected to write some of the small letters and to count and add using ball frames. Five-year-olds were expected to know three and four letter words, six-year-olds to read from a primer. Addition, subtraction and tables were taught. Object lessons were given on a variety of subjects ranging from an elephant to a knife and fork. Not much interest was shown in these topics but there was a better response to drill and to singing, described by an inspector as 'sweet and pleasant'.

Work on the basic subjects included composition, letter-writing and spelling. The time-table included geography, singing—from notation if the master was competent—poetry and drawing. Later, drill, mostly Ling's exercises, history and science were introduced. The inspectors set a number of lines to be learnt from such poems as *The Wreck of the Hesperus*, *Lord Ullin's Daughter* and *Llewelyn and his Dog*. Mrs Pinder asked that her son might be excused from learning poetry 'as he was not strong'; others may well have been daunted at the idea of learning 150 lines from *Julius Caesar*.

Pupil-teachers

Pupils and pupil-teachers were given homework. This was especially important for the latter as each year they had to sit an examination at Blackburn. By 1878 they were making some progress. Elizabeth Nowell was said to be 'very industrious and will make a successful teacher.' She did. In 1881 as a certified teacher, she was appointed assistant mistress at the school with a salary of £26 a year. Two years later this was increased to £30. When she left in 1890 she was given a 'nice present' of a silver breakfast and tea service from the managers, parents and scholars. Joseph Oddie, the other pupil-teacher, eventually became master at the school.

Less successful was Ada Cording who became a paid monitor in 1881 and a pupil-teacher in the following year. Although she was given lessons at 8.15 in the morning and after school, a week seldom passed but the head complained about her work. In 1883 her examination result was not satisfactory and a warning was given that should she be required as a member of staff and fail to the same extent next year the grant would be reduced. By contrast, Harry Danson, although he had neglected Euclid, passed first class, gained a five-shilling grant for the school and went as a Queen's Scholar to train at St Mark's College, Chelsea. Provision was made eventually for the pupil-teachers to attend classes at Blackburn on Friday afternoons, half the fees being paid for them.

Headmasters

Between 1875 and 1901, there were seven headmasters at the school. Following George Turner's resignation, James Butterworth, who had trained at Caernarvon Training College, was appointed and remained at the school for two years. The 1878 report noted that 'The change in teachers has in no way affected this School ... It has few equals amongst the schools of like character in my district.' His successor, William Hitchin of Burnley, selected from 150 applicants, was also college-trained. In 1885, his last year at the school, ninety-two of the 140 pupils were examined. There were seven failures and two exemptions. Arithmetic received much praise and, for a country school, the inspector thought it deserved to be called excellent. Hitchin had included scripture lessons in the timetable for which he received a commendation from the vicar and a £10 salary increase. As the children had been working well for the year Hitchin had no hesitation in asking the managers to close the school for a week when he married. The managers, for their part, had no hesitation in complying.

When Hitchin left to teach at Whalley, Joseph Oddie, a former pupil-teacher and son of one of the managers, was selected from over a hundred applicants. His salary was fixed at £70 plus one third of the government grant. (The last grant made had been £97 14s. 3d.) The managers, like the government, believed in payment by result. Oddie maintained discipline 'occasionally with some harshness' and in 1888 the inspector could 'just pass the upper classes as excellent but shall hope to find increasing attention given to the cultivation of a pleasanter and more expressive manner of reading and reciting the poetry. Gallery lessons show some improvement but are not yet more than fair.' The infant section was also 'only fair. Interest has not been awakened.'

One November Friday in 1891 the headmaster left the school having first written to the secretary of the managers to say that he was unwell. 'He took to his bed. Inflammation of the bowels [appendicitis] set in and he gradually grew worse.' Within the week he was dead.

After this the infant teacher and one pupil-teacher ran the school for some weeks as it was not until the following January that Henry Rookes, Head of the National School in Newtown, took up his duties in response to an advertisement asking for 'a thoroughly earnest churchman expected to attend Sunday School as former masters.' On his arrival the new master complained about indiscipline and backwardness. By the following month he was satisfied that discipline at least had improved. The inspector, however, whilst accepting that the death of the previous head and the delay in appointing his successor had caused 'a great deal of weakness', found discipline to be weak and hoped that the new teacher would improve the condition of the school. His introduction of clog inspection after morning prayers was not appreciated by those boys who had to clean out shippons and then walk to school across the fields.[1]

Rookes had a difficult year. There had been a tremendous snow storm in March, an outbreak of fever in June, storms in October with only twenty children present on one day, and heavy snow which forced the school to close in December. The pupil-teacher resigned and a monitor had to take his place. Rookes must have been relieved to be able to write in the log book on 27 January 1893 'Nothing of importance occurred during the week.' A week later, amidst much speculation, he left the village giving no reason for his sudden departure.

The managers as soon as possible appointed Edwin Woodcock of Clitheroe temporary headmaster and later made this a permanent appointment. Although he began well and restored order, in his final year there was a serious decline and the children became listless and inattentive.

The appointment in 1897 of Harry Danson, former pupil-teacher, was somewhat unusual, if not irregular. The managers' proposal that from four to six applicants should be interviewed was defeated by the Chairman using his casting vote. The vicar then proposed that Danson, of Calder Vale School, be appointed and the proposal was carried by five votes to one. A letter was afterwards written to the Revd G. Wilson, Vicar of Christ Church, Mirfield, informing him of Danson's appointment 'in compliance with your wishes.' Both Wilson and Danson may well have been known to the vicar of Waddington who had previously been at Mirfield. Wilson visited the school two years later and found that satisfactory progress had been made. The report for 1900, however, found the condition of the school 'far from satisfactory.' 'Spelling and

[1] J. H. W. Fishwick, *In and around Waddington*, p. 17.

Arithmetic are both weak, discipline needs to be strengthened. [The master had only one young pupil-teacher to help in six standards]. The staff ought to be strengthened without delay. More reading books are wanted. The porch needs repairs.' Shortage of money was the basic problem but, in view of the report, the managers found sufficient money to appoint an assistant, Miss Beatrice Brennand, in July 1900.

Discipline

Most of the masters were disciplinarians and followed the example of Turner who kept children in until 5 o'clock, even in winter time, if they had been noisy or had not learnt their homework. Mistakes in dictation had to be written out ten times at home.

Girls were punished for running about the room in the dinner hour. They were spoken to severely on the wickedness of quarrelling and using foul language. The whole school was spoken to on the evils which might arise through deception when sums had been marked right instead of wrong.

Boys were punished for stealing and then lying, for refusing to repeat the creed and for bullying. In 1900 an old man asked for protection from two boys who had used bad language towards him as he walked along the road from Waddington: the boys received corporal punishment.

Only in exceptional cases did parents complain about the punishments, as when a parent protested at her daughter's being given ten strokes on the hand for bringing the wrong material for sewing. After this, punishments were left to the head.

There were rewards as well as punishments. Prizes of books and cards were given for homework, for regular attendance and for the best grown hyacinths. Before breaking up at Christmas, nuts and sweets were 'squandered' and a Tea Festival was held. Holidays were given to allow the children to visit the circus and to attend a festival in Waddington given by Lady Holker. May Day celebrations, including dancing round the maypole, took place.

The headmaster's duties were not confined to teaching children, training pupil-teachers, collecting school pence and maintaining discipline. He was expected to attend church twice on Sunday—absence was soon remarked upon by the vicar—and teach in the Sunday school. He was to teach the Evening Classes and provide his own light when doing so. He was expected to join in village activities. One headmaster became secretary of the Reading Room Society; another was secretary of the Foresters' Sports Committee and Rookes, during his short stay, was secretary of the newly formed Cricket Club. Danson could be relied upon for a few solos whenever there was an entertainment. For all this, twenty years after opening of the school, the headmaster's salary was just over a hundred pounds. After 1897, there was a school-house rented for £5 a year, rates and outside repairs included.

The vicars, Edward and Francis Parker, frequently visited the school. They taught the catechism (during which time the Wesleyans read the Bible) and saw to it that the children attended services on Ash Wednesday and Ascension Day and were well supplied with hymn books.

Problems

With only one assistant, a pupil-teacher and someone to teach sewing, the head-master's work was not easy. There were other difficulties, many of which arose from the shortage of money. But for the generosity of the Burton family who had already played an important part in the building of the school it might not have survived. Members of the family paid for the additional classroom built in 1893, built the schoolhouse, helped in the provision of a water supply and new heating system and made a further bequest of £100. In some years the school ran at a loss. In 1889 after furniture had been replaced and other expenses met, there was less than a shilling a head to be spent on books and slates. Although at the opening the school building was commended by inspectors, inadequacies became apparent. Unless the caretaker could be prevailed upon to light the fires early in the morning the rooms were cold. It was not until 1895 that a hot water system of heating replaced the open fires. There were problems because of the lack of lighting. In winter 'it was awkward seeing during sewing lessons' and though an earlier afternoon start was arranged it was sometimes so dark that the children had to be sent home early. Until the new classroom was built, sewing lessons were cancelled or reorganised to allow the managers to use the infants' room for their meetings. Inspectors recommended better ventilation, pegs in the porch and the more frequent emptying of the privies, smells from which were obnoxious.

Rats were another nuisance. 'We were disturbed all morning as on several mornings last week by rats crossing the floor after the children's dinners.' Traps were set but the rats, outwitting ferrets and dogs, proved 'too sly to be caught'.

In spite of financial difficulties the head arranged to have the school photographed in 1876, set up a museum with a display of Horrocks' cotton, and put up pictures and a notice about wild birds. He also invited the police constable to speak on 'Kindness to Dumb Creatures.'

Managers

The Managers, who included Captain Parker, James Walmsley, secretary, Edward Burton, Edward Burton, Junior, Newstead Garnett and Robert Walker also kept an eye on the school. Their position had been defined in a Deed of Trust dated November 1875 which conveyed the land and school to the minister and church wardens. A committee of eight, already in being, and the minister were to act as managers. Robert Walker refused to sign the deed. Edward Chester later asserted that Walker refused because, when collecting subscriptions for the school, he had assured donors that the money was for an undenominational school; the managers did not refute this statement. Walker's widow said they did well to leave Chester's statement alone, it being 'as near right as could be.'[1] Others contended that Walker's reason for not signing was that he felt the vicar had too much power.

---

[1] *Clitheroe Times*, 22 April 1898.

New managers, who had to be members of the Church of England, were elected by subscribers to the school. Usually it was a case of co-option. In 1885 Wilkinson Boothman successfully claimed the right as churchwarden and ex-officio trustee to vote at meetings. There were occasional differences of opinion as when the vicar contended that he and the wardens should decide whether the school should be used for outside activities such as the Flower Show, or when two managers, believing that the vicar had assumed more control than the others, resigned.

Finance

At their quarterly meetings the managers dealt with the school's finances. The main sources of income were the government grant and school pence paid by the parents. Income fell when payment of school pence was first reduced, and then, officially at least, abolished in 1891. The government grant was based on the principle of 'payment by result' and meant that a child under six could earn for the school a grant of 6s. 6d. if the inspector's report was satisfactory. Older children could earn 4s. for a minimum of two hundred attendances and general merit and 8s. for a pass in the three Rs. As a result of the 1891 Education Act a grant of 10s. per child in regular attendance was paid. The managers sent a circular to all parents urging them to make sure their children attended and pointing out that for the last seven years the school had run at an average loss of £9 a year. Scholars not paying their penny a week were to be sent home. In addition each member of the committee paid a minimum subscription of £1 and a few others also subscribed. The collection taken at the annual sermons, about £20, went to the school. Money left over form the Cotton Famine Relief Fund (£170 and £90 interest) was transferred to the school and invested. Although the Reading Room Society was not at first allowed to hold a concert at the school, in later years the building was let to various organisations for 2s.6d. with an additional charge if the piano was used.

   1888 was a typical year as regards finance. Sixty-seven boys and fifty-five girls were then on the register and ninety-six was the average attendance.

Income	Government Grant	£ 91	9s.	od.
	Subscription	£ 23	6s.	od.
	School Pence	£ 64	2s.	4d.
	Collection	£ 13	4s.	3d.
	Interest	£ 14	17s.	3d.
	Total	£206	18s.	10d.
Expenditure	Head's Salary	£110	9s.	8d.
	Assistant Teacher	£ 46	0s.	od.
	Pupil-Teacher	£ 13	3s.	4d.
	Fuel and Cleaning	£ 18	15s.	od.
	Rates and Insurance		16s.	3d.
	Replacement of Furniture	£ 11	5s.	7d.
	Books and Slates	£ 4	5s.	5d.
	Total	£204	15s.	3d.

The caretaker

The managers were responsible for appointing the caretaker whose duties were clearly stated in 1896:

Thoroughly sweep the school floors and dust all desks and seats, window bottoms and hat rails each day.
Light the boiler fire each morning so as to have the School warmed for the scholars during the winter months.
The cloakroom and the closets to be washed weekly.
The windows to be cleaned each month.
The room floors to be washed and scrubbed twice yearly.
The Managers to find all brushes, cleaning materials and firewood and pay the same rate per week during holidays.
Payment for the year—£12

The managers were responsible for carrying out the inspectors' recommendations with regard to the building. They arranged for the school to be whitewashed and painted, for the long desks to be varnished and the place to be 'beautified' generally.

Evening classes

For those who had been unable to attend school there was the opportunity to attend evening school classes. These were first held by Butterworth who charged the twenty-one pupils fourpence a week for their two weekly sessions. Rookes had evening classes for younger pupils on Tuesdays and Thursdays and on Wednesday for older ones and these were fairly well attended. By the end of the century there were Evening Continuation Classes in writing, drawing, arithmetic and sewing. These were so well attended that the head needed an assistant. It was suggested that the meetings should be held in the newly built Church Sunday school as the majority of those attending came from Waddington.

The Reading Room

For some time before 1882 Edward Chester had thought that there should be a Reading Room in Waddington. Not everyone shared his opinion: 'Let them as wants one get one' was the reaction of one villager. In spite of this, an architect was instructed by Chester to draw plans and land was rented from William Garnett at 1½d. a yard. He built two houses adjoining those south of the Sun Inn and the Reading Room completed the row. James Walmsley, expecting the venture to 'fizzle out', provided furniture, but only on loan. The headmaster became secretary and on 21 July 1883 was enrolling members on payment of a two shilling subscription. Entertainments were arranged to cover costs, pay for newspapers and start a circulating library. From 1891 there were lectures at the Reading Room on subjects ranging from the formation of rocks to insects.

Both church and chapel had Mutual Improvement Societies. The church formed theirs in 1896 and held weekly meetings at which papers were read. One, about 'Some Marvels of Modern Engineering', dealt with the Manchester Ship Canal. A man from the *Clitheroe Times* spoke on 'How a Newspaper is Got Out'. Free use of the chapel with heating and lighting provided was allowed to the society which began there in 1892. The main aim was to encourage reading and writing. Talks were given on Cromwell, Bunyan and other subjects. For the more ambitious there was the technical school in Clitheroe where Joseph Oddie, when headmaster, had furthered his own education by attending classes in agriculture and botany.

The Reading Room.

Although, as Francis Parker recognised, most children in 1900 left school with only 'a bit of knowledge' most could read and write. Some who continued their studies became teachers themselves. James Fishwick, preferring to follow Wordsworth's advice of 'Let Nature be your Teacher', seldom attended school but from one source or another learned enough to write on the history and natural history of Waddington.

Secondary education

In the 'sixties and 'seventies several local families sent their sons to the Grammar School. Amongst them were three of the vicar's sons, Peel Dewhurst, John Sagar, two sons of Eli Tucker and, later, two Rushtons from Colthurst. Some of them were boarders at a cost of £40 a year, £42 for seniors. By 1889 the school had three departments, Classical, Commercial and Junior. The ordinary course included reading, writing, arithmetic, geography, history, English grammar, composition, literature, mathematics, Latin, French, natural science, drawing, vocal music and drill. The course was £4 a year for Juniors, £6 for Seniors. Greek and Latin were available for an extra £3. The outfit included '1 school cap, 1 black felt hat, 1 handbag for occasional use'.

From the Grammar School the vicar's sons went to university. Most Parkers went to Oxford or Cambridge but Francis Parker went to King's College, London, and his brother Arthur to Durham.

At the vicarage the girls were taught by a governess. They acquired the social graces which helped then entertain and carry out their duties in the parish. Two of them became accomplished artists. For the majority of the village girls a little reading and writing and some sewing were considered quite sufficient education.

At the village shop the local newspaper sold for a halfpenny. (The repeal of the paper duties in 1861 had brought the price down from 1½d.) That most people could now read the news for themselves instead of awaiting the arrival of the coach at the Swan Inn, Clitheroe, for the news-sheet to be read to them is a measure of the progress made in their education during the century.

8

The Hospital

WADDINGTON was fortunate in that in the late seventeenth century Robert Parker of Carleton, younger son of Edward Parker of Browsholme, built a hospital and chapel for ten 'necessitous widows'. In 1700 the Hospital and certain estates at Carleton, Keighley and Manningham were conveyed to Edward Parker and five other trustees who were to use the rents from the estates to maintain the Hospital, to pay a reader £10 a year to read divine service and to give an allowance to each widow.[1] Further provision was made for the Hospital in the founder's will.

By 1801 there were sixteen widows living at the Hospital, the latest addition of cottages having been made in 1796. Their 'particular rooms' or apartments consisted of a living room and a bedroom, each about nine feet square. With the chapel they formed a row facing south towards the West Bradford road. In front of them were gardens and a pump which is still to be seen in its original position.

The widows were chosen from 'the poorest and most deserving widows inhabiting Whitewell, Waddington, West Bradford and Grindleton and, if necessary, Slaidburn and Newton.' With the increase in population it was not difficult to fill vacancies and in 1825 the conditions regarding selection were strictly enforced. Upon entering the Hospital the widows accepted the ten orders drawn up in 1700 whereby they agreed to attend the services, to obtain the Reader's permission for an absence longer than twenty-four hours and to live peaceably and quietly amongst themselves. By 1809 the original document which set out these rules had been filled with the names and marks of those who had taken up residence. In addition to a £4 allowance the widows may have been supplied with milk: the Hospital accounts mention wheat and straw being bought 'for our cow'. Even with these allowances life was hard at a time when prices were rising. Mrs Clarke of Waddow was moved to write to John Parker of Browsholme on the widows' behalf:

> To my knowledge several of the widows in the Hospital from infirmity has last winter and I believe do now suffer greatly for want. They were not only unable to work but required attendance. One I believe had a regular assistance from her parish, and accept the governors are agreeable to fix something in case of sickness above what they now receive others must come to their parishes or want the absolute necessaries of life. Had I not been a witness of the truth of the above

---

[1] Browsholme Archives, Indenture 12 William III.

I would not have given you the trouble.

[Written shortly before 1801 but applicable in the early nineteenth century.]

In 1825 the allowance was increased to £18 5s. od.

The Trustees saw to the maintenance of the Hospital, calling upon Thomas Boothman and members of the Pye and Hanson families to act as carpenters and masons. Repairs included fitting new windows—both casement and box—at a cost of 6s. a window. In 1805, though door-frames and chimneys were renewed, 'the evil of chimneys given to smoke' remained a problem. Two cartloads of slates and flags for repairing the roof and paving at the back of the Hospital were brought from Clitheroe for 5s. These and other costs of plastering, glazing and painting with chocolate-coloured paint, were entered in the account book.

Interior work included whitewashing and putting in new grates and cupboards. Whenever a cottage became empty it was well aired and cleaned in readiness for the next occupant; fourpence was paid for the chimney to be swept.

The chapel also had to be maintained and cleaned. There was a coal stove for heating: coal was bought for 2s. 6d. a load in 1820, and chips for kindling were supplied by the clogger. For keeping the chapel clean, lighting the fire and other duties Hannah Smith was paid one shilling a week. Items which were bought for the chapel included wicking paper, a coal box, oil, brooms, a rubbing stone and 'cocoa' matting.

During the century, extensions were made to the Hospital. In September 1822 work had begun on four more houses which were ready for occupation by the following February. Included in the costs were:

	£	s.	d.
Mr Chaffer of Burnley, architect, for drawing up the plans	3	13	6
Bricks and cartage from Blackburn	5	12	0
Stone and cartage	15	2	8
Lime and sand	11	7	4
15 yards flags	1	10	0
Wood and carpenter's work	50	17	10
Removing old garden walls	1	2	6
Making a sough [drain] and digging foundations	3	18	9
Building garden walls	2	0	0
Plastering and hair for plaster	5	3	10
Slating and flagging	27	19	4½
Fire grates and ovens	8	3	7½
Glazing and painting doors	7	19	1
Mason's work	73	5	10
Longstone from Longridge	4	7	11
Blacksmith's work	1	4	2
Pavior's work	1	17	3
Rearing	1	16	6
Cost of new houses and repairs to old	300	0	0

The Hospital as it was at the beginning of the nineteenth century.

The Charity Commissioners noted in their report in 1826 that six new houses were in the course of being built and that widows had already been selected to live in them. Shortly afterwards twelve of the ancient dwelling houses were found to be in such a bad state of repair that 'the widows could not remain in them with safety to their health and comfort without being new roofed and repaired'. Repairs were carried out. In October 1853 a contract was made with William Hanson for the building 'with the very best of materials of four houses with pettys'. He was given six months and £300 to complete the work. There was no shortage of occupants. Seven widows were admitted in 1846, three in 1850 and five in 1851. Most of them were sixty or older, though a cripple of only 49 was admitted in 1841.

During the next thirty years, new sewers were put in (1873), a retaining wall built at the west end of the Hospital (1882) and a piped water supply laid on at a total cost of £230. In spite of these improvements, in 1889 the Rural Sanitary Authority condemned the cottages as insanitary. A surveyor's report stated that the closet accommodation was insufficient and at a considerable distance away from the cottages. The Trustees themselves declared the cottages unfit for the elderly and beyond adaptation; even one of the widows complained. As a result, the Charity Commissioners came to inspect the buildings and held a public inquiry relating to the proposed alterations. Colonel Starkie, a Trustee, thought they ought to provide houses for two nurses, a dispensary and baths. He proposed utilising the good houses, throwing two into one and improving them. The chapel was said not to be large enough as there were three times the original number of widows using it. The vicar, in view of 'the satisfactory longevity amongst the inmates' did not think it necessary to rebuild all the cottages. James Walmsley was concerned about the provision for burials as 'St Helen's churchyard was getting too small.' The Trustees eventually supported Captain Parker who, having declared that he would not like to live a month in any one of the cottages, proposed a complete re-building.

'A flutter of excitement' was reported 'amongst the old women in the almshouses as they anticipated with pleasure the erection of better and handsomer houses.' Not all lived to see their new homes. The winter of 1890–91 was exceptionally severe and five of the widows had died before the foundation stone was laid in June. There were lengthy discussions including proposals for forty houses to be built in brick before plans for thirty houses, a chapel and a dispensary were agreed upon. Ninety pounds was allowed for each house and seven thousand pounds was set aside for the whole project although in fact more was needed before John Bleazard, contractor, completed the work.

On 13 June 1891 the stone-laying took place at a great Masonic ceremony. A procession of about fifty masons in full regalia set out from the Lower Buck Inn. The Tyler with drawn sword walked at the head, followed by brethren from various Lancashire and Yorkshire lodges carrying a cornucopia with corn, ewers containing wine and oil, mallet, square, level, plumb-rule and Bible. The Grand Masters and Grand Officers went on the platform along with the vicar and local worthies and they sang the Hundredth Psalm. The stone was raised and a bottle containing copies of local papers and coins was

The Tyler's Coat.
This coat, made in 1829, was worn by
the Tyler when the foundation stone
was laid in 1891.

placed in a small cavity which had been chiselled in the lower stone. Brother Edward Parker produced the plate, read the inscription on it, and placed it over the cavity containing the bottle. The stone was then lowered a few inches. Mr Bleazard handed a handsome trowel to Mrs Parker who laid it on the cement and the stone was lowered into its place. It was tested with plumb-rule, level, and square and declared well set, level and true. Mrs Parker having been presented with a mallet, struck the stone three times and said 'I declare this stone to be duly and truly set.' Brother Smith sprinkled corn and salt, poured on oil and wine, and swung a censer of incense round and about it. There followed a vote of thanks, a prayer and the National Anthem.

In September 1893 over seventy men who had been employed in the rebuilding of the almshouses were given a sumptuous repast at the Lower Buck in celebration of the completion of the work and toasts were drunk to the Trustees. There was indeed reason for general satisfaction. All the materials used, including stone from the fell, Accrington brick, Westmorland slate, and asphalt for the paths were the best of their kind. The widows had more spacious accommodation, hot and cold water, water-closets and bathrooms. The building had been done in blocks and some of the residents had been accommodated in the village while the work was carried out but they had not been greatly disturbed. According to a Charity Commission report:

> The new building forms three sides of a quadrangle and is so arranged that the completion of the quadrangle will double the extent of the building. On the principal side, facing south, and remote from the road, the centre is occupied by the chapel and the flanks by the dispensary and waiting room, the board room and five cottages on the west, and the nurse's house and five cottages on the east. The two sides of the quadrangle consist each of a block of ten cottages, each block containing a common laundry and bathroom. The boardroom is above the dispensary. The nurse's house contains on the ground floor a sitting room and kitchen, and on the first floor two bedrooms.
>
> Each cottage contains a sitting room entered by a porch having double doors, and in the rear of this room a passage giving access to a bedroom, a scullery and a small yard in which are a coal-hole and conveniences. Ashes are emptied through a door in the yard into a roadway which encircles all the buildings and is shut off from them by a stone wall. The ashes are frequently removed by carts.
>
> In the upper corners of the quadrangle, next to the laundries, are drying grounds. The rest of the close is laid out for the most part as ornamental grounds.[1]

A further £132 was spent on papering and decorating the almshouses and 'the widows were well satisfied with their new homes.'

Meanwhile, however, dissatisfaction had been growing about the selection of the widows for the almshouses, and charges had been levelled against the Waddington Hospital Charity:

> The Chapelry of Whitewell is thinly populated and its inhabitants consist almost exclusively of substantial farmers. It rarely happens that a poor widow resides within the district.
>
> On the other hand the Township of Waddington cum Bradford and Grindleton have a comparatively numerous population and have always inhabiting within them many poor and deserving widows.
>
> For many years past the inhabitants of Waddington cum Bradford and Grindleton have complained of the administration of this Trust.

Complaints alleged that some of those chosen were not eligible as they came from Blackburn and other places in Lancashire; that widows in possession of considerable property were admitted while the poor and deserving were passed over; others, well able to maintain themselves by their own labour, were admitted, whilst those unable to do so were not admitted and became chargeable to the parish; favouritism was

---

[1] Charity Commission Report, 1896, p. 19.

The new Hospital.

sometimes displayed. Robert Walker, Felix Leach, and James Rushton gave instances of these irregularities including that of a widow who was often away for five or six weeks while acting as cook for a relation of one of the trustees. In 1867 solicitors prepared a case concerning such appointments made by the trustees.

By the time of the rebuilding, widows who lived in the Hospital cottages were more carefully selected at the trustees' meetings. Vacancies were advertised, applications made and testimonials presented before interviews took place. By the end of the century there were on average three applicants for every vacancy and, as one resident said, 'to secure a residence is looked upon as extremely desirable.' The area from which the widows were selected was extended in 1885 to include twelve more villages, though preference was still given to widows from the townships stipulated by the founder: there were always several Waddington widows in residence. For a while, when it was discovered that people were coming, particularly from Low Moor, to settle in Waddington in the hope of being allocated a cottage, a period of five years residence was stipulated as a condition of selection.

This requirement, like others, was made in 1885 by the Charity Commissioners in the 'Scheme'. This laid down that the widows should not have received poor law relief during the five years prior to their admission and should be 'unable to maintain themselves by their own exertions because of age, ill-health, accident or infirmity.' Preference was given to those reduced by misfortune from better circumstances. Usually the widows were sixty when they entered the Hospital: in 1895 the average admission age was 64½ but occasionally widows in their fifties were admitted. Many lived there for over ten years and for even thirty.

The longevity of the widows was in part due to the medical attention which the Hospital provided. In 1858 it was decided that some 'medical man be appointed and a chest for medicine placed in the chapel.' Though in one year more was spent on wine for sick widows than on drugs for the chest, the 'medical gentleman' visited the

Hospital two or three times a week and received £10 a year for his services. By 1894, his salary was £50. Medicine and appliances were provided for him. When Nanny Alstone incurred a surgeon's bill for over £2 'in consequence of an accident sustained by her in the exercise of her duty in cleaning the chapel' the bill was paid for her.

As far as possible, the widows looked after themselves and their cottages in which they had their own furniture and possessions. Amongst these were pewter plates and wine-glasses, oak Bible boxes, even churchwarden pipes. Iron bedsteads had to be used. Those who wished could cultivate a small garden plot. With permission from the trustees they could have someone to share their rooms: in 1881 one had a daughter living with her and another a grand-daughter.

There were various restrictions and regulations: the gates were locked at night and the widows could be suspended or dismissed for insobriety or other offences. Widow Dugdale lost a fortnight's allowance 'she having misconducted herself'. In 1861 both Abigail Silverwood and Betty Pinder had thirteen shillings deducted from their allowance for their non-observance of the rules. A further breach would have meant expulsion. Three years later Sarah Whitaker had twelve shillings deducted as 'a consequence of her mis-conduct'.

The 1885 scheme, while renewing most of the original ten orders, stated that widows of good character were to be elected: immoral or unbecoming conduct would lead to their removal. There was to be 'no run on the score' and they were not to obtain goods or provisions on credit. Old age, and in one case intemperance, caused some of the widows to run into debt. The Reader then had to deal with their finances. The Reader or the nurse chose widows to clean the houses, light the fires and cook for those who were sick. If they refused, a substitute would be found and one shilling a day 'be taken from the former party'.

Their 1825 allowance of a shilling a day was increased at intervals if only by a farthing a week. In 1871 they received 8s. 9d.; in 1896 they were receiving nine shillings and a Christmas payment of 1s. 6d. Up to 10s. weekly was payable by the 1885 scheme—sufficient for food, clothing and a little drink and tobacco.

The widows attended two services daily, originally at nine in the morning and three in the afternoon; later, an evening service replaced the afternoon one. On Sundays they attended the parish church, where their pew was provided with a straw mat and cushions, tailor-made for £2 11s. 6d. For a time John Pinder was being paid £2 12s. 0d. a year to check their attendance. Failure to attend on two consecutive Sundays, unless sick, meant a financial penalty.

By the mid-'fifties there was a library for their use: in one year £3 was spent on religious books. Rather than read or knit, some, no doubt, preferred to talk of the past, of weavers, bull-baiting and of the celebrations at the time of the Queen's coronation when thirty shillings was allowed for tea, of the days when farms were so cut off in winter that no visitor appeared till Easter to 'let in' the New Year. One, whose mother had been at Peterloo, could tell of the bloody massacre at St Peter's Field, Manchester, four years after Waterloo. Towards the end of the century, when a month's holiday was allowed, some took a week's holiday at the sea-side; others worked in the hay fields and on one occasion all were invited to tea at Browsholme.

Many of these facts appear in the Hospital account and minute books. A more detailed description of life in the almshouses, however, was given by Thomas Dent when he wrote his reminiscences of the Hospital in 1848. Dent, Reader there for seventeen years in the 'twenties and 'thirties, knew that 'interesting asylum of age and infirmity' well.

On Founder's Day, for example, he found 'the cottages cleaned, the furniture and other apparatus in regular order so that when the worthy Trustees according to ancient custom kindly pay a visit to each there may be found among them no cause for blame or reproof.' Should Founder's Day fall on the Sabbath 'a postponement very properly took place', as there was secular business to be transacted.

Elections to fill vacant cottages were on average two a year and led 'not infrequently to animated scenes' as the widows speculated upon the appointments. 'Their furniture cannot be sufficient for a cottage like this.' 'Their habit of snuff and tobacco will consume no small portion of the allowance.' Such remarks were heard by the Reader.

The widows, who greeted him with a bow or a curtsey, wore shawls or short cloaks and bonnets. Some carried a stick and snuff; several wore spectacles. Most took pride in keeping their cottages tidy and their gardens, in which they grew tulips, onions and potatoes, were just as neat.

Amongst the inhabitants were Elizabeth Titmarsh and Milly Hudson. Of the former Dent wrote 'curiosity was the very bane of her comfort. Whatever happened … nothing was lost for want of a reporter.' Milly carefully made preparations for her own funeral deciding which friends were to be invited, the material of the coffin and the psalm to be sung. Dorothy Whittam, 'The Old Mother in the almshouses' was renowned for her constant visiting; Betsy Hopkins for her superstitious beliefs. Betsy had been brought up on a farm and remembered the inverted horseshoe over the shippon door placed there to stop witches from tainting the milk. She remembered, too, the rowan tree under which the oxen which she had driven took shelter. She believed they knelt on Christmas day. Grace Jepson had a caged bird and happily fed those that came to her garden.

Two of the widows, Margaret Fisher and Matty Simpson taught a few children how to knit and read. Matty was the mother of seventeen children though only two or three were alive when she was at the Almshouses. Nicholas Gibson was one of her more promising scholars. Returning home one day at noon he was about to pass the thatched cottage where Mary Ibbetson lived when, for some reason, he entered and was never again seen alive. When Mary's husband returned from work he found the boy battered to death with an iron poker and axe and Mary sitting unconcernedly by the fire. She said that Jesus Christ had told her to do it 'though it should have been a girl'. Gloom fell over the school and it was closed. (The parish register records that in July 1837 George Burgess, aged six, was killed by an axe by Elizabeth alias Betty Read in a state of insanity.)

It was to elderly ladies such as these that Thomas Dent ministered, reading the lessons slowly and deliberately, and basing his sermons on their foibles.[1]

The widows, grateful to Robert Parker, founder of the Hospital, commemorated his birthday on 13 June when a special service was held in the church. The preacher

---

[1] *Clitheroe Times*, Articles published under the name 'Clericus', May to August 1905.

for the occasion was paid three guineas and the ringers, singers and clerk were also suitably rewarded.

The Trustees appointed the Reader, whose main duty was to read divine service twice daily according to the liturgy of the Church of England. His salary was increased from time to time. In 1885 a stipend between £60 and £80 was decided upon; a clergyman in Holy Orders might receive £120. Francis Parker was given £150 when he became Reader in 1895.

With the exception of Richard Parker, the nineteenth-century Readers were clergymen who also served as curates. James Dewhurst, appointed in 1801, was Reader for almost a quarter of a century.

His successor, Thomas Dent, was appointed in 1824 and remained in Waddington until 1841 when he became vicar of Langho and, in 1846, first incumbent of Grindleton. He married Mary Anne Sleading and their only child, Mary, born in 1829 married Mr Lancaster, the Hospital doctor.

Richard Pearson from Doncaster, chosen from eight applicants, succeeded him. During his Readership two visitors to Waddington wrote an account, not entirely accurate, of the Hospital:

> Just beyond the bridge is an enclosure of almshouses, entered by a good archway, bearing an inscription to the effect that the hospital was built and endowed in the year 1700 by Robert Parker of Mosley [sic] Hall, Yorkshire, for the reception of poor widows. They consist of twenty-seven small but comfortable dwellings, with a large garden in front, and a chapel in the centre, where prayers are read by Mr Pearson, who lives in the village. At present there are twenty-three widows dwelling in the place, one is absent from illness. The widows assist each other in sickness. They are divided into two classes; one class receives £10 a year, the other £18. It would be difficult for anyone to view the place, marking the neatness and propriety which reign there, and the kind of inmates which it has, without gratefully admitting that Mr Parker had made a wise as well as a benevolent use of his superfluity in founding this pious retreat.[1]

Richard Parker was the nominee of his relation, John Fleming Parker, Vicar of Waddington. A lay person, he had to appear at the Hospital in a black cloth gown. On being appointed Reader in 1853 his salary was increased, work was done on his house, the pig-cote converted into a stable and a new pig-cote built. When he died three years later £40 was paid to his family for the fruit trees which he had planted.

The vicar then nominated Eugene Perrin MA to succeed him. Born in Dublin, Perrin became curate at Whitewell and at the age of thirty-three, Reader. His wife came from Clitheroe and their three children were born at the Reader's old house. A new house for the Reader was completed in 1876, the year in which Perrin left to become rector of Ribchester. When he left he was given £60, a year's salary, 'in consideration of his long and faithful services.' Eighty-eight people applied for the Readership; the new house may have been an attraction. There were three short

---

[1] C. Redding, *An Illustrated Itinerary of the County of Lancaster, England in the Nineteenth Century: Lancashire* (How and Parsons) p. 214.

The eighteenth-century Reader's House.

Readerships before Thomas Augustus Parnell, late Fellow of St John's College, Oxford, was appointed in 1886 at a salary of £100 a year. He read prayers in the morning and evening and accompanied the widows to church. During his ten years as Reader he was held in high esteem and was given an additional £10 to compensate for the disturbances caused by the rebuilding of the Hospital. Afterwards, the two brothers Francis and Ernest Parker were appointed before James A. Burton became the last of the nineteenth century Readers.

In addition to carrying out their duties at the Hospital some of the Readers showed an interest in gardening and farming. The trustees had the shippon re-roofed, the milk-house flagged and new outbuildings provided.

The Readers enjoyed various perquisites. A 'suit of black clothes' was bought for Dewhurst in 1820. A folio Bible was obtained from the SPCK for use in the chapel. The Bible, with carriage, cost over three pounds. A large Common Prayer Book with red lines and lettering was bought. The Reader's pew rent in Waddington Church was paid, as was his window tax—£1 in 1815; even his surplice was washed for him. A new one, bought in 1879, cost £2 10s. od.

The Reader's House up the Fell Road often needed attention. Slates, flagging and floors had to be replaced. In 1848 it was rough-cast and shortly afterwards, instead of the usual whitewashing, some of the rooms were papered. A kitchen with slopstone and a bacstone on which oat cakes could be made was put in. The pantry was repaired and new parts fitted to the pump. Outside there were new gate-posts, gravel for the garden walks and a rain-tub. Money had earlier been spent on the 'little house' when it was sparred and provided with a new door and seat. The house had a sitting room or library and

The Reader's House: 1876.

a dining room into which the front door opened direct. Both rooms were only 7 feet 2 inches in height and the kitchen 6 feet 6 inches. There was a scullery but no larder. The bedrooms were 'of a most indifferent character'; the smallest was only 4 feet 9 inches high at the sides. In 1863, a report on the house stated that 'the roof timbers are all exposed and the rain and snow penetrate through the interstices of the slates. It is totally unfitted for human habitation and incapable of substantial repair: nothing short of an entire rebuilding of the house can remove the present defects.'[1] The house was situated near to a brook liable to overflow and a further report from the family medical adviser in 1864 referred to the dampness and lack of ventilation. In 1867 £63 was spent on plans and estimates for a new house; five years later work began. The house was built in the close opposite the almshouses. It was 'a large substantial building, containing on the ground floor three large sitting rooms, butler's pantry, kitchen and scullery and on the first floor four bedrooms, bathroom etc.'[2] The estimated cost was £1,287 10s. od. but before the work was completed in 1876 the contractor for the masonry had gone bankrupt and further money had to be found. Expense was not spared. A piped water supply was provided for £500. Plants and shrubs were bought in Colne for the garden and grounds. Venetian blinds and bell pulls were fitted.

The old house was let for five shillings a week. Improvements were made and in 1900 the back premises were pulled down and a new breakfast room and kitchen with bedrooms over were built at a cost of £100.

---

[1] Report on the state of the Reader's house, Browsholme Archives.
[2] Charity Commission Report, 1896, p. 19.

Initially, six trustees were responsible for all this work and for letting the land, the main source of income. In the early nineteenth century, the trustees were Thomas Lister Parker, Thomas Clarke of Waddow Hall and John Brocklehurst of Colthurst. Later, William Brocklehurst, Edward Parker and his sons Thomas Goulborne and Ambrose became trustees. By 1825 the increasing amount of business which they were called upon to transact led them to apply to Parliament for modification of the terms of their appointment and powers. They secured an 'Act for more effectually vesting the Estates of Charity in the Trustees and for enabling them to grant leases ... sell part of the Estates and appoint new trustees.' The sales and appointments already made were sanctioned. The legislation was costly; £500 had to be paid for the Act, £30 each to three trustees for their coach fares and expenses in London and nearly £80 for witnesses' fares and expenses.

As early as 1811, property in Long Preston and Hellifield had been sold and land near Twitter Bridge and some 'contiguous to the Hospital and very convenient to be held therewith' had been bought from T. L. Parker for £2,100. The nearby clough and wood originally owned by the Parkers was also bought. The enclosure award allocated to the trustees 5 acres 1 rood 16 perches on the fell. In 1820 they made a further purchase from T. L. Parker when they bought the Buck Inn and farm for £3000, 'a very desirable investment' of the Charity's surplus income. Land in the Keighley area near to large and developing manufacturing towns was sold or leased at considerable profit. The rental, which was £254 at the beginning of the century and £1,290 in 1873, had risen to over £2,000 by the end. Although in 1850 the trustees failed to purchase Chancery Farm they then owned 63 acres in Waddington as well as land in Clitheroe. Later purchases included Chapel Meadow and Higher Field (11 acres 27 perches) and the Nook (3 roods) bought for £880 in 1866. They made an unsuccessful bid for Leemings but in 1896 bought the three Leawood cottages from the vicar's trustees for £362. They had been valued at £200 and described as 'old, out of repair, damp, with very small windows, dark sculleries, closets nearly down and in an insanitary condition.'

The transactions involved a considerable amount of legal work, much of which in the early part of the century was dealt with by Martin Richardson, Steward of Clitheroe Castle. For drawing up a conveyance he charged £1 10s. 0d., 'it being long and special' and 15s. for engrossing two skins of parchment 'close wrote'. On another occasion he was paid nearly eighteen pounds for parchment duty and two days' work registering the transaction at Wakefield.

The trustees proved good landlords, supplying their tenants with lime, drain pipes, clover seed and a mole catcher. A new farmhouse was built at Carter Fold, farm buildings and fences repaired, brooks cleared and footbridges mended. The customary allowance was made to tenants when they paid their rent at the half year.

The woodland was well managed and occasional sales of timber brought in extra income. Action was taken against trespassers who were cutting down trees in the clough. The allotment on the fell was drained and planted with nearly four thousand Scotch firs.

To deal with these matters the Trustees met twice a year, then quarterly, as their work increased. They employed a clerk to collect the rent and to make such payments as the land tax, highway and poor rates, window tax and tithe. The clerk was given an extra allowance in 1860 for his additional work in negotiating with John Holgate concerning a new mill and water-wheel in the clough. In 1885 the Charity Commissioners' Scheme increased the number of Trustees, one of whom was to be the vicar, to ten. They were empowered to appoint a clerk and treasurer at a reasonable salary. In the late nineteenth century the Trustees included Ralph Aspinall, William Peel, William King-Wilkinson, Henry Worsley-Taylor and Nicholas Le Gendre Starkie.

The Trustees, like the widows, honoured the founder. They bought a case for his family tree and had an inscription carved on his tombstone. In commemoration of his birthday, after checking the accounts and examining the Hospital, they attended a service in the church and had dinner at the Buck. There was refreshment at their other meetings: four dozen bottles of wine from Lancaster in 1821, four dozen Madeira in 1822 and five dozen port wine and a case of wine from Leeds in 1844.

There were occasional problems. When John Parker was away fighting in South Africa the vicar was obliged to write to him that 'the nurse too, is a little trying when she begins to give away to her unfortunate habit of drinking. The latter is a periodical scandal.' More seriously, Kay, the agent, took advantage of Parker's absence. The vicar, suspecting irregularities, found that he had 'been playing ducks and drakes with our money. Betting I suppose. We should have been bankrupt almost if he had got hold of the May rents. His last balance sheet was cooked.' Kay promised to repay the money—£1,500—but when he later kept the money intended for some out-pensioners he was dismissed. This outcome may have given a certain satisfaction to Charles Parker, solicitor, who had unsuccessfully applied for the position of clerk and afterwards wrote to the Charity Commissioner to complain because the post had not been advertised. Kay, he said, though educated at public school and Oxford, was not the best qualified of those applicants who had heard from private sources about the post. Parker more than hinted at nepotism and concluded 'Not only did he receive the clerkship but upon appointment his salary was spontaneously raised to £100.' After Kay's departure the trustees took care to advertise the post: they received over a hundred applications.

Not all their meetings, particularly those attended by Edward Parker, vicar, were amicable affairs. Disappointed at not being made a trustee when he arrived in Waddington in 1863 he stopped the Reader from taking services in the Hospital chapel for a time. When after nearly twenty years of waiting he was finally appointed he found that his proposals were seldom seconded. In his frustration he complained to the Charity Commission, refused to sign the accounts and at one meeting declined to hand over the minute book.

When Parker's nephew died the Trustees wrote of 'the sense of obligation which the trust had been under to him for the zeal and ability which he had always displayed in all matters relating to its administration.' When the vicar himself died, they simply expressed their regret.

Once the new almshouses had been built the Trustees, in the happy position of having £2,000 in the bank and a clear annual income of £600, prepared to implement the 1885 scheme by making annual pensions to men (single, married or widowers) and to women 'who are not or have not been married'. In December 1895, twenty-four men (one from Waddington) and five women (two from Waddington) were given pensions. Four male pensioners were requested to appear before the trustees when it came to their notice that they had certain means of their own: after interview two of the pensioners were struck off the list. So many men applied, however, that the pensionable age was raised from sixty to seventy-five.

When applying for a pension, a certificate of baptism and testimonials filled in by the parish clergymen had to be produced. Insistence upon membership of the Church of England led someone to write to the *Clitheroe Times* suggesting that 'Noncon-formists must try to derive consolation from the passage in the Old Book which says "Lay not up for yourselves treasures on earth".'

The trustees also decided to appoint a trained nurse. For some years they had relied upon the widows to look after any invalids. In 1872 Mary Bleazard, aged fifty-six, was appointed on condition that 'she shall act as nurse to the invalid widows so long as she is able.' Ann Coates and Hannah Smalley were admitted on a similar under-standing. Several of the widows with extensive knowledge of the healing properties of such plants as eye-bright and gentian had their own remedies for illness.

The first trained nurse was not sufficiently caring. The Trustees wanted a 'lady of culture, a member of the Church of England and not only with good practical knowledge of nursing but also likely to take an interest in the spiritual and general welfare of the widows.' She was to be allowed about £1 a week, a free house and fuel. That was in 1894. One applicant withdrew after seeing the place, believing that it was too quiet.

In 1897 Nurse Ford took up residence. She soon made an impression. The houses were numbered, a lamp was placed over the gate, two wringing machines were bought, a charwoman was appointed and one of the widows was given eight shillings 'to wait on the nurse'. £61 14s. od. was paid on furniture for her; £32 5s 11d. was paid for carpets and house linen. Her pay, originally £6 13s. 4d. a month was soon raised to £8 6s. 8d. In the following year a bath was put in the nurse's house and a bath-chair was provided for those widows unable to get out. Even when there was a nurse the occasional tragedy occurred: one of the widows was found burnt to death when the nurse made her morning round.

A happy event was the celebration of the Hospital's two-hundredth anniversary in June, 1900. The event was heralded in the morning by special peals of bells which continued later in the day. At 10.30, a service was conducted by the vicar. Later, dinner was provided at the Hospital and about seventy widows and male and female pensioners sat down. The vicar remarked that he was sure it would have been a far more elaborate affair had Colonel Parker been at home. The proceedings terminated with the singing of 'God save the Queen'.[1]

By then there were thirty widows comfortably housed and as many men and women were receiving an annual allowance: nearly £1,500 was paid out each year in pensions and salaries. The Reader, too, had a new residence. The Chairman of the trustees, Colonel Parker, was shortly to return from South Africa. There was good cause to celebrate the birthday of the founder, Robert Parker.

---

[1] *Clitheroe Times*, June 1900.

9

Local Government

A<small>T THE BEGINNING</small> of the nineteenth century the Vestry was responsible for local government. At the end the Vestry dealt only with church matters: secular ones, if not taken over by outside authorities, had become the responsibility of the parish council.

The Vestry

Every parishioner had the right to attend meetings of the Vestry until the Vestries Act of 1818 limited attendance to ratepayers. By common law the vicar chaired the meetings which dealt with such matters as the appointment of the churchwardens, one of whom was the vicar's choice, the fixing of the church rate and maintenance of the church. Minor church officials were also appointed (see page 102). These matters were settled at the Easter Vestry. Other meetings dealt with secular affairs, in particular with the election of local officials whose nomination had to be confirmed by the magistrates.

Magistrates

The magistrates, nominally selected by the Crown, were in fact the choice of the Lord Lieutenant and came mainly from the gentry and clergy. They administered justice in quarter and petty sessions, sometimes in their own homes: more serious cases were referred to the county assize courts. The magistrates were responsible for prisons and workhouses in the early part of the century. They licensed ale houses at the Brewsters Session and made orders for the removal of paupers and the apprenticing of poor children.

As could be expected, Thomas Weddell, Lord of the Manor, had been a JP, but after his death in 1788 there was no lord of the manor until 1879. Though William Brocklehurst of Colthurst was a magistrate, there was no magistrate in the village until 1874, when James Garnett of Waddow and William Dewhurst of Brungerley were made JPs.

By then a further duty had been imposed upon magistrates—that of granting exemption certificates to those who objected to their children being vaccinated. Other duties, however, were being curtailed and much of their administrative work was transferred after 1888 to the newly established county councils.

The men whose election they confirmed were the overseers of the poor, the constables and the surveyors of the highways. Although there was initially some reluctance to hold office because of the time involved and the ill-feeling created, in later decades, people were prepared as a matter of prestige to be re-elected year after year.

Overseers remained throughout the century but their importance decreased after 1834 when Boards of Guardians became responsible for the new Union Workhouses. The office of constable was abolished in 1872, by which time a police force was being paid to keep law and order. The need for better roads meant more work for the surveyors until the rural district and county councils assumed some of the responsibility.

For the appointment of these officials, there was a formal procedure which was used, for example, when a constable was appointed for Waddington in 1841. A notice from the magistrates relating to the appointment was fixed to the door of the church and at the ensuing meeting the overseers drew up a list of men to serve as constables (their calling or business had to be stated). The list was then returned to the justices and at special petty sessions held at the Courthouse, Bolton-by-Bowland, they appointed either one or two constables. 'Substantial householders' like Robert Walker and John Dugdale were appointed. Overseers were appointed in a similar way. Having made the appointments and agreed upon the rates the townspeople left matters to the officials until, at the end of the year, their accounts had to be checked.

Vestry meetings

A Vestry meeting held at the Sun Inn in 1867 'for the purpose of allowing the accounts of the Surveyors of Highways' was the last one presided over by the vicar apart from Easter and special church Vestries. The minute book in which decisions made at that and subsequent meetings survives and covers local government until 1894.

Attendances at the meetings, which were held at one of the inns, varied. In 1867 only four people were present and on one occasion the three who attended considered it advisable to adjourn. Forty-seven attended when the pay of the roadworkers was discussed in 1887. The average attendance at the annual meetings was twenty. As, during the 'seventies, these were still held in the afternoon presumably many of those who attended were self-employed or men of independent means. Prominent amongst them were William Dewhurst who took over not only Felix Leach's farm but his role in local government, Felix Grimshaw, Leach's great-nephew, and Robert Walker, owner of New Hall and the tannery. Several farmers—John Parkinson, Francis Clarke, Richard Harrison and John Sagar were regular attenders as were John Dugdale, shopkeeper, Richard Pinder, shoemaker and William Redmayne. In the 'eighties James Collinge, William Slinger, farmers, and Joseph Banks, joiner, seldom missed a meeting. At least half the meetings were attended by seventeen or more ratepayers. There was deference to position in the choice of chairman. William Garnett, Lord of the Manor, was elected whenever he attended: on the one occasion when Captain Edward Parker of Browsholme, one of the Hospital Trustees attended, he was elected. Usually William Dewhurst or James Walmsley was in the chair. Felix Grimshaw, and after his death, William Dewhurst, almost without fail, were elected to the Poor Law Board of Guardians. Dewhurst, Sagar, Henry Rushton and Collinge were the usual choice for overseers. Joseph Banks was the main surveyor with Calverley and Clarke his assistants. John Dugdale, Richard Pinder and Edward Chester, an accountant, were often elected as assessors and collectors of the rates.

The annual general meeting had to be held by 22 March. A typical meeting in 1889 was reported in the *Clitheroe Times*. William Dewhurst was in the chair: thirteen others attended—forty according to the minute book. The surveyor and his assistant were appointed. The former's salary was fixed and he was also appointed to collect the rates, then 10d. in the pound. Dewhurst was re-elected poor law guardian. Four names were submitted for the office of overseer: it was thought that the first two nominees would be chosen by the magistrates.

At most of the meetings there was some consideration of roads, footpaths and bridges. Though they expressed readiness to 'consider any other business conducive to the welfare of the inhabitants' this did not mean that action would result. When it was suggested that the village should be lit by means of paraffin lamps they 'let the matter rest'. Steps were, however, taken to improve the water supply and to collect refuse.

The minutes of the meeting which elected Waddington's first parish council state that

> consequent upon the local government Act of 1894 coming into effect the first Parish Meeting for the parish of Waddington was held in the Waddington and West Bradford Church of England School on the fourth day of December, 1894, at 7 o'clock in the evening. Upwards of 60 of the electors were present, also a number of non-electors who were allowed to remain in the room by permission of the Electors though sitting apart from them. James Walmsley, overseer, opened the proceedings.

Of those nominated, seven were declared elected by a show of hands. Conscious of their new rights, however, the electors insisted upon a poll in spite of the warning that it would cost money. With an eye to economy the election was arranged to coincide with the rural district council elections. Twenty women were qualified parochial electors but there is no evidence of their having taken part in local government.

The councillors met in the following month and having elected Walmsley to be chairman and clerk proceeded with the business of the meeting, fixing an 11d. rate and deciding to exclude reporters.

On 1 April 1895 the annual general meeting attended by the council and some twenty others was held. Henry Rushton and James Walmsley were elected overseers, the date of the intended Charity Commission Enquiry was given and the need for a better water supply was acknowledged. During the year the Clitheroe Corporation and others were approached to see on what terms they could provide a water supply. Two members were appointed to distribute the Ellen Wilkinson Charity. Subsequent meetings followed this pattern.

At the meeting held in March 1897 the celebration of the Queen's Jubilee was discussed. The clerk caused some surprise when he reported that Mrs Duckworth of the Sun Inn had handed over an old oak chest which had been in her attic for a considerable length of time. 'From examination,' he continued, 'it appears to have been the parish chest though the lid was broken and part wanting. The contents were of a very interesting nature. They included the annual accounts of the churchwardens, the overseers of the poor, the surveyors of the highways, the constables, as well as sundry other papers regarding settlements. The papers dated from between 1736 and 1800 but were not complete.'¹ The clerk was instructed to get the lid repaired and to hold on to the papers.

Shortly afterwards, William Garnett, Lord of the Manor, claimed the chest and contents but the clerk was again instructed to keep them. Following Walmsley's death in 1898 a new clerk took over responsibility for the papers and the chest was 'put into proper order'. The county council made enquiries about the documents when the matter came to their attention, but it was not until 1977 the documents were deposited at the Lancashire Record Office. The whereabouts of the chest are unknown.

Amongst the documents are some relating to the early nineteenth century. They provide evidence of how the poor were treated.

Care of the poor

The main task of the overseer was to provide for those unable to support themselves and their families. Gilbert's Act of 1782 allowed relief to be given to the poor in their own homes and after 1795 the Speenhamland system, which related payment to the price of bread, size of family and wage, was widely adopted in calculating the amount to be paid. Such payments were needed in Waddington, for the Muster Roll of 1803 listed eleven infirm men between the ages of seventeen and fifty-five. In years of depression increasingly large payments in money and in kind were made to the poor. House rents were paid; coal or peat, meal, clothing and clogs were provided; funeral expenses were paid. Overseers knew that they could be cited for manslaughter if a pauper, having been refused help, died of want. Vagrants—people without a settlement—were not entitled to help and could be removed, usually by the constable, to their place of legal settlement, often their place of birth, once they had become chargeable on the parish. People who had a pass and were travelling to their place of settlement were given financial aid.

In the early nineteenth century there are instances of people being returned to Waddington, their place of birth or legal settlement. Others acquired a settlement: the names of three people doing so are mentioned in the parish register. A settlement could be acquired by apprenticeship, by holding office, paying rates, being hired for a year, by five years' residence without relief or by renting a £10 tenement. In 1810 the overseer consulted John Parker, a Clitheroe solicitor, as to the place of legal settlement of Thomas Leeming, pauper. In the following year Parker was consulted as to Widow Chippendale's settlement. She was examined and Slaidburn was ordered to remove her. Slaidburn appealed and a notice of respite was granted. The costs for both cases came to £1 6s. 8d. This was a small payment in comparison with the costs involved when dealing with James Pye, his wife, Ann, and three children.

A lengthy examination of Pye was followed by the questioning of his wife, his mother, the overseer and various witnesses. An appeal resulted in a journey to the

---

¹ Parish Council Minute Book.

Midsummer Sessions at Skipton in July 1812. Parker's bill, finally settled in 1814, came to £30 14s. od. to which 9s. for a subpoena and a further 6s. 8d. were added. These details relating to Pye show the lengths to which overseers were prepared to go to prevent settlements liable to increase the poor rate.

The folly of this policy has been pointed out by Tate. 'Half the business of every quarter sessions consisted in deciding appeals on orders of removal at an expense which would in many cases have covered the entire cost of the pauper's maintenance several times over and still left the contesting parishes a handsome profit.'[1]

Other cases throw light on attitudes towards the poor and the work of an overseer. In 1802 Alice Gardner, a widow with three children, went to live in Clitheroe, where she failed to gain a settlement. As she was with child and likely to be chargeable, the churchwardens and overseers made complaints to the magistrates, who 'upon due proof and examination' found that Waddington was her lawful settlement. The Clitheroe churchwardens and overseers were required to 'convey the said Alice Gardner (and children) out of Clitheroe, and deliver them to the churchwardens and overseers in Waddington'.

James Read, who had moved to Slaidburn, sent his four children back to his mother in Waddington when his wife died. He was paying £5 rent for some land in Waddington, worked on the roads, washed at his mother's house and slept there on Saturday or Sunday. He later re-married and, with children, lived at Whalley, but paid no rent. He decided to remove to Waddington and insisted that his settlement should be tried at his own expense. On the grounds that he had lodged for more than forty days—it did not matter that they were not consecutive—in Waddington, had not worked in Whalley and had not forty days' residence elsewhere, he gained his settlement.

The workhouse

Although the office of overseer remained until 1929 its importance diminished after the passing of the Poor Law Amendment Act in 1834. The Act was intended to stop the increasing amount of money being paid in outdoor relief. In 1802 five and a third million pounds had been paid to the poor in England; in 1817 almost twice that amount. The result of such payments was that wages remained low and some preferred to rely upon relief rather than look for work. The Act ordered those needing help to enter a workhouse. Many handloom weavers in Waddington believing that they would soon have to chose between starvation and the workhouse petitioned unsuccessfully against the Act. Waddington was one of nineteen Yorkshire parishes which, along with fifteen Lancashire ones, formed the Clitheroe Union responsible for providing work-houses.

A representative from each township formed a board of guardians which, in 1837, began holding weekly meetings in Moor Lane, Clitheroe. Felix Leach, overseer, was the first guardian for Waddington. He attended board meetings at which they

---

[1] W.E. Tate, *The Parish Chest*, p. 199.

inspected the accounts kept by the masters of the union's two workhouses, Holden and Aighton. Medical reports and those from the inspectors on dietary requirements, buildings and education were considered. Waddington's contribution to the union funds was £110 in 1840 and £90 in 1859.

From the first, the board made it clear that they were prepared, regardless of the Act, to pay outdoor relief. At a meeting in 1837 Leach, in the chair, noted the great distress prevailing in manufacturing areas and in the following year informed the Poor Law Commission in London that 'in consequence of the low state of trade in the neighbourhood it would be inexpedient and injurious to the whole district forming the union if the Act were to be carried into full operation during the coming winter.' A relieving officer, appointed by the board, made weekly payments to those outside the workhouse who applied for help. The Poor Law Commissioners in London who supervised all workhouses, satisfied that the required administrative arrangements had been made, allowed the payments to continue. In 1888 'actuated by a humane feeling' the guardians gave money to two men working only three or four days a week. They believed that it was 'better to give a little outdoor relief than to send these large families to the workhouses and thus make them regular indoor paupers.' In any case, the latter course cost more.

Some payments, including a doctor's payment, went to people in Waddington where, in 1851, two children, two women and two men were stated to be paupers.

In spite of the stigma attached, a few elderly people whose children had left Waddington spent their last years in 'the house'. In 1851 two men who had been factory workers, one unmarried and one a widower, were in the Holden workhouse. In 1861 an eighty-one-year-old widower, formerly an agricultural worker, was there but most elderly people if their families remained in Waddington were supported by them.

Though the inspectors were satisfied with the management, the workhouses— converted cotton mills—needed constant repair. In 1859, when the number of 'inmates' had fallen to sixty, the Poor Law Commissioners proposed their replacement by one new workhouse but it took them until 1873 to establish it.

While plans for this new workhouse were being discussed an unprecedented strain was imposed on the Union resources by the Cotton Famine of 1861-5. The seventy-five millworkers in Waddington suffered when the supply of American cotton failed and craftsmen and trades people were also indirectly affected. Wisely, the board stuck to their policy of providing outdoor relief for temporary unemployment. It was recognised too that factory workers could not easily adapt to outdoor work even if it were available.

In these exceptional circumstances a special relief fund was opened in Waddington and raised £294 7s. 7d. From this, payments were made to twenty-three people in 1862 and to nearly as many in the following year. The amounts paid varied from three to seven shillings a week but more than half the money remained in the fund when the end of the American Civil War ended the Cotton Famine in Lancashire.

Generally the Waddington guardians found their duties to be light. This was partly because there were other sources of help in the village available to the poor. Indeed, Waddington was considered to be 'rich in charities practically beyond estimation'.[1]

By 1853 the Hospital Trustees were providing almshouses and pensions for thirty widows. Twelve of the residents in 1894 were from the village and this was not exceptional. By the end of the century annual pensions of £20 were being given to needy men and women living in their own homes.

Throughout the century the Simon Chapman Charity provided money for the poor. In 1893 no payment was made as the vicar 'found no-one poor enough' but the following year he paid out two sums of five shillings and one of ten. In accordance with the terms of the Ellen Wilkinson Charity, in one year alone eighty yards of calico were given to eight men and five women. A widow and two men each received three yards of blue flannel.

There were other gifts as well. In 1856 it was reported that 'Mrs Parker distributed to the children of Waddington Church School the following useful and welcome articles—to each girl a pair of hose and a petticoat; also to the poor of the village about 85 yards of strong calico for shirts and seventy yards of blue flannel for petticoats, 60 pairs of stockings and a number of flannel vests.'[1] When the parish council was set up they and the overseer continued the distribution of money and material. The villagers were also ready to help each other. A widow and her seven children who had lost their home were taken in by neighbours and friends until another house was obtained. The Wesleyan Sunday school collected for an invalid and garments were given to the needy, and the church had a collection for the poor. When the Charity Commissioners were in Waddington in 1895 James Walmsley was able to assure them that 'Waddington is very well off; very few are in receipt of Poor Law Relief.'

Care of the sick

The Ancient Order of Foresters gave help to its members in times of sickness and unemployment. Branch Number 604 had been started in Waddington in 1838. At a time when trade unions had little power and state pensions and other benefits did not exist workers throughout the country were largely dependent upon friendly societies such as the Foresters. An admission fee of sixpence for a child, paid soon after birth, and a contribution of 2d. a month, increasing at intervals, was usual. At eighteen, probationary members became full members of the Court which was organised by the Chief Ranger, Sub Chief Ranger, Secretary, Treasurer, Woodwards and Beadles. The Woodwards visited the sick, paid benefits and ensured that they did not receive sick pay without cause. Medical attention and medicine were supplied to members, their wives and children; funeral expenses were paid. Members 'in distressed circumstances' were granted relief and assistance when they were compelled to search for employment. Some families took out life insurances.

When the Foresters celebrated their Jubilee it was reported that during their fifty years of existence £3,828 15s. 0½d. had been contributed, £2,424 2s. 2d. had been paid out in sick allowances and £574 for death payments. In his report the Secretary stated that in the past five years sickness was considerably above average and there had been one death per annum from 1881 to 1885. There were then 160 members.

9 *Clitheroe Times.*
1 LRO, DDX/28/286.

The Foresters' Banner.

In the year 1888–9, 3,349 days of sickness were recorded, an average of twenty-one per member. (Average age forty.) In 1889, £149 3s. 8d. was paid for sickness, £55 for funerals and £2 2s. od. to Blackburn Infirmary.[1]

Apart from medical payments made by the Foresters, the Hospital and the Board of Guardians—these last paid 14s. 6d. in 1851 to the doctor who attended Benjamin Wilson's wife—there was no financial aid for the sick. Some, like Edward Parker dismissed doctors as 'mere dolts' and relied upon their own remedies. Others tried to 'work themselves well'. By the time the doctor was sent for it was often too late. PC Greenwood had influenza for a fortnight before leaving work and died shortly afterwards. When Joseph Oddie, headmaster, a man in his prime, eventually gave in to illness he was dead within days.

As the century advanced, more was done to prevent, or at least contain, the spread of disease. With the passing of Public Health Acts, especially that of 1876, local authorities were obliged to take action. In Waddington the Rural Sanitary Authority condemned the Almshouses in 1888 as damp and insanitary and they were rebuilt. The Medical Officer, appointed as a result of the 1876 Act, visited the school and ordered the cleaning and emptying of toilets. In cases of infectious disease children had to stay at home and sometimes the school was closed. Vaccination centres were set up and parents were penalised if they failed to have their children vaccinated and had no exemption certificate. When cases of suspected typhoid were reported and complaints were made about

---

[1] *Clitheroe Times*, 1889.

overcrowded houses, inspection followed. In 1892 the occurrence of three cases of scarletina led to a house-to-house inspection. An Inspector of Nuisances, of Dairies and Cowsheds was appointed and when in 1869 a Nuisances Committee was set up, Felix Grimshaw represented Waddington, West Bradford and Grindleton.

Water supply

The problems of refuse disposal and of an adequate water supply gave increasing concern. It was common practice to throw rubbish into the stream from which water was drawn. In 1879 at a meeting of ratepayers called 'to consider a report made by the medical officer of the Clitheroe Union as to the defective and impure water supply to the village' it was resolved that 'it is desirable to have a better and purer supply of water to the village.' When the Rural Sanitary Authority made it clear that it was more than just desirable, a committee was set up to consider the best course to be taken. Within a short time the Hospital had agreed to allow water to be taken from the clough and the route for bringing the water had been selected (giving a fall of one foot in 36 yards over 248 yards). A weir and tank were constructed and pipes and a hydraulic ram were bought. William Garnett, the new owner of the manor, undertook to raise £150. He donated £50 and arranged for four of his tenants to pay £10 each and twelve to pay £5 each. Ratepayers paid the rest.

This did not solve the problem completely. Water was not supplied to all houses and there were continued complaints about pollution especially in 1898 when there was a suspected case of typhoid. The brook below the kennels was declared to be 'somewhat offensive'. Overflow from tanks at the almshouses and elsewhere went directly into the brook and refuse was still being deposited there. It was suggested that the brook should be cleared out and that there should be more settling tanks. There was even talk of a general sewerage scheme. The parish council complained to the rural district council about the state of the lodge or pond at Feazer, the source of the water supply which, it was contended, was polluted by ducks. On inspection, the Nuisance Officer said that only ten ducks were to be seen; he was assured that in the breeding season there were two hundred. A mild letter of complaint was sent to the owner of Feazer.

Children at the school were accustomed to drink water from the nearby stream or from a well. In 1895 the threat of caning was used to discourage the former practice though there were those who in 1899 claimed that the 'water was of excellent quality'. With help from Edward Burton, water was piped to the school and afterwards at the Medical Officer's insistence a filter was provided.

In 1892 the Nuisance Officer reported that certain farmers were without a proper water supply as the brook from which they took water was polluted with sewage. Following this the Rural Sanitary Authority met the agent of the two most important landowners to consider the supply of water to Leemings, Gannies, Hollins and other farms above the village. The agent said that nine out of ten farms in the country had their water supply from open drains. He was smartly told that 'requirements are now very different'. The government inspector and county councils insisted on a supply from Rushy Well through iron pipes, and an outlay of £500 was made. (It was not, however, until 1912 that one of the farm cottages received piped water.)

Refuse

Meanwhile there was the problem of refuse disposal. The vicar took the matter up in the parish magazine in 1896, advising people to burn what they could and give what was suitable to the pigs. 'If not attended to we will be compelled to provide public scavengers who will, of course, have to be paid out of the rates.' Four years later that happened. Following complaints about ashes and wood being left in front of houses, a scavenger was appointed in 1899 to remove waste. He was paid £15 by the district council. For this he was to empty all pails every fourteen days, to clear all ashes and find his own tipping place. 'The contractor does not recognise any closets that are not on the pale [sic] system.' Some attempt was made to secure the removal of old timber and carts—'an eyesore to nearly all the villagers'—from near the wheelwright's shop. The scavenger scheme evidently worked: Bolton-by-Bowland was soon applying to adopt a similar plan.

In 1899 the West Riding Sanitary Committee called attention to the offensive smells coming from Waddington brook and urged the necessity for improved sanitation, notably the provision of a proper system of sewerage and sewage disposal. This proved to be a twentieth century matter.

Law and order

The maintenance of law and order was at first the responsibility of the constable, who also dealt with vagrants and many other matters, as indicated in the constable's accounts for 1803. John Myerscough, yeoman, constable for that year—the year in which war against France was renewed—had to draw up the Muster Roll. On two occasions he attended the balloting of the militia when men were chosen by lot from those liable to do compulsory military service. Those selected were then 'viewed by the doctor' and sworn in.

In September and in March of the following year Myerscough went to Settle to pay £21 9s. 7½d. and £21 0s. 11d. as estreat money to the chief constable. The estreats were the county rates fixed by the West Riding magistrates at quarter sessions and divided by them between the eight wapentakes and their townships which formed the Riding. Waddington with West Bradford was in the Ewcross and Staincliffe wapentake along with eighty-four other townships. An increasing amount of money was needed for construction and repair of county roads and bridges. To raise the money the constable fixed the notice with details of the escheat to the church door. He then had thirty days in which to collect the money.

Another of the constable's duties was to present the freeholders' list containing the names of those entitled to vote in parliamentary elections. With it he presented a duplicate of the land tax returns so that the voters' qualifications could be checked. He also had to supply the names of those assessing the land tax and state the duties levied on servants and windows. He supervised alehouses and called township meetings. Before the assizes, the constable made his return under the Fourteen Articles by supplying details of the number of felons arrested, the number of drunkards, and other information as requested.

In 1803 nearly sixty pounds was needed for the estreats, the constable's expenses and other matters. This was almost three times the annual amount spent in the previous decade. For enforcing law and order the constable was given a small salary as well as expenses. When the office ceased to exist William Taylor was the first police constable for Waddington, followed by John Tomlinson.

Various offences, including several cases of trespass, were committed in the village. Thomas Hayhurst, farm servant, was charged with trespassing in search of game in Tan Pit Meadow. The Hospital Trustees put up notices in their woods offering rewards for information leading to the arrest of trespassers and the chapel trustees gave warning to trespassers. They also decided to write to the Home Secretary about the bad behaviour outside the chapel and Sunday school during services. On more than one occasion they asked for the village constable to be on duty after the Christmas Day celebrations. In 1895 at the entertainment given at the day school 'a dialogue was ruthlessly stopped by the police authorities'; the next year the constable was there lending assistance. During the Cotton Famine one of the villagers was charged with receiving stolen goods from Low Moor Mill. Surprisingly, perhaps, there was no great increase in crime while the Cotton Famine lasted.

In the later part of the century many cases involved dogs. In 1890, the police were having 'a raid on dogkeepers'. PC Greenbank charged Edmund Hartley, the butcher, with keeping a dog without a licence. At the Bolton-by-Bowland Petty Sessions his pleas of forgetfulness did not save him from a shilling fine and costs. There were many cases of owners being fined for allowing dogs on the highway without a muzzle. Fear of rabies—there were 438 cases in the country in 1896—had led to legislation. A Clitheroe man who pleaded that he thought a muzzle was not required in Yorkshire was fined, as were James Garnett, Isabella Frankland and John Hartley. Hartley, rather than risk another fine, drowned his dog. Lady Holker was fined a shilling when her servant broke the law.

Thomas Hayhurst was again involved with the law when, one Good Friday evening, he started quarrelling with a Chatburn man at the Sun Inn. When John Walmsley intervened Hayhurst 'took hold of him by the whiskers and threw him down in the middle of he room.' PC Greenwood, hearing the row, found the two scuffling on the floor amidst broken glass. A number of local farmers and Thomas Wallbank, the carter, were present. As well as their drinks, they were enjoying the contents of the jug which was being passed around. Hayhurst was fined 10s. A man who 'was laid in front of the Higher Buck and could not stand' was fined 2s. 6d. and costs, or seven days' imprisonment, for being drunk and incapable.

There was an 'impudent theft' at Waddow Hall when three men, ostensibly begging, appeared there. While one was at the house the others took three rabbits from an outhouse, though they dropped two when servants gave chase. Arrested by the constable, the men were taken back to the Hall. James Garnett, who was a JP, agreed to let them off if the rabbit was restored.

Adulteration of food was a common practice in the late nineteenth century. Two of the grocers in the village were fined £2 and costs or one month in prison for selling under-strength malt vinegar and impure camphorated oil. There were several cases concerning vehicles, usually traps, without lights.

County courts for the hearing of civil cases had been established in 1881. The Deans of Gannies took a Padiham innkeeper to court when he failed to pay the full amount for the horses they had fed for him. Tomlinson, the local wheelwright, appeared at Blackburn, having failed to pay for work which he considered to be defective.

'A Vicar's son and his Tailor' made the headline in the local paper when Edward Parker's youngest son had an action brought against him for failing to pay for a suit of clothes; he was ordered to pay within a fortnight. Although served with a subpoena, Parker had failed to appear in court. The plaintiff's lawyer drew the attention of the judge to this contempt of court but no further penalty was imposed.

Roads and bridges

The local official responsible for maintenance of the highways was the highways surveyor. Responsibility for bridges was shared with the West Riding who built and maintained the bridge near the Hospital and repaired Wetter (Twitter) Bridge. With the passing of the Highways Act of 1862 other agencies, first a board and then the county council, became involved.

The surveyor and his assistant had to ensure that work on the roads was done. Failure to do so could lead to complaints, even to an indictment. In 1890 the surveyors were summoned by the police constable for neglect of duty in not having a stone fence removed from the highway. The chief surveyor said in court that he had not wished to cause any ill-feeling about the fence and preferred being summoned himself to summoning the builder.

Until 1835 the surveyor could rely upon householders to work for six days a year on the roads or pay composition money. With more money in circulation people increasingly chose to pay rather than suffer the inconvenience of statute labour. In 1800 £6 15s. od. was collected as composition money, Thomas Clarke of Waddow paying £2 10s. od. Four others paid 2s. each. Twenty-two men supplied labour, cart and horses. In addition, some men were paid for fifty-five days' work at 1s. 6d. a day. Whenever these arrangements proved insufficient a 'sess' book was prepared. Property was assessed and a rate, usually 6d in the pound, was levied. In 1811 eighteen people were paying composition money in amounts varying from £4 5s. od. to 1s. 3d. This and the rates brought in £110.

The surveyor's accounts for the years 1811 to 1814 show:

	Collected:			Spent:		
1811	£111	7s.	3½d.	£100	10s.	9½d.
1812	£ 56	16s.	10½d.	£ 52	11s.	10d.
1813	£ 42	15s.	3½d.	£ 42	9s.	7d.
1814	£ 42	12s.	3½d.	£ 41	17s.	7½d.

These were exceptionally large amounts, especially when compared with the £6 15s. od. raised in 1800.

During these years, in accordance with the enclosure award, one road had to be constructed from the Moor Gate over the fell to the Newton boundary and another to the Cob Castle quarry. These roads, verges included, had to be thirty feet wide. Bradford Lane was also widened.

In 1811 James Read did 79½ days' work at 1s.4d. a day and 101 days at 1s.8d. Eighteen others who supplied horses as well as labour received sums varying from £5 4s. od. to 5s. In 1812 even more men were working on the roads. Money was also spent on liquor, the repair of tools and a wheelbarrow.

The late eighteenth century practice of assigning sections of roads, usually to farmers, for upkeep had completely replaced statute labour by 1835. It necessitated an annual rate. One of the early account books, begun in 1844, shows the work executed, by whom, payment made and cost of material. In that year £41 14s. od. was spent on the fourteen lots of contract work and £2 10s. od. on materials. By 1856 it was usual to have seventeen lots. Nine farmers, one of whom had four sections, undertook the work for which they received £4 5s. od. Their work, which involved leading the stone from the quarry, breaking and spreading it, was inspected. If not properly carried out no payment was made and the surveyor himself took over.

At the end of each year the surveyor's accounts were 'laid before the Township in Vestry assembled', perused, 'allowed' and then submitted to two magistrates at a special Highways Session at Settle for final approval. In the first half of the century generally less than £50 was collected each year: in 1863 £63 was raised. A rate of 6d. to 9d. was usually levied.

Some stone was obtained from Brungerley Quarry and sand and lime from Robert Walker. In 1879 there was concern about the supply of stone when James Garnett refused to allow any more rock 'to be laid bare' at Brungerley. Negotiations took place, however, and gunpowder was supplied to Edward Chester so that he could obtain the rock. He used his locomotive traction engine to move the stone, damaging the road surface while doing so. There was further discussion about the supply of stone, and some from the workhouse, available at a cheaper rate, was used.

In 1877 the surveyors, assisted by a committee of five, were responsible for making a footpath from the village to Waddow Gate. A sough (drain) had to be made at Fields Farm and 1080 yards of kerbstone costing £113 15s. od. and eight cast iron grates costing £4 4s. od. were needed. Mrs Ramsden gave the gravel; 3s. 6d. a day was paid for labour. The immediate cost was met by a 4 per cent loan from Robert Walker.

A township meeting decided not to repair the road near the old vicarage as requested by Miss Susan Garnett, but various footpaths were attended to. These included the paths from Belle Vue to Hammond Hey, West Bradford Road to Brungerley via Coplow and from the village across the fields to Eaves House. Improvements were made to the wall opposite the Sun Inn to below the waterfall and rails were placed near the church croft steps. To prevent flooding, in 1880 a culvert was constructed below Altham's barn in Low Moor Road.

Bridges had to be repaired. Both at the beginning and end of the century there was concern about the one at Brungerley. The early state of affairs was set out by a Clitheroe lawyer in preparation for a possible case:

> There is a certain King's highway leading from the market town of Clitheroe over and across the River Ribble ... which proceeds to an adjoining village called Waddington upon which and thro' which said Road and River all his majesty's liege subjects have time immemorially been in the habit of using both on foot, horseback, cart and carriage at all times of the year when the state of the River

would so admit them as formerly there was no Bridge whatever over or across the same which at particular times in wet seasons and from great inundations was entirely rendered unfordable and impassable. [Edisford Bridge had then to be used.] But for the convenience of foot passengers to trip across the said river there was a lineable and formal set of Hippins or step stones placed in a regular frame at suitable and convenient distances. The initials B.C. were carved on the midstone [the boundary 'mere']. About 24 or 25 years ago the said road across the said river in great measure was occasioned to become useless.[1]

This was the result of Livesley and Co. being allowed to construct a weir nearly a quarter of a mile below the usual ford. This raised a head of water which was diverted by canal to their Low Moor cotton mill. As the hipping stones were several feet under water, the road was useless.

This occasioned much dissatisfaction. 8 or 9 years ago a subscription was entered into to erect a Wood Bridge placed on 3 stone piers upon the old foundation of the frame part on which the hippins or trip stones were originally placed. The inhabitants of both townships repaired the bridge for a time. After a period of neglect, it was dangerous and unsafe for man and horse to pass.[2]

The case under consideration was whether the lessee of the weir could be ordered to take it down: whether the inhabitants should repair the bridge as they had previously maintained the hipping stones; could the county be held responsible; or could a new subscription be raised.

The document is not dated, though it has an 1810 watermark. As the lease was made to Livesey in 1782 the wooden bridge must have been built early in the nineteenth century. A stone bridge was built, possibly in 1816, by public subscription.

Towards the end of the century, negotiations took place to transfer the responsibility for Brungerley Bridge to Lancashire and West Riding. The latter was only prepared to take action if the copings were first made good by Waddington. As this meant an outlay which the parish considered unnecessary the matter remained under discussion.

Horsehey Bridge near the school was repaired and, rather than have setts put down, as originally suggested, a cartbridge was built near Brook House Farm. Frequent accidents at the Sun Inn Bridge led to the district council's being asked to help with its widening. In reply Bolton-by-Bowland simply told the parish council 'to do the best they could.' Throughout the century 'doing the best they could' appears to have been the policy of those in local government.

---

[1] LRO, DDX/8/92.
[2] LRO, DDX/8/92.

10

Parliamentary Elections

EARLY NINETEENTH-CENTURY ELECTIONS were the concern of a small minority of Waddington inhabitants as only forty-shilling freeholders were entitled to vote for the two county members who represented them in parliament.

A new parliament had to be elected every seven years, but not all the elections for Yorkshire's county members were contested. In 1802 and again in 1806 the withdrawal of candidates unlikely to succeed allowed the uncontested return of their opponents. When in 1807 an election was finally held, four men made the tedious journey from Waddington to York in order to vote. They were Richard Calverley, farmer; Edmund Chippendale, woodturner; John Myerscough, yeoman; John Whalley, shopkeeper. John Altham of Grindleton and Thomas Taylor of West Bradford, as owners of land in Waddington, also voted.

The High Sheriff presided over the proceedings at York which were usually exciting, often lengthy and always expensive affairs. The 1807 election was no exception. Three people had been nominated before 20 May when the election began. After a show of hands the High Sheriff declared a majority for Lascelles, and for Milton, son of Earl Fitzwilliam; Wilberforce, the third candidate, demanded a poll. The poll, taken in the Castle Yard, began that same day and continued for fifteen days from 9 a.m. until 5 p.m. It was a tremendous contest—the first contested election for the county since 1742. Remarkable scenes were witnessed as voters were brought in from far and wide regardless of cost. Totals were announced at the end of each day and towards the end of the election when results were running close, arrangements were made to bring the Yorkshire freeholders living in London to York by private carriage.[1] Harewood and Earl Fitzwilliam each spent more than £100,000 in support of their candidates. In the end Wilberforce had 11,806 votes, Milton 11,177 votes and Lascelles 10,989. The Waddington freeholders voted for Wilberforce and Lascelles— an odd combination as the former was already campaigning against slavery and Lascelles' wealth came mainly from sugar plantations dependent upon slave labour.[2]

When another election was about to take place in 1812 Lascelles was promised £50,000 by his friends. His opponent thereupon withdrew and no election was held. It was this kind of arrangement that made county elections a rarity.

---

[1] *Letter to the Gentlemen Clergy and Freeholders of Yorkshire occasioned by the late election for that county*, W. Wilberforce, 1807.
[2] Yorkshire Poll Book, The Poll for the county of York, 1807.

The Great Reform Act of 1832 increased the number of county members and extended the franchise to include £10 copyholders and £50 leaseholders. This raised the number of Waddington voters from four to eleven. The Clerk of the Peace was made responsible for the compiling of the electoral register which put an end to the practice of relying on Land Tax Duplicates to establish the voters' claims. At the Knaresborough Quarter sessions in 1832 the justices decided on new polling stations, necessary now that the number of county voters had doubled. Waddington and other townships in the wapentake of Ewcross and Staincliffe were included in the Settle polling district.

A bye-election in 1835 for the new West Riding constituency gave the newly enfranchised in Waddington their first opportunity to vote. There were two candidates for the seat: George William Frederick Howard (Viscount Morpeth) wearing the orange favours of the Whig Party, and the Hon. John Stuart Wortley with the blue Tory favours. Voting was spread over two days and took place at fifteen voting centres.

On the electoral roll for Waddington were: William Brocklehurst of Colthurst; Isaac Corbridge, cotton manufacturer; Francis Holgate of Hollins; Matthew Ellison of Mitchells; James Grimshaw, schoolmaster; Felix Leach, Brungerley; Thomas Leeming, Sen., Old Hall; John Fleming Parker, Vicar; William Pinder, shoemaker; Stephen Whalley. Joseph Whittle, owner of the Moorcock, although non-resident, was also included. Eighty-five per cent of the West Riding voters exercised their right to vote. Morpeth was returned with a substantial majority of 2,807.

When the next election took place in 1841 there were 30,998 registered voters in the West Riding as compared with 18,063 in 1835. The number of Waddington voters had increased to twenty-seven, ten of whom were non-resident. Twenty-five polling stations had been provided in the constituency: that at Gisburn, only ten miles away, was used by Waddington voters.

Six nominations had been handed in at Wakefield. The sheriff declared after a show of hands for the two Whigs, Morpeth and Milton, but was obliged by the Conservatives to have a poll. Two other candidates, assumed to be Chartists, made no speeches. When the election took place Waddington, favouring Robert Peel and the retention of the Corn Laws, voted solidly Conservative with the exception of the two Leemings, father and son, who voted Whig and one other who voted for a Whig and a Conservative.

Early in 1846, Morpeth, a Whig Free Trader, was returned unopposed in the West Riding bye-election. His removal to the Lords on the death of his father led to another bye-election in 1849. Of the thirty on the Waddington electoral roll (sixteen were non-residents), twenty-five voted, twenty-four of them voted Conservative.

Most of the non-residents were Lancashire men who, having bought small farms or cottages in the village, were qualified to vote in the West Riding constituency as well as in the constituency in which they lived. Amongst them were: John Fenton of Bury, owner of Feazer House and mill; Elijah and Henry Helm of Padiham and the Reads of Whalley, owners of cottages in Back Fold; Edmund Howard, whose wife had been left Waddow Lodge by her father; R. H. Hutchinson, cotton-spinner and owner of a cottage; Robert Stewart of Clitheroe, owner of Baileys; Robert Whittle, owner of the Moorcock.

The resident voters were:

James Boothman	freehold cottage, house and smith's shop adjoining the Methodist chapel.
Edward Chester	Mitchells—£50 leasehold.
James Grimshaw	freehold property near Belle Vue.
John Harrison	freehold property.
Thomas Herd	Carter Fold—£50 leasehold
Felix Leach	Brungerley: freehold building and land at Lillands.
Thomas Leeming	Fields Farm—£50 leasehold.
John Fleming Parker	Freehold glebe estate.
William Robinson	Fields House Farm—£50 leasehold.
James Rushton	Cuttock Clough—£50 leasehold.
John Tattersall	Hollins—£50 leasehold.
Henry Taylor	Gannies—£50 leasehold.
Robert Walker, jnr.	New Hall—£50 leasehold Bonny Bar Gate.
Stephen Whalley	Old Hall: Owner of Buck i'th' Vine.
(Thomas Lancaster	qualified as a Mitton voter.)

The Second Reform Act of 1867 mainly benefited the boroughs, where all male householders were enfranchised. In the counties the franchise was extended to £12 householders with a resultant electoral roll in Waddington of forty. This was more than doubled in 1884 when the Third Reform Act allowed all male householders the right to vote. There were eighty-five voters in 1886, fourteen of whom were ownership voters (eight of them non-residents), while the rest were 'occupation' voters (that is, occupiers but not lodgers). By the end of the century there were 102 on the electoral roll.

In 1885 new county constituencies, amongst them Skipton, were created. Stretching sixty miles from north to south and forty miles from east to west it was still an extensive area. Waddington, part of this new constituency, became the polling centre for West Bradford, Grindleton, Bashall and Mitton. Every year the revising officer in the presence of representatives of the Conservative and Liberal parties 'held court' at one of the inns in the village to check the list of voters. Usually half an hour was sufficient for this, though sometimes objections were raised, as when William Garnett's name was struck off 'it being stated that he occupied the kennels only as trustee of the Pendle Forest Hunt'.

After 1872 voters were protected by the Secret Ballot Act. Bribery and intimidation by employers offering jobs or threatening dismissal were no longer effective. Not all voters were convinced that the Ballot Act gave them the promised security. During the election campaign of 1892 Morrison, the Conservative candidate, repudiated assertions that Liberal tenants on his estate dared not avow their support and that one of them had been turned out.

Whether they had the vote or not, there were times when Waddington people turned to parliament for help. The weavers petitioned against the Poor Law Amendment Act of 1834 and the tanners petitioned against the Nuisances Removal Act of 1855.

In the closing decades of the century the Irish Question was an important, if not the main, political issue. It roused considerable local interest when in 1880 Irish extremists murdered Lord Frederick Cavendish of Bolton Abbey, MP for the constituency and Chief Secretary for Ireland, in Phoenix Park, Dublin where only ten years earlier a statute had been erected to Lord Morpeth, commemorating his work for the Irish. Gladstone proposed Home Rule in order to pacify Ireland; and in 1890, when rival speakers appeared in Waddington, this was the main topic.

At the first meeting the Liberal speaker emphasised the consistent policy of his party and, in an illustrated lecture on the Glengarry evictions, attacked the landowners. The following evening the Conservative supported the Unionist policy, maintaining that the Irish people had more freedom than the English. The Liberal candidate himself appeared later in the year and at a well attended meeting stressed that Home Rule did not mean separation from England, nor did it mean 'Rome Rule'. One of his supporters, an Irish Protestant, spoke mainly on the poor law and free education and remarks were made about Mr Balfour's playing golf in Scotland instead of dealing with a potato famine in Ireland. In the ensuing election, the Conservative, Morrison, was nevertheless elected. As another election was anticipated, the supporters of Morrison held a meeting in March 1891. Tom Garnett as chairman alluded to 'certain little adventures of Mr Parnell' and asserted that it would not do to hand over Ireland or any part of it to the Home Rulers. He spoke of the calm and successful statesmanship of Mr Balfour and of the Conservative party.

When, as expected, parliament was dissolved in 1892 further campaigning took place. Roundell, the Liberal candidate, addressing a meeting in the Wesleyan schoolroom, avoided the Irish question and concentrated on 'one man one vote', temperance reform and village councils. When a resolution was proposed in his favour a majority of the audience left the room. Later, Morrison at a short but enthusiastic meeting was given three cheers when he spoke in favour of Union.

Although only one day was allowed at each polling station for the election a general election was still a long-drawn out affair: not every polling station had the same voting day. In 1892 voting was on Wednesday at Skipton and on Friday at Chatburn. Plural voters could exercise their second, even a third vote. After a heavy poll it took over an hour and five minutes to count the votes at Skipton Town Hall. The Liberal, Roundell, was declared elected with a majority of ninety-two. Gladstone, prime minister for the fourth time, again tried to secure Home Rule. A Conservative meeting in Waddington claimed that this would lead to civil war and if Ireland were lost the colonies would follow 'and we should lose the whole of our trade with them.' Only two people at the meeting doubted that this would be so. The proposal to pay MPs at a total cost of £670,000 received little support, one speaker contending that 'so long as we can get this paid by the candidates themselves, it would be madness to impose such expenditure on the ratepayers'.

After Gladstone's final defeat the Conservatives returned in 1894 and soon had to deal with trade competition, famine in India and the Boer war. Locally there were other issues. In 1900 the Liberal candidate opposed the payment of 'doles' to landlords and spoke in favour of board schools—hardly a vote-catching speech in Waddington. Morrison, again a contender and enjoying the support of Lady Holker, Captain Horsfall, William Garnett and Councillor Sagar, spoke mainly in defence of the government's conduct of the war in South Africa. In November 'polling passed off very quietly. The Conservative colours were very much more in evidence than the Liberal'.

Regardless of party differences there was one matter at the turn of the century on which most men seemed to agree: 'For a woman to be able to elect a member of parliament seems a heavy task'—a task they had no intention of imposing upon her.

11

Waddington People

WADDINGTON was not without class distinction. Money, education or a well-planned marriage helped those with ambition to rise to a higher class though it took time to gain acceptance within it.

There were no gentry living in the village. The Parkers of Browsholme Hall, owners of the advowson, were sometimes seen at church in the Parker pew and they had their relations at the vicarage. They entertained the Garnetts and Brocklehursts, not so much as equals but as the nearest in rank. Cotton manufacturers even of the third generation were hardly of the same class: certainly not if they sold game. 'I think there is very little difference between the gentleman and the poacher when we hear that Mr Townley, Mr Taylor and even Mr Brocklehurst regularly send game for sale to Manchester' wrote one of the Parkers in 1838.[1] At the end of the century when the Parkers were about to sell Newton Hall one of them 'thought it a pity some cotton spinner should get hold of a place that had been so long in the family'.[2]

Edward Parker, attending a Vestry meeting, automatically was the chairman. When he and other Hospital Trustees needed to appoint new trustees they first considered the local landowners. Like it or not, the manufacturers, increasingly powerful in parliament, were establishing themselves in local society. In the village, the Burtons, the Garnetts and the Brocklehursts were treated with the respect due to members of the upper class. It was not only tenants and mill workers who showed deference to William Garnett, Lord of the Manor: the Vestry, in need of stone for road repairs, addressed him in the most obsequious terms. These families provided the JPs and were determined to preserve the social structure. Their ladies took round the trays on social occasions and presided over missionary and mothers' meetings. These were the 'carriage' families with servants and governesses, conscious of their position and such obligations as heading subscription lists. Although their privileges gave rise to some resentment, expressed by some in persistent poaching, John Chester was genuine in his respect for William Brocklehurst—'a good sample of a country gentleman'.

Below them were the successful farmers and business men who by their acumen and force of personality accumulated wealth, invested in property, lent and banked money and played a leading part in village affairs. They became the overseers, guardians, members of the parish council, churchwardens, managers of the school.

[1] Browsholme Archives.
[2] *Ibid.*

Amongst them were the Walkers, Felix Leach, William Dewhurst—leading members of the Anglican Church, supporters of the Conservative party.

The Nonconformist–Liberal element included small farmers, craftsmen, shopkeepers, members of the Wesleyan chapel—the Whalleys and Dugdales, Robert Foulds and David Speakman—people of rather less importance. Some bought property and after the 1832 Reform Act were able to vote. They too had a hierarchy: only certain ladies presided over the chapel teatables. Education and determination helped men like Edward Chester to enter the 'professional class'.

Mill workers and labourers formed the working class. Many of them had the vote before the century ended and some had become literate. On occasion the economic situation was to their advantage.

> Labour of every description is awfully high in these manufacturing districts and it is further increased at present by the extra demand for labour for the extension of the Clitheroe railway to Gisburn which is just commenced.[1]

So wrote Sir John Ramsden's agent in 1875 when considering building a new barn and shippon at Brungerley. Soon, however, trade fluctuations and the agricultural depression made it difficult to escape from poverty.

Whatever 'class' people belonged to, they tended to find their marriage partner in the same class, even in the same occupational group, and in the same church or chapel. The result was tight-knit sub-divisions in the village of inter-related families: offend one, offend many.

Some details of the more important, and of representative families are given.

Some local families

Jane Clarke and her relations, the Leaches and Grimshaws

Jane Briggs was born in 1754 and lived for some years at Higher Standen. She appears to have been well educated, though the vicar, while acknowledging her ability, was critical of her writings. Her marriage by licence in 1777 is recorded in the Waddington Register: 'Thomas Weddell Esqr. and Mrs Jane Briggs both of this par. mar. 3 July by Robt. Smith, Curate.' The term 'Mistress' suggests some social standing. She married well, for her husband, Thomas Weddell, was Lord of the Manor of Waddington and owner of Waddow Hall. He vastly increased the size of his estate but in doing so incurred huge debts. These, along with some private property, a yearly income of £400 and a life interest in the manor he left in 1788 to his widow. When the Master of the Rolls made their repayment a matter of urgency, several farms had to be sold.

In 1793, Jane married Thomas Clarke of Mellish, Suffolk, a cousin of her late husband. After Cambridge he entered the Coldstream Guards in 1777, became a major and served overseas. Robert Smith's reference to Clarke 'sprawling with a foot on each

---

[1] WYAS, Leeds, RA 65/12, Ramsden Papers.

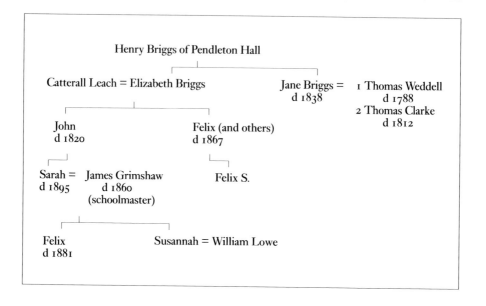

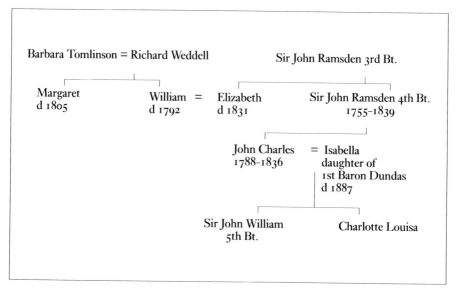

Thomas Weddell, Lord of the Manor, left his wife a life interest in the estate. After her death, according to his will, the manor was to pass to his cousin William or, in the event of his death, to another cousin, Thomas Clarke. Clarke gave Margaret Weddell, his cousin, his reversionary rights in return for the settlement of his debts. William Weddell had died in 1792, and as a result the manor passed to John Charles Ramsden. A year before he died, in his will of 10 February 1835, he left the manor to his wife for her life, then to his son, John William, on condition that he paid his sister £5,000 when he came into possession of the property. Thus, when Jane Clarke died in 1838 the Hon. Isabella Ramsden became Lady of the Manor.

Waddow Hall.

hod end' suggests a life of ease at Waddow after his marriage. It was then that he gave up his claims to the estate in return for the settlement of his debts. Among the portraits at the Hall, one showed Clarke wearing his hair in a 'queue' or pigtail. He disliked being called 'major' and hated the puns which their acquaintance, Dr Wilson, head-master of the grammar school, was so fond of making. When he died in 1812, at the age of seventy, Mrs Clarke's nephew, John Leach, acted as her agent.

John Leach, one of the twelve children of Elizabeth (Betty) Briggs, Jane's sister, and Catterall Leach, had been born at Pendleton Hall in 1774 and continued to live there after his marriage. He moved with his wife and family to Fields House Farm, Waddington, soon after his widowed mother bought Cuttock Clough (1801) from the Clarkes and was given 'out of sisterly affection' the small farm, Leemings, and Lord's Moss. He advised about the enclosure of Lord's Moss to such effect that the vicar declared 'the blood-sucking leeches had left scarce enough to feed a goose.' He served as churchwarden for a number of years before his early death in 1820.

Jane Clarke then turned to his younger brother, Felix who for some years had lived at Brungerley. She gathered together her silver and books and joined him there in 1820 having first leased Waddow Hall to B. N. R. Batty. She showed concern not only for her nephews and nieces but also for her great-niece and great-great-nephews and nieces, the widows at the Hospital and the poor children in the village. She paid her share of costs for chancel repairs during the restoration of the church. Edward Parker wrote of her to his son Ambrose in May 1838:

> Poor old Mrs Clark [sic] of Brungerley was buried at Waddington last week. She will be a great loss to her poor neighbours. It is said that two claimants have

already sprung up for Waddow, namely Sir John Ramsden in right of his infant grandson and Earl de Grey your cousin Lister Parker's great friend. For my own part I am much surprised as it was always understood the state would go to the Ramsden family at the old lady's death.

And so it did.

Felix Leach

Felix Leach, 1787-1867, farmer, lime-dealer, surveyor and cotton manufacturer, became one of the most important men in the village—partly because of his own ability and partly because of his connection with the manor. He rented, first from his aunt and then from Mrs Ramsden, Waddow Farm, Brungerley and Proctors Farm—some 300 acres—an exceptionally large amount for the district. He also bought 100 acres of moorland. In 1851 he was employing eight men to cultivate over 50 acres of arable land and attend to sheep, cattle and pigs. Ten years later Leach had given up Waddow Farm and was concentrating on dairy farming. In addition to farming he had an interest in cotton. He was a partner of the Canal Mill, Clayton-le-Moor. When he bought out his two partners in 1856 he paid each one £8,666 13s. 4d. In 1861 there were 700 hands at the mill.

From the beginning of the century he supplied lime from the Brungerley kilns to local farmers and builders. Many people, including the Hospital, turned to him for land surveys and valuations. In 1850 he made the survey of Waddington for the tithe award and helped in the valuation of houses, mills and land in Clitheroe for the poor rate. For many years he was churchwarden, poor law overseer, chairman of the Vestry and the representative of Waddington on the Board of Guardians responsible for the two workhouses in the Clitheroe Union. He and other guardians received threatening letters when the workhouses were first established. Forty years later his suggestion that the two workhouses should be replaced by one was acted upon. He was Captain of the 2nd Lancashire Rifle Volunteers and a generous donor to such causes as the Cotton Famine Fund and the Wesleyan chapel.

An outspoken man, he was critical of the Hospital over the choice of residents and had no hesitation in telling the new vicar, Edward Parker, that he did not care for his 'delivery'. He was soon afterwards involved in disputes with him over the Waddow pew, the schoolmaster and control of the school. These arguments led to his leaving St Helen's and attending St Mary's, Clitheroe, where he was buried in 1867.

In 1821 he had married Hannah Sanderson of West Bradford. The eastern extension to the house may have been made then and the garden with lawn, shrubs and greenhouse laid out. It was at this time that a few acres were bought from the Parkers and Lillands cottage was built.

At least two of his four sons attended the Grammar School in Clitheroe. One of them, Frederick Sanderson Leach, went into the cotton business in Manchester and later bought property in Waddington—the cottages in Back Fold and the Moorcock Inn. After 1867 he kept part of Brungerley and underleased the rest and the farm to William Bolton Dewhurst. Improvements were made to the coach house and harness room. Like his father he was a keen member of the Rifle Volunteers, became a captain and declined to become a churchwarden because of his regimental duties. After his death in 1892 a considerable time was needed to settle up all matters relating to Leach property in Waddington.

James Grimshaw

James Grimshaw, 1791-1860, did very well for himself when he came to Waddington to be schoolmaster (c.1819), married the great-niece of Jane Clarke, Lady of the Manor, and made the school a 'private-enterprise', charging fees and taking in boarders who lived at his Belle Vue house. It was a successful school with boarders from various parts of Lancashire: Stephen Clarke even described it as 'famous'.

As schoolmaster he was called upon to copy the church registers and measure and map the churchyard. He could afford to buy a row of cottages and 4 acres. These Mascar Row cottages went to his daughter when she married William Lowe, a manufacturer from Rawtwenstall, in 1858.

His wife, Sarah, (1802-1895) daughter of John Leach, was born at Pendleton Hall shortly before the family moved to Fields House Farm. She married in 1826 and, after the birth of six children, taught in her husband's school. When her husband died she remained at Belle Vue with her son, Felix. Her last years were spent at Stalybridge with her daughter and son-in-law William Lowe.

Felix Grimshaw, (1832-1881), named after his great-uncle, became a land agent and, like his namesake, was active in local affairs. He was the first secretary for the managers of the Waddington-West Bradford School and for over ten years represented Waddington on the Board of Guardians.

William Bolton Dewhurst, JP

William Dewhurst, Clitheroe watchmaker and jeweller, moved to Waddington c.1870 having taken over the lease of Brungerley. He soon established himself in the village and in 1874 was one of the four collectors of subscriptions for the new school; he later became one of its managers. In 1882 he succeeded Felix Grimshaw as Waddington's representative on the Board of Guardians for the Clitheroe Union and chaired their fortnightly meetings. He gave prizes to the Rifle Volunteers at their competitions, was president of the Clitheroe Agricultural Society and arranged the ox-roasts held on special occasions.

Poor health led to his giving up some of this work, selling his farmstock in 1900 and retiring to Cleveleys at the age of seventy-seven.

Ramsdens and Garnetts: later owners of the manor

Isabella Ramsden became lady of the manor in 1838 following the death of Jane Clarke. Her husband, John Charles Ramsden, who had inherited the property from his relations the Weddells, had predeceased her. Although she spent most of her time at her London home, she had close connections with Yorkshire where she held the manor of Buckden as well as that of Waddington.

She was interested in the activities of the village and gave generously to the Cotton Famine Fund. She was prevailed upon to support those inhabitants who thought James Mattinson was not a suitable schoolmaster and in 1866 became involved in the ensuing lawsuit. There was trouble when the vicar ordered the local blacksmith to cut down her pew and though she wrote to the proctor of York about a faculty for its replacement the matter was eventually dropped.

In 1870, when a school had to be built for the village, Mrs Ramsden considered donating a site and money but eventually gave up the idea. She had many of the old thatched cottages pulled down and new houses built in Katey Lane, Ramsden Terrace and at the smithy. In 1879, when she was nearly ninety and her health was beginning to fail, she and her son Sir John Ramsden sold the manor to William Garnett. Like many other industrialists who had done well in cotton, Garnett invested some of his wealth in land and bought Waddow Hall and nearly 600 acres for £60,000. Though William Garnett lived at Bashall Eaves as lord of the manor he took an interest in Waddington. He donated land and the old school to the vicar and churchwardens—a questionable act in view of the uncertain ownership. He repaired the stocks, paid the customary £1 6s. 8d. each year to the vicar, became a manager of the Waddington-West Bradford School and in 1894 was elected to the parish council.

James Garnett was better known to villagers. He was a keen fisherman—his diary records catches of salmon and grayling in the Ribble. In 1869 he was anxious to give evidence to a select committee on salmon, not only because he understood their habits but because he believed that 'Many who legislate don't understand the question at issue.' [1] His interest in education led him to supervise the studies of his own children and to give evidence to the Taunton Commission. In support of the Temperance Movement he spoke at public meetings on the 'Beauties and Blessings of Teetotalism.' Both he and William were mayors of Clitheroe. Unlike his brother, James, an admirer of Gladstone and Cobden was for many years a Liberal. He and his wife presided over many of the village's social functions and with customary generosity he welcomed many visitors to Waddow. He died there in 1913.

Robert Walker

Robert Walker, tanner and farmer (1774–1868), was another successful businessman. Just before the turn of the century, he left Newhurst Farm, Bolton-by-Bowland, and settled in Waddington. He first rented, then bought, the tannery and New Hall, one-time Parker property, and a few acres of land. He rented Bonny Bar Gate and the Elms Farms (62 acres) before buying them from the Bradshaws in 1866. Some of his employees lived at the cottages adjoining New Hall.

In 1804 Robert Walker married Edith Earnshaw (1778–1863), a West Bradford girl. Only three of their seven children survived infancy. Betty, who was born deaf,

---

[1] WYAS Leeds, Ramsden Papers 64/15.

was not taught to speak. She became a dressmaker and remained at home until her mother's death. Her last years were spent with her married sister at Bury where she died in 1875 aged sixty-eight.

Her brother Robert, born in 1821, married Ann Whalley in 1849. When her father, Stephen Whalley, moved to the Old Hall, they took over his grocer's shop. Within six years the shop had become the post office; Walker was the agent for *Whewell's Family Paper and Clitheroe Monthly Advertiser*, price 1d. After his father's death he took over New Hall and full responsibility for the tannery and farms.

Both Walkers served as churchwardens: Robert Walker Senior held office during the 1824 restoration. As an old man he gave evidence in the Leach *v* Parker case and firmly maintained that the chancel pews had not been moved during the rebuilding. His son, when churchwarden, refused to carry out the vicar's instructions to cut down the Waddow pew: he also refused to vote for a church rate.

When the new school was to be built Robert Walker, Junior, took the initiative, called a meeting of ratepayers, collected subscriptions and was chairman of the managers. There was further conflict with the vicar who was wanting too much control over the school. Walker did not live long enough to be able to reply to Edward Chester's letter in the *Clitheroe Times* asking 'Whose School Is It?'[1] Had he done so, he could have settled the controversy as to whether subscribers were or were not told that the school was to be undenominational. He died intestate in 1879.

His widow remained for a time at New Hall with her niece, Winna Whalley, as her companion before moving to one of the houses in the Square. James Walmsley, Walker's nephew, as the new owner of the tannery and other property moved to the Hall.

James Walmsley, son of Mary Walker (1813–83) and Henry Walmsley, a confectioner in Bury, was born in 1842. After moving to Waddington he not only took over his uncle's work as tanner and farmer but also became a churchwarden and obtained for St Helen's the choir stalls from Bury Church. He gave some help to the Reading Room, was chosen by the ratepayers to be the poor law overseer and chairman of the first parish council meeting. He soon became one of the school managers and was their secretary after the death of Felix Grimshaw. Considerable interest was aroused in 1889 when his men, digging for gravel at Pinder Hill, found two cinerary urns.[2] He died in 1898 and the church clock, whose chimes were first heard at 12 noon, 25 July 1901, was given by his widow in his memory. Their son, James, born at New Hall in 1886, inherited the property.

The Brocklehursts of Colthurst

Colthurst, known as New House when it was built in the late eighteenth century, is in the parish of Bashall Eaves. The owners, however, had strong connections with Waddington as much of their property lay within its boundaries and they 'owned' pews in St Helen's Church. At the beginning of the century the owner was John

---

[1] *Clitheroe Advertiser and Times*, 11 March 1898.
[2] A. Raistrick, reprinted from *Yorkshire Archaeological Journal*, 1932.

Tomlin, a cotton manufacturer from Little Harwood, but by 1802 the vicar was writing 'Mr Brocklehurst has gone to the New House, Tomlin to Clitheroe'. John Brocklehurst, already owner of Gannies and owner occupier of Hollings Farm, was one of the freeholders who objected to Mrs Clarke's encroachment upon the common land. He died in 1805 before that dispute was settled and his trustee, Richard Grimshaw Lomax, received the 10 acres of common land allotted by the Enclosure Award and bought out some small freeholders.

His son William, who took over the estate, was keen on shooting and rented additional shooting rights from the Parkers. A magistrate, he dealt severely with poachers. John Chester, who was a keeper at Colthurst thought 'the Squire was a good sample of a country gentleman and would worship at Waddington Church. He kept a pack of harriers and three or four hunters.'[1]

Colthurst, a Georgian house, overlooked a rose garden, extensive lawns, an eight-hundred-year-old yew tree and woodlands. It was elaborately furnished, mainly with walnut and mahogany; more modern pieces, the semi-grand pianoforte and a whatnot, were rosewood. The bed and dressing rooms were said to be 'replete with lofty mahogany and birch four-poster bedsteads with chintz hangings and drapery'. There were Spanish mahogany dressing tables and washstands with marble tops; handsome sets of chamber services, night commodes and bidets. The domestic quarters had up-to-date equipment—for example, patent double-geared wringing, washing and mangling machines in the wash-house and laundry. There were plate warmers in the kitchen; papier maché trays, bronzed tea-urns and a patent knife cleaner in the butler's pantry; meat safes in the pantry. For the family there were 'sets of expensive and modern China Tea and Coffee services and a capital selection of rich cut glass'.[2]

William Brocklehurst was severely injured by a fall from his horse and seldom, if ever, hunted afterwards. When he died suddenly at Colthurst in 1855, the estate passed to his sister Sarah, wife of Samuel Holker, a Bury manufacturer, and afterwards to their son, John. Colthurst was let to a Mr Potter, MP for Darwen, and for a short time to Mr Blair before Adam Sykes was tenant for some twenty years.

John Holker, born in 1828, eventually became Solicitor General and was knighted by Disraeli in 1874. Later, as Attorney General, Sir John earned £22,000 in two consecutive years. Gladstone also appreciated his abilities and made him Lord Justice of Appeal in 1882. Locally, he served as a Hospital trustee.

Sir John was described as 'a tall, plain, lumbering Lancashire man who never seemed to labour a case nor to distinguish himself with ingenuity or eloquence, but through whom the justice of his cause appeared to shine as through a somewhat dull but altogether honest medium.' At the time of his death in 1882 he was 'by universal consent in the very first rank of his profession.'[3] He spent his last years at Colthurst where he had an extra wing built on for a billiard room. The workmanship was first-class: nothing was too good for Sir John.

---

[1] *Clitheroe Advertiser*, 7 December 1906.
[2] LRO, DDX/28/286, *Whewell's Family and Clitheroe Monthly Advertiser*, May 1855.
[3] *Dictionary of National Biography*, p. 1027.

His widow had a memorial window placed in St Helen's Church. When the rebuilding took place Lady Holker ensured that this and the Colthurst pew were retained. As a subscriber to the school she was entitled to vote for managers but usually entrusted the chairman with her vote.

When she married Henry Beaufort Inglefield in 1894 there were great celebrations in the village, where a knife and fork tea was provided for the inhabitants. The *Clitheroe Times* gave the event full coverage and even printed pictures of Colthurst, the village and Waddow Hall, to mark the occasion.

The closing years of the century were hard times for landowners and tenants and rents at Mitchells and Leemings and other farms on the Colthurst estate had to be reduced.

Thomas Taylor

Thomas Taylor, Gent., 1753–1828, lived for most of his life at the fine eighteenth-century farmhouse known as Eaves House on the Waddington–West Bradford boundary. This, and Lane End Farm, he had inherited from his father. Over the front door of the house are the initials T. C.—of Thomas, and Catherine Rimington of Mitton, whom he married in 1778. She died childless at the age of fifty-six in 1808.

Some years before this Mr Thomas Taylor, as he is designated on the 1803 Muster Roll, had been extending his estates. He bought Feazer Farm with the old walk mill as well as land in West Bradford. During the dispute over the common he readily supported Walmsley and the other freeholders against the encroachments of the lady of the manor whom he referred to as 'Mrs Boneparte'. Taylor acquired 23 acres of the common by allotment and purchase and at the same time gained part of West Bradford common. The land Taylor held in West Bradford was copyhold: it was as a Waddington freeholder that he qualified to vote and made the journey to York to vote in the 1807 election.

Not much is known about Taylor as a person. He had a knowledge of Latin, a good library and counted the schoolmaster of Wray among his friends.

In 1824 he decided to move to Waddington with his housekeeper and three-year-old daughter. He bought 4 acres, originally part of the Parker estates, and built Waddow Lodge for 'near £1,000'. The date 1624 over the door of the house is misleading: the carving is certainly not seventeenth-century and there is no certain evidence of an earlier house on the site. Eaves House Farm and Feazer he sold before building the new house. Later he bought Walmsley's three farms.

Thomas Taylor did not enjoy his new possessions for long, dying suddenly of apoplexy in 1828 without making the intended revision of his will. The words 'Boast not thyself of Tomorrow for thou knowest not what Day may bring for thee' were chosen for his tombstone. Legal arguments about his property, most of which went to his niece, Mrs Brennand, followed. Jeremiah Horsfall of Waddow Hall and James Grimshaw became guardians of his daughter Mary, who was left Waddow Lodge.

Mary and her mother lived in Spring Gardens where three houses had been built by Taylor: the Lodge was let to Captain Ryan. In 1850 Mary married Edmund Howard, the chemist from whom the Hospital bought its medical requirements, and went to live in Clitheroe.

Fentons and Burtons, manufacturers and landowners

Thomas Taylor sold Eaves House Farm and Feazcr to the Fentons of Bamford Hall, Rochdale. When in 1838 they also bought the land left by Taylor to his niece they owned 375 acres in Waddington; they bought other property in the area. One of the Fentons, Roger, was *The Times* photographer during the Crimean War. Local knowledge enabled him to get a supply of horn drinking-mugs from Chipping at the request of Florence Nightingale. Apart from being on the electoral roll and drawing the rents, the Fentons seem to have had little contact with Waddington.

In 1867 they sold their land to the Burtons, another family of manufacturers who came from Tillsley, near Bolton. John, and then Edward, Burton made their home at Eaves Hall where, for a time, they kept a staff of eighteen.

They proved to be great benefactors to the village with their donations to the church and school. Edward Burton also gave generously to St Catherine's, the new church at West Bradford, and gave land for the churchyard. When he died in 1889 (aged seventy-three) he was the first to be buried there. In Waddington a row of lime trees was planted in his memory near St Helen's Church.

Robert and Susannah Foulds

Both Robert Foulds, farmer and Wesleyan local preacher (1799–1862) and his wife Susannah were born in Waddington. After their marriage they moved to Brook House Farm, which Foulds ran with the help of a farm servant. In 1850 they had 5 acres of arable and 19 of pasture and meadow. After Robert's death his wife and one labourer continued to run the farm.

Foulds was one of the first members of the Wesleyan chapel and one of the first local preachers in Waddington. He preached at a number of chapels in the Clitheroe circuit taking more services than any other lay preacher. Possibly he helped with the Sunday school and certainly found its library a great help. A shoemaker—also a local preacher—lodged for a time at the farm.

Susannah Foulds was a dressmaker and had two apprentices, one from a Wesleyan family in Rimington, living at Brook House. She was a Sunday school teacher renowned for her good works, her prayers and hospitality.

The Speakmans

Jonathon Speakman (1818–80), son of a weaver, came from Preston and worked as a chairmaker in Waddington. He married Mary Ormerod in 1851 and trained John, her six-year-old son, to become a chairmaker. They first lived in one of the thatched cottages with workshop in what is now Waddow View. In 1869 they moved with their six daughters and son to Ramsden Terrace. The two houses, one with a workshop, had been built in 1869 by William Hanson for £400 for Mrs Ramsden. Outside there was a walled garden, petties and a pig-sty. It was known before the houses were completed that Speakman, one of the last of the village chairmakers, was to live there: the workshop floor was left

Post Office Row.

unflagged so that benches could be fixed up. Speakman died in 1880: his widow spent her last years at the Hospital where she died in 1902 at the age of eighty.

In 1871 four of Speakman's daughters were working at the mill; the other children were 'scholars'—this may mean that they were attending the Wesleyan Sunday school. David, his son, became a grocer's assistant and later had his own shop and bakery and kept hens at the back. Like his rival David Wilkinson, another Wesleyan, he developed his business and by the turn of the century had a café to which wagonettes from Blackburn and Accrington brought customers (but not on Sundays). By 1900 his name was on the electoral roll as an ownership elector.

John Dugdale

John Dugdale was born in 1819 in Waddington and spent his early life as a shoemaker in Bury. He came to Grindleton for the haymaking one year and met and married Hannah Frankland, three years his junior. She was not without money, as her father owned the cotton mill at Grindleton.

They lived at Bury for a time. Their first child, Henry, was born in 1842. By 1866 twelve other children had been born, the first Waddington one in 1848. According to the 1851 census he was married, a 'visitor', living in Waddington and working as a shoemaker employing one man. The term 'visitor' may have been used instead of lodger. When the children became old enough they went to work at Low Moor Mill, starting work at 6 o'clock and finishing at 5.30. John Dugdale took over the grocer's business from John Pinder but kept his shoemaker's tools in the attic and made and repaired the family's shoes and clogs. He started collecting eggs and butter from the farmers and took them weekly to Accrington. His son Benjamin started the corn business in his father's name. At first he used a spring cart and horse and had a small warehouse and stables north of the shop.

With the money made in business and with his wife's money, John Dugdale was able to buy the property in Post Office Row and the land behind the houses.

Golden Wedding of John and Hannah Dugdale.

He was a great worker for the Wesleyan chapel. For nearly fifty years he was a circuit steward and he was also a class leader. In the Sunday school he was treasurer, teacher and superintendent. During these years the school flourished. For a few years there was no other school in the village and Edward Parker was later to observe that 'but for John Dugdale the children in the village might have grown up heathen.' So impressed was the vicar by Dugdale's work that he promised to use his influence to secure for him the position of post master. With or without this help, John Dugdale had become post master by 1887.

A photograph of John and Hannah shows them with their family at their golden wedding in front of the shop/post office. This was shortly before his death in 1893. His work at the shop and post office and the corn dealing business were carried on by his son Benjamin, as was his work in the chapel.

John Chester

John Chester was born on 14 September 1828 at Harker's Farm, Eastington, about a mile out of Slaidburn. He attended the grammar school, where he was taught by the curate. When he was about fifteen the family moved to Mitchells Farm, part of the Colthurst estate. His father, a Congregationalist, held monthly services for the family and neighbours (see page 123).

The farm lies to the south of the Moorcock, which had not long been built. The walls on the fells also were newly built following the enclosure award of 1819. In his reminiscences, recorded in 1906, John Chester recalls:

Before they were built an old man enclosed a bit of land and grew some potatoes, then some wheat. Somebody pulled up his fences and nothing else was grown. We used to pick cranberries near Cob Castle, but an old man called Thomas Hanson, a coal-dealer in Waddington, used to stand about the Moorcock and used to demand sixpence apiece from th'lads before he'd let 'em gather 'em. [Chester believed they were on 'the Poor Lands'.]

Richard Walker went with his donkey across the fells delivering letters, then John Jackson, who only had one arm, took on the job. He used to ride th' donkey when it would let him, but at times it turned stupid and he had a job to get it forward. Before there was a post office in the village it took a fortnight or three weeks for a letter to land out of the south of England. Only one newspaper came to Slaidburn and three people joined at it. Swales, from Clitheroe, had a huntsman's horn which he used when he went round hawking barm.

Chester worked on the farm and 'did a bit of walling for folk'. Later, he became assistant keeper at Colthurst Hall working for 'Squire' Brocklehurst. When he was about twenty-four John Chester married Sarah Rushton from the nearby farm of Cuttock Clough.

The biggest half of the houses in Waddington were thatched then. Hand-loom weavers were going out in them days. There was only one i'th' district; Maria Whitehead had it. She lived at th' cottage next to Thornber's Farm where Mrs Pye now is. Rev. J. F. Parker had the living when we first came. He was a bit of a sportsman. I have his gun.[1]

There were seven children in the family; one died in infancy. When Sarah Chester died in 1868 after a long illness John Chester moved to Chancery Cottage and spent his final years at Leawood with one of his married daughters, Dorothy Evans. Before his death in 1906 he worked as a warder at a private asylum near Billingham. For fifty-five years he was a member of the Foresters—its oldest member after the death of William Lawson.

His children had attended the Wesleyan Sunday school where they received their earliest education. One of his sons, Edward, was for some years a master stone merchant. He employed eight men and used a traction engine to move the stone. He became an accountant, was the enumerator for the 1881 and 1891 censuses and built the Reading Room and two adjoining houses. A stalwart of the chapel, he wrote its history to celebrate its centennial in 1924.

Ellen Brown

Among the poorer members of the community was Ellen Brown. Life was hard for her. Born in the year of Waterloo, she lived in West Bradford with her unmarried mother before moving to Waddington with her sister Mary. In 1841 they were sharing a house with Alice Baxter and her seven-year-old son. In the following year Ellen's

---

[1] *Clitheroe Advertiser*, 7 December 1906.

son, John, was born. Thomas was born in 1843. In 1851 Ellen, now a power-loom weaver, and John were still living with the Baxters; Thomas, a scholar, was lodging with neighbours in Back Fold.

In 1861 Ellen and John were both weavers, presumably at Low Moor. Another son, Robert, born in 1853, was a scholar in 1861. They still shared house with Alice Baxter, whose son had recently died at the age of twenty. She had been working as a washerwoman for over ten years. This was the time of the Cotton Famine with little or no work at the mill. From the Special Relief Fund which had been set up in the village Ellen was receiving 3s. a week at the end of 1862. In January and February she received 5s. In March the amount was cut to 2s. and no further payments were recorded.[1]

Ellen was away from home when the next census was held, though John, a weaver, and Robert, a carder, were there. She died in 1876. John left Waddington. Robert, with a responsible job as a grinder at the mill, married. Two of his seven children died at an early age.

---

[1] LRO, PR 2993 1/7.

12

Waddington, 1901

'A QUAINT, pretty looking village'—at the end of the century this was still a true description of Waddington. A writer in the *Clitheroe Times*, however, thought it was 'waking up from the lethargy which has surrounded it for so long. This is most encouraging and gives promise of better days for the old village. Its situation and surroundings are such that if it once gets on the move, I should not be surprised if it developed into a popular place of residence.'

It retained its rural aspect, though changes in agriculture had had their effects. Stone walls on the fells marked the allotments made in the enclosure award. Corn had not been grown for some years; meadow and pastures, moorland and woodland remained. The farms, with their relatively new owners, had more machines and fewer men.

Some of the old industries—quarrying and tanning—and old crafts survived. Blacksmiths, wheelwrights and joiners were fully employed but shoemakers and tailors were going out of business. When Feazer Mill and the chair factory ceased to operate men looked outside the village for employment and found work in the Clitheroe mills and in a widening variety of service industries. It was accepted that women should work outside the home; for them, too, there was a wider choice of occupation. The unemployed relied for help chiefly on the Foresters, 'an organisa-tion,' according to the Chief Ranger, 'of working men to help working men who did not cringe and cry for assistance from the state but relied on their own efforts.'

Travel had undoubtedly become easier. In fifty years people had become accus-tomed to trains. Roads and bridges were being improved by parish and county councils. Gigs, charabancs, bicycles, even the occasional car, were to be seen. Many still had to walk to work but at least they had a footpath, though no lights, from the village to the stone bridge at Brungerley.

There were the same three inns in the village, and an additional one, the Moorcock, up the fell road. Opening hours had been curtailed and a closer check was kept on the contents of their drinks. The police constable in his tall hat and his coat of Melton cloth with crown-embossed buttons used his truncheon to good effect should fights occur there.

In the Square there was much evidence of new building. Francis Parker, although he had been vicar for barely five years, had already arranged for rebuilding work at St Helen's. He had also started a number of activities for his 'old fashioned' congre-gation. In 1889 the Wesleyan chapel, whose exterior had not changed since 1824, had had its gallery removed and the interior spruced up when the Sunday school was built. To the south of this was an adjoining house for the caretaker; the Beech Mount Row of six houses and bakery was built in 1900.

Opposite were new houses built on either side of the Sun Inn: one was for the wheelwright, who also had a new 'shop'. The smith had been equally fortunate in that Mrs Ramsden had replaced the pair of cottages and the smithy by a new, larger house and smithy shortly before selling the manor to William Garnett. The pinfold and stocks, recently repaired by him, were becoming items of antiquarian interest rather than of practical use. Criminals were severely punished, however. The hanged Ribchester murderer seen by James Garnett as he returned by train from Liverpool in 1863 was a reminder of this.

There were at least three shops in the Square selling an increasingly wide range of goods—cloth, medicines, paraffin, bread and tea. The post office had been established in its present position for some twelve years. Lower down the village, Stones' sold newspapers. Cigarettes and snuff were on sale; those who bought tobacco were asked not to chew it when attending functions in the Sunday school. A weekly delivery van from Clitheroe also supplied goods.

Since 1881 the population had begun to rise as people found Waddington a desirable place for retirement. In the last decades the thatched cottages had disappeared to be replaced by stone or brick houses with slate roofs, and a few substantial houses like the Reader's House and the School House had been built. There were thirty new houses at the Hospital, and the Old Hall, 'sombre, deserted and unattractive', was about to be saved from decay. Even so, though the population was greater than that of 1801, there were, in fact, fewer houses than at the beginning of the century.

As new houses were built and old ones modernised, they were fitted with grates and kitchen ranges. Peat was no longer burnt. Cheaper glass encouraged people to have larger windows. Wooden floors and papered walls were replacing the stone flags and whitewash. Most of the houses had running water, even if it was not pure; a few had baths and indoor lavatories. More attention was being paid to personal cleanliness. A local optician maintained that 'Spectacles and eye-glasses are as much benefited by a Bath now and again as people are.'

In the majority of houses candles and oil lamps were used, but these were lit by matches now that the horror and consternation caused when they first appeared had been finally forgotten. A few people were using acetylene gas, and one family had its own generator.

Not only were people better housed, they were better fed and had a longer life expectancy. By the late 'eighties it was said that a labourer 'dresses better, eats more butchers' meat, travels more, eats more, drinks less'.[1] Though wages were low, low rents and low prices meant that real wages had risen and in 1885, when bread prices still ruled country budgets, bread was cheaper than in 1850. Cheese also was cheaper; tea ('magnificent' tea cost 2s. 6d. a pound) and sugar much cheaper; bacon at least no dearer.[2] People grew more vegetables. There were innovations like tinned fruit and ice cream for those with money; for others a sheep's head simmered with vegetables for one and a half hours made a cheap Sunday dinner. Cloths appeared on many tables;

[1] C. M. Chapman, Assistant Commissioners 1893–4, XXXV 44.
[2] J. H. Clapham, *An Economic History of Modern Britain 1850–86* (Cambridge, 1952), p. 296.

crockery and cutlery were in general use. The few dined off Spode and Wedgwood, and if the middle class could not afford solid silver, electro-plated was available.

Fashion in dress had changed. On rare occasions, as in 1894 when Lady Holker was in Waddington, the latest fashions in bustles were to be seen. Most villagers had simplified versions of these styles. With dressmakers and bonnet-makers in the village, sewing machines and fashion books, it was easier for the ladies to acquire 'Sunday best'. Not many villagers could afford velvet, brocade and lace, but their cottons were easier to wash; and if they aspired to kid gloves, these could be bought for 1s. 9d. The men wore billycocks, bowlers, or beavers made of rabbit skins, trousers and coats of cloth rather than of fustian and moleskin. Wigs had long ago disappeared with the powder tax of the French Wars; whiskers were in fashion.

Improvements in social conditions and increasing medical knowledge contributed to improvements in health. Leeches, still being used in the 'forties, were no longer applied. When James Garnett had teeth extracted in 1866 he had had the benefit of chloroform. There were still those who had no choice but to try and 'work themselves well' rather than pay the doctor or go to the infirmary at Blackburn. Vaccination was helping to stamp out smallpox, but measles and diphtheria caused many deaths, and scarlet fever and whooping cough were accepted as inevitable. Spectacles were increasingly used: £2 2s. 0d. was paid for a pair for one of the Hospital widows. Advertisements offering to buy used false teeth might offend, but such teeth were preferable to the 'Waterloo teeth' extracted from soldiers killed on the battlefield.

Attempts were being made to clear away the refuse from the village after complaints had been made about rubbish left outside the wheelwright's shop or thrown in the brook. Even though there was no proper sewerage system and drains still emptied into the brook, the claim was made that 'in spite of the insanitary state, Waddington contains more old men and women than any other village for fifty miles around.'

There was rather more leisure time, even a few holidays. Bull-baiting in the Square had been replaced by billiards at the Reading Room. People gathered for the Foresters' annual celebrations, when members assembled with band and banner to process through the village. There were Whitsuntide processions and carol singers at Christmas and on New Year's Eve.

Weddings were more elaborate affairs than in the past when many had only been able to take a short time off work for the ceremony. The old customs of throwing rice and 'scammering'—throwing coins to the children who had gathered—survived. In 1893 a spectator wrote in disgust to the *Clitheroe Times* about the children who, disappointed at not receiving money, pelted the couple with clods. More respect was shown whenever a funeral took place. Work stopped, men stood bare-headed, curtains were drawn.

At weekends, there were cricket or football matches. At Brungerley there were pleasure boats and a variety of entertainments. Young ladies were advised to 'pass no day without invigorating the circulation by exercise more or less energetic'.

Women had little spare time and were not expected to play a prominent part in village life. Even when mangles and wringers were available, washday meant hours of hard work. The death of children in their infancy was accepted as the norm. Though a few women were qualified county and parochial electors, they had not received the right to vote for MPs—unlike the majority of men. The ballot box and a polling booth in Waddington were of no advantage to them. Those who went out to work were becoming

more independent: some joined in the Foresters' sports. Races—100 yards for single ladies—80 yards for the married ladies, were organised. Social distinctions were maintained. The lord of the manor was asked with due deference 'if it would be agreeable and convenient to him to meet some of the ratepayers to discuss the privilege of getting stone'. Only certain ladies expected to be, and were, asked to preside at social functions.

At the end of the century, as at the beginning, England was at war—this time against the Boers in South Africa. Continental wars, apart from the Crimean, had been avoided during the century and an *entente* with France, the ancient enemy, was about to be made. When wars did occur the press brought events nearer home. Letters written during the Napoleonic War show an awareness of Napoleon's ambitions, though news was somewhat out of date by the time it arrived. *Whewell's Paper*, during its short run, contained illustrations and graphic accounts of events during the Crimean War. When that war was over there were celebrations at Waddow and a camp was set up near Longridge. During the Boer War extracts from the diary of Major Parker appeared in the local paper with details of events soon after their occurrence.

In peace time, church, chapel, school, the friendly society and the cricket club relieved the tedium of village life. But as the century came to its end, and as the queen's long reign was drawing to its close, it was evident that, though many changes had occurred since 1801, some things remained the same and

> Yet this will go onwards the same
> Though Dynasties pass.

> Thomas Hardy.

Glossary

backboard	a thin board on which meal was riddled for oatcake dough.
bacstone	a slate, later an iron plate, over the fire on which oatcake was baked.
barkham	a collar made of bark.
barm	yeast.
besom	a bundle of twigs, heather or broom bound round a long handle and used for sweeping.
castor	a little box—pepper castor.
chandler	dealer in candles, oil, soap, paint and groceries.
deviller	workman in charge of a machine (known as a devil) for shaking rags.
forty shilling freeholder	person owning land valued at this amount.
fulling mill	mill in which cloth was thickened by beating with wooden mallets. Soap, or fuller's earth, was used to clean it.
gaffer	master or foreman.
gallery lesson	object lessons usually given to large classes.
glebe	land assigned to a clergyman as part of his benefice.
hey	an enclosure.
hipping stones	stepping stones.
kip	leather—the tanned hide of a stirk.
kit	pail or wooden vessel, sometimes with a lid, for milk or butter.
knur and spell	a *knur* (a wooden ball) was placed on a *spell* (a block of wood). When the spell was struck the knur flew into the air, to be struck by a bat.
laith	barn.
lead	carry, draw a load.
lonks	Lancashire sheep noted for their wildness and excellent wool.
lurry	lorry, cart
merestone	a stone to mark the boundary of a property.
pavior	paver, road-worker.
petty	privy, 'little house', lavatory.
rearing	the laying of timber on a new building.
riddings	clearings.
riddle	coarse sieve
shadray	a two-wheeled cart on springs.
silo	pit—or air and water—tight chamber for the storage of green fodder.
sneck	latch of a door

Speenhamland system	the calculation of poor relief in accordance with a person's wage, size of family, price of bread, made by the magistrates of Speenhamland in 1795. The practice was widely adopted until 1834.
tackler	overlooker
tenter frame	a wooden frame on which cloth, after being milled, was stretched so that it would dry evenly and without shrinking.
terrier	book recording items (in church); a register of landed property.
trencher	platter of wood with a scooped hollow.
tyler	doorkeeper (Masonic).
walk mill	a fulling mill—a term mainly used in the north.
windle	a basket; a measure, usually of wheat—about 3 bushels.
wisket	a basket of plaited hazel with a hole at each end for the hands; used for carrying grain.

For several of these terms see *Carr's Dialect of Craven with a Copious Glossary*, 2 volumes (London, 1828).

Sums have been given in pre-decimal currency: twelve pence (12d.) = one shilling (1s.); 20s. = £1. With conversion, 100p = £1. Christopher Hibbert suggested, as a rough guide, multiplying eighteenth-century sums by at least sixty to have an idea of their worth in 1986.[1] A multiplier of seventy might be applied to nineteenth-century figures to give a 1994 approximation of worth.

[1] C. Hibbert, *The English: A Social History 1066–1945* (London, 1988).

Main Sources

Lancashire Record Office, Preston

Local government records

Enclosure and tithe awards

Archives of the Wesleyan Methodist Church, Waddington: account books; Sunday school registers.

Browsholme Hall Archives: letters; papers relating to the Waddington Hospital; land sales.

W. Yks. Archive Service, Wakefield

Land Tax returns

Land registrations

Electoral rolls

Trade directories

W. Yks. Archive Service, Leeds

Waddington Hospital Archives: account books; minute books.

Ramsden papers

Leeds University Library

Census returns

Parliamentary papers

Election results

Charity Commissioners' reports.

Clitheroe Library

Census returns

Ordnance Survey maps

Trade directories

Local history collection

Photographic collection

Newspapers

Blackburn Library

Blackburn Mail

Harris Library, Preston

Preston Guardian

Office of the Clitheroe Advertiser and Times

Newspaper collection

Borthwick Institute of Historical Research, York

Wills

St Helen's Church, Waddington

Parish register

Parish magazine

School log book

Managers' minute books

Letters

Sales catalogue

Leach *v* Parker case

Select Bibliography

Ashmore, O. (ed.), 'The Diary of James Garnett of Low Moor, Clitheroe, 1858–60, 1861–5', reprinted from *Transactions of the Historical Society of Lancashire and Cheshire*, CXXI 1969, CXXIII 1972.

Ashmore, O., 'Low Moor, Clitheroe: a Nineteenth-Century Factory Community', reprinted from *Transactions of the Lancashire and Cheshire Antiquarian Society*, Vols 73, 74, 1963–4, Manchester 1966.

Bamford, S., *Passages in the Life of a Radical* and *Early Days* (London, 1905).

Briggs, M. (ed.), 'Journals of a Lancashire Weaver, 1856–60, 1860–4, 1872–5' in *The Record Society of Lancashire and Cheshire*, CXXII (printed for the Society, 1982).

Bythell, D., *The Handloom Weavers* (Cambridge, 1969).

Chester, E., *History of the Wesleyan Chapel, Waddington* (printed by *Clitheroe Advertiser and Times*, 1924).

Clarke, S., *Clitheroe in the Old Coaching Days* and *Clitheroe in its Railway Days* (2nd edn) (printed by *Clitheroe Advertiser and Times*, 1929).

Field, J., *English Field-Names* (David and Charles, 1972).

Fishwick, J. H. W., *In and Around Waddington* (printed by Clitheroe Advertiser and Times, n.d.).

Harland, J., and Wilkinson, T. T., *Lancashire Legends, Traditions, Pageants, Sports* (London, 1873).

Hartley, M., and Ingilby, J., *Life and Tradition in the Yorkshire Dales* (Dalesman Books, 1985).

Langshaw, A., *How Cotton Came to Clitheroe* (Borough Printing Co., Clitheroe, 1953).

Raines, F. R., 'Miscellanies. Memoirs of the Life of Rev. Thomas Wilson' (Chetham Society, Vol. 45, 1857–8).

Raistrick, A., *Regions of Britain: Yorkshire Dales* (London, 1968).

Redding, C. (ed.), *England in the Nineteenth Century, Vol. VI: Lancashire: An Illustrated Itinerary of the County of Lancaster* (How and Parsons, 1842).

Rothwell, M., *Industrial Heritage: Guide to the Industrial Archaeology of the Ribble Valley* (Bridgestone Press, 1990).

Tate, W. E., *The Parish Chest* (Cambridge, 1946).

Turner, W., *Riot! The Story of East Lancashire Loom Breakers in 1826* (Lancashire County Books, Preston, 1992).

Watts, S., *The Facts of the Cotton Famine* (London, 1866).

Waugh, E., *Home Life of the Lancashire Factory Folk* (London, 1863).

Whitaker, T. D., History and Antiquities of the Deanery of Craven (3rd edn, edited by A. W. Morant) (London, 1878).

White, W., *History, Gazetteer and Directory of the West Riding of Yorkshire, Vol. I* (Sheffield, 1837).

Index

The index is arranged under the following subdivisions: 1. Persons: 2. Occupations: 3. Locations in Waddington: 4. Other locations: 5. Miscellaneous.

1. Persons

4. Other Locations

5. Miscellaneous